Dinner at The Lighthouse

Recipes from families who served at Piedras Blancas Light Station

by
Beverly S. Praver

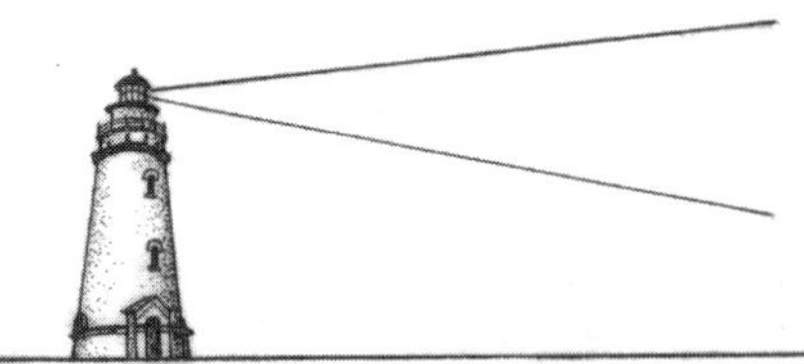

For information contact:

Beverly S. Praver
P. O. Box 894
Cambria, CA   93428

Design and Layout - Beverly S. Praver

ISBN 1-930401-51-5

Illustrations:

Top of Pages - Lynn Rathbun

Front and Back Covers: Judy Lyon

Pages 5, 14, 15, 33, 37, 38, 40, 41-43, 56, 61, 62, 65, 71, 73, 75, 76, 103, 113, 115, 119, 123, 128, 131, 133, 136, 154, 159, 160, 163, 167, 169, 172, 174, 181, 194, 198, 203, 208, 210, 231, 256, 258, 281, 287 - Fred Richter

Pages 57, 139, 144, 147, 150, 170, 175, 180, 185- Beverly S. Praver

Pages 53, 60, 81, 89, 93, 99, 105, 143, 188, 192, 204, 207, 226, 239, 243, 248, 265 - clipart

Photographs:

Title page -Thorndyke family and friends having dinner at the lighthouse prior to 1906, Courtesy of Gerald "Dick" Thorndyke.

Pages 212 and 276 - courtesy of Pat Inabnit

Page 214, courtesy of U.S. Rep. Lois Capps

Original cookbook page and all other photographs, courtesy of
Donna Jean Thorndyke Schneider

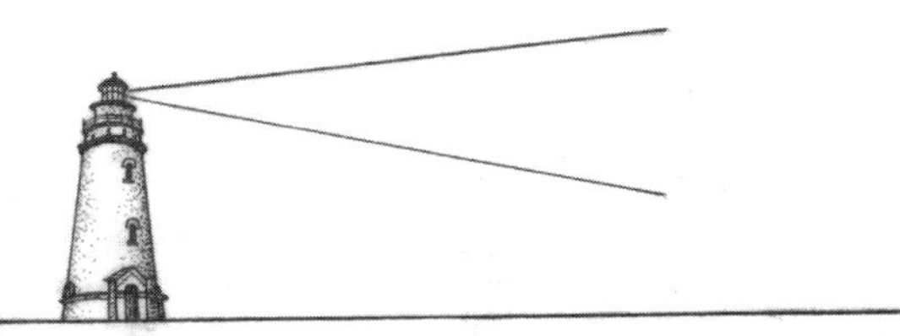

Acknowledgments

I thank the following people for their help and encouragement during the writing of this book: John Bogacki, Kathe Tanner and Consuelo Macedo.

Thank you to all who contributed recipes to this book: members of the Thorndyke family, former members of the U.S. Coast Guard and their families, U.S. Rep. Lois Capps and her staff, and the Bureau of Land Mangagement and their volunteers. Jim Lilly, who I interviewed in November 2003, passed away before this book was published. His contribution added valuable insights to the section on the U.S. Coast Guard.

I owe a particular debt of gratitude to Donna Jean Thorndyke Schneider who brought her great-grandmother's cookbook and family pictures to share with us. Without her generous permission to use these treasures, this book would not exist.

Finally, thank you to my husband, Jerry Praver, for checking the historical facts and for never complaining about the many hours I spent writing and compiling this book.

---Beverly S. Praver

Women of Piedras Blancas
L-R, Back row: Margaret Jarmon Thorndyke, Mary Jarmon Evans, Sarah Williams
Front row: Helene Van Gordon, Kate Van Gordon (Mary's daughter), and Gladys Van Gordon

Dedicated
to
The Thorndyke and Jarmon Women

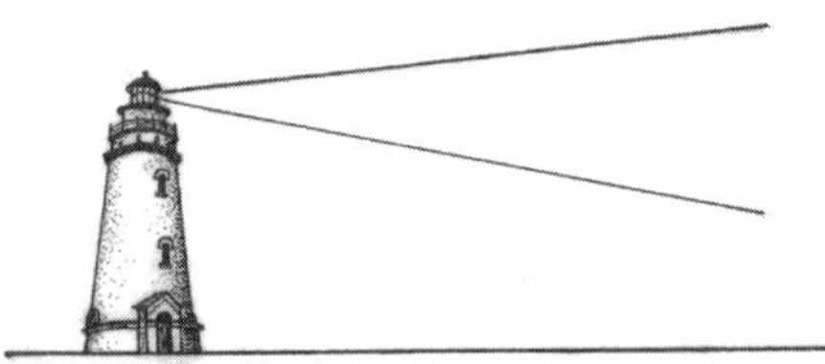

Contents

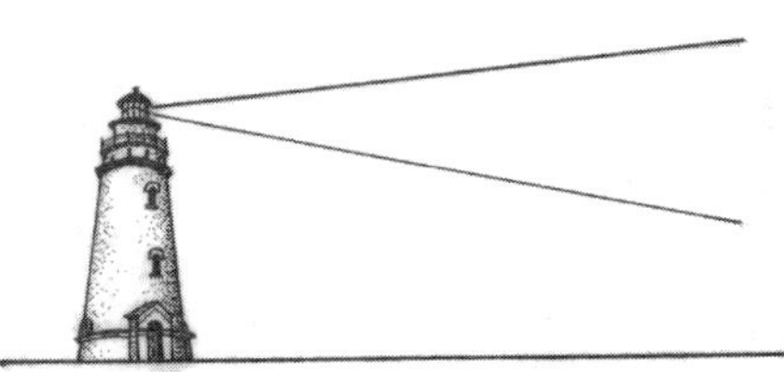

An early photograph of Piedras Blancas Light Station

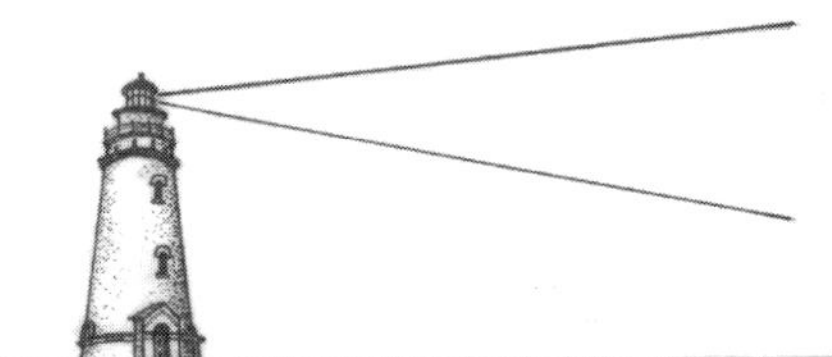

Preface

The idea of creating this cookbook came into being when Donna Jean Thorndyke Schneider came to see the Piedras Blancas lighthouse for the first time in October of 2002. She brought with her an old handwritten cookbook started by her great-grandmother, Elizabeth Jarmon Thorndyke. Elizabeth began the cookbook in 1879 when she became the first wife of Capt. Lorin V. Thorndyke, the head keeper at the Piedras Blancas lighthouse from 1879 to 1906. Elizabeth died in 1886.

To the best of my knowledge, the Captain's second wife, Francis (Frank) E. Clark, did not make any entries in Elizabeth's book.

Elizabeth's sister, Margaret Jarmon continued the cookbook in 1897, when she became Capt. Thorndyke's third wife. John Bogacki, the Piedras Blancas site manager for the Bureau of Land Management in 2002, copied the pages and subsequently asked me if I'd like to compile a cookbook from the copied pages. I quickly agreed and began

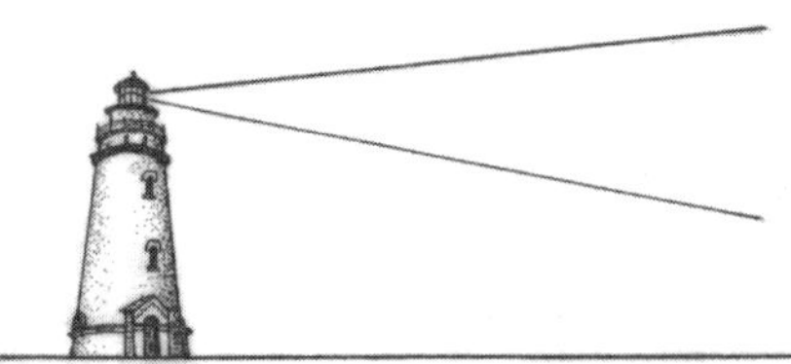

transcribing the recipes. It soon became clear that this wonderful old cookbook contained primarily dessert recipes and that others would be needed to make a complete and interesting cookbook. So I contacted all of the Thorndyke descendents we knew of plus the lighthouse personnel and researchers who worked there during the Coast Guard years. I asked for favorite family recipes from the Thorndykes, the Coast Guard personnel, the Bureau of Land Management personnel and BLM volunteers along with any reminiscences they had of their time at Piedras Blancas.

I have also included recipes from Margaret Jarmon Thorndyke's copy of "Crumbs from Everybody's Table" a community cookbook compiled in 1907 by Mrs. Arina L. Porter and Mrs. Eva B. Ball for the Ladies of St. Paul's Guild, in Salinas, California.

Some of the recipes came from a small book which belonged to Maud Rogers Thorndyke, Lorin V. Thorndyke Jr.'s wife. She clipped recipes from newspapers and magazines and pasted them into a small, paperback-ledger book.

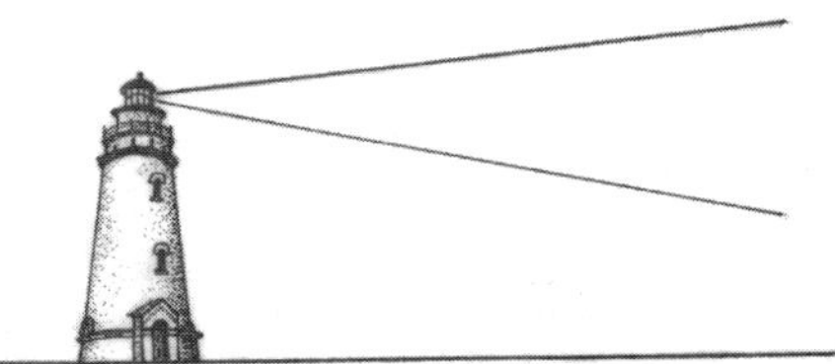

A Note to the Reader

I have presented all of the recipes as I received them. I have *not* corrected spelling, punctuation, capitalization or the recipes themselves, but have left history as I found it. Ingredients listed in the oldest recipes were not listed in neat orderly columns as modern recipes are. At times ingredients and instructions are interspersed and you must read carefully to follow the recipe.

Remember that these recipes were written down only for the personal use of Elizabeth or Margaret. In some cases I have added notes or modifications below the original recipe. Many of the early recipes are incomplete or lack cooking instructions. When you come across such a recipe, I suggest that you find a similar recipe in this cookbook, or another, and try using those directions. When you keep in mind that the women who wrote these recipes were cooking on wood stoves you can understand that each woman knew her stove well enough to know how long to bake cookies or cakes without having to write it down. The incomplete recipes in Elizabeth's and Margaret's portions of the book are presented

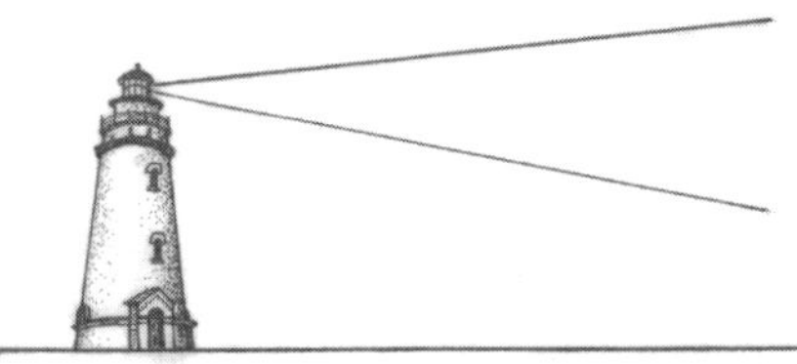

the at the end of each of their sections for historical interest. The incomplete recipes in Maud's section of the book are left in their original context since her book was arranged by categories. I have indicated registered trademarks even when they were not included in the original recipes. (Do you put that mark next to ingredients when you write down a recipe for your own use?)

L.-R. Maud Rogers Thorndyke, Richard Thorndyke, Capt. L.V. Thorndyke, Margaret Thorndyke and Lorin V. Thorndyke, Jr.

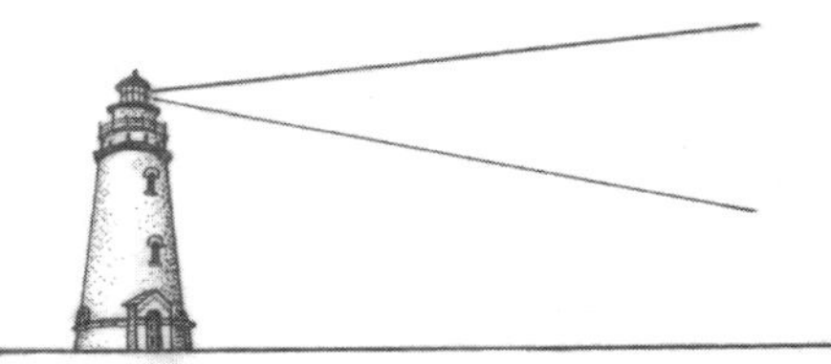

The older recipes in this book direct the cook to dissolve the baking soda in cream, milk, or even vinegar in one case before adding to the other ingredients. This is because prior to the arrival of baking powder on the American market in 1839, baking soda came in solid or lump form. It then had to be painstakingly crushed and measured and mixed before it could be used.

Baking soda, formerly known as saleratus, was used for baking and for cleaning butter churns and other household articles.

American saleratus was packaged in a bright red wrapper, each pound with its free recipe card for the ladies. It quickly became a strong competitor for soda imported from England. This was a colorful era of salesmanship. Imagine the delight of all onlookers as the soda salesman drove into town in a colorfully decorated wagon drawn by plumed horses. One of the most memorable, and surely one of the most successful, salesmen was Colonel Powell. He was a former Barnum giant, who stood nine feet tall with the aid of a very high hat and a pair of thick-soled shoes.

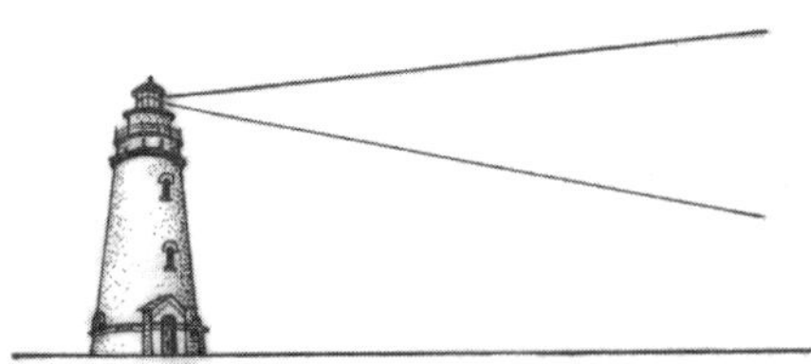

If you make any successful modifications to these recipes and would like to share your creativity with us, please send your recipes to us so that we can include them in our next edition.
Send to:

PBLS Association,
P. O. Box 127
San Simeon, CA   93452

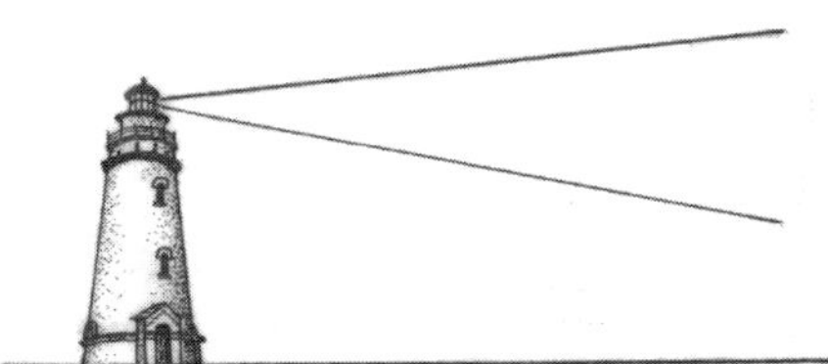

The Thorndykes

Capt. Lorin Vincent Thorndyke arrived at Piedras Blancas Light Station in August of 1879 and served as head keeper until August of 1906. There is no record of any shipwreck near Piedras Blancas during those years, which could be considered a testament to his devotion to duty.

Capt. Thorndyke, a native of Maine, claimed to have sailed around Cape Horn five times. He married Elizabeth Jarmon in November of 1879 and they had two sons, Lorin V. Thorndyke, Jr. and John Emory Thorndyke.

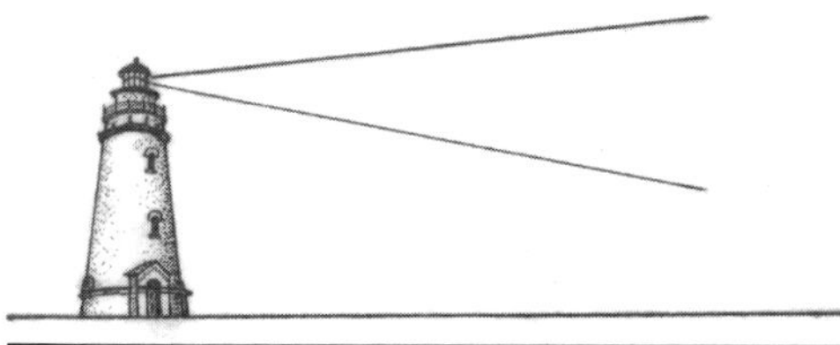

Elizabeth died in 1886 and the captain married Frank (Frances) E. Clark in 1889. After Frankie Ruth Thorndyke was born in 1891, Mrs. Thorndyke left the captain, deciding that the lighthouse was much too lonely a place to live. She took her baby back to San Francisco, where she had lived prior to her marriage.

After Frank E. left, the captain lived alone with his sons until September of 1897 when he married one of Elizabeth's younger sisters, Margaret Jarmon.

Mary Jarmon, Elizabeth and Margaret's sister, was the first of the Jarmon girls to come to California from Wales, Wisconsin. She married a local rancher, Thomas James Evans, when he went back to Wisconsin to visit his family. Thomas' brother John was already married to another of the Jarmon sisters, Ann. Mary Jarmon Evans brought her sisters, Elizabeth and Martha out to California to meet and marry the local bachelors. Martha Jarmon married Benjamin Muma.

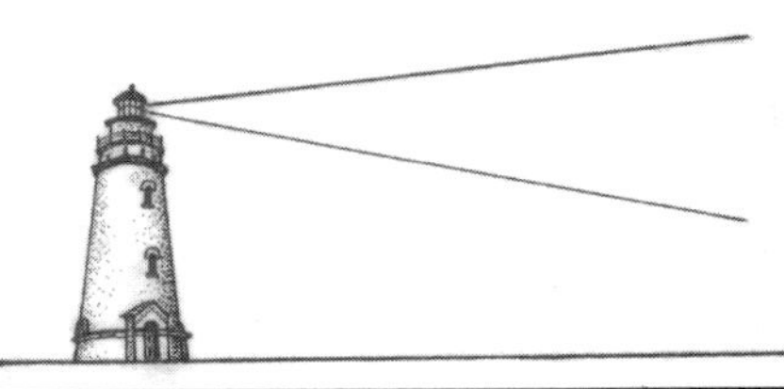

Elizabeth Jarmon Thorndyke

Margaret Jarmon Thorndyke

Capt. Thorndyke married sisters, and his sons, Lorin Jr. (known as Lo) and John Emory (known as Em) Thorndyke, also married sisters, Catherine Maud(known as Maud) and Clara Erma (known as Erma) Rogers.

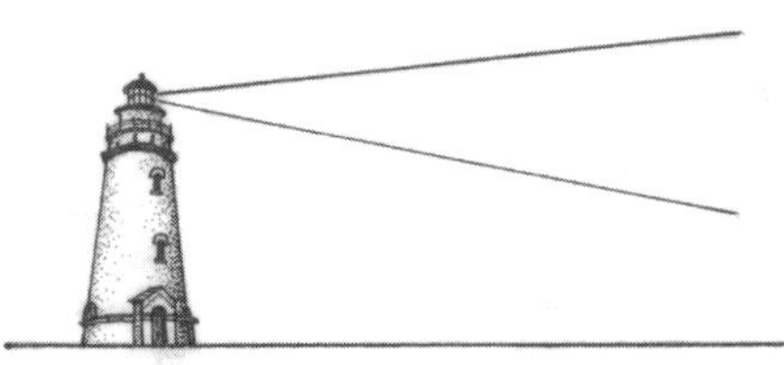

Elizabeth started her cookbook in a small ledger book. When Margaret married the captain she turned the book over (front to back <u>and</u> top to bottom) and started putting her recipes in it. Both women asked their friends and relatives to put their recipes in the book and, as a result, I have identified at least nine different handwriting examples. Some recipes had the names of the contributors next to them. I have endeavored to credit the recipes to the original authors whenever possible.

Many of these recipes came to me incomplete and I have presented them to you as they were received.

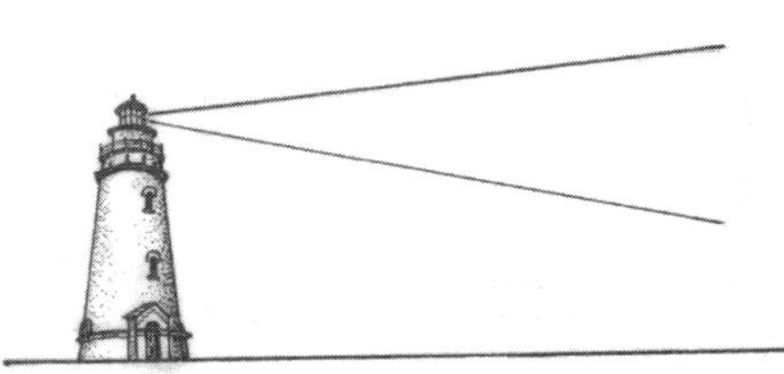

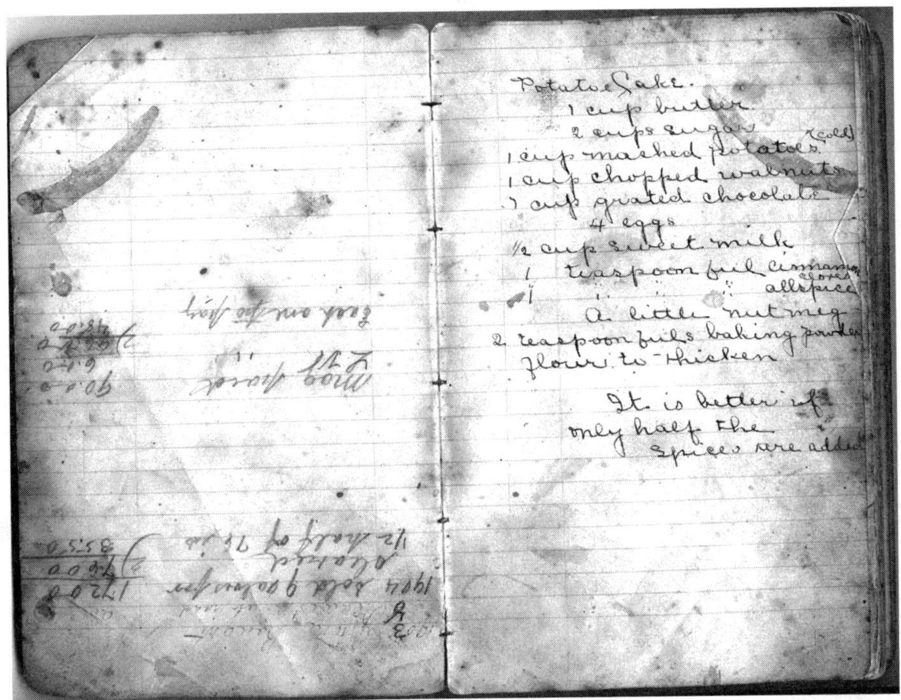

An example of writing in two directions. See pages 24-25 for a typed version of this example.

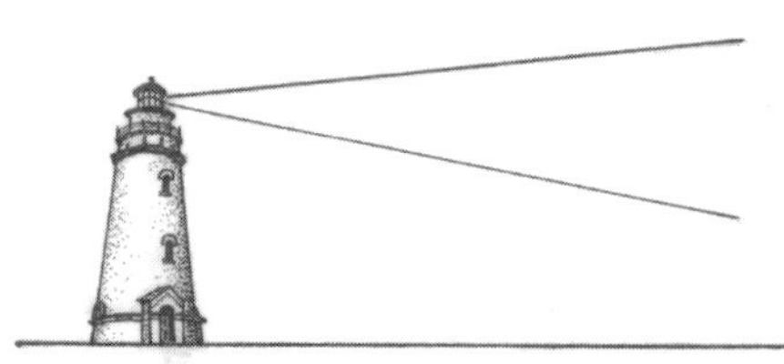

Capt. Lorin V. Thorndyke
and
Margaret Jarmon Thorndyke
on their wedding day, September 24, 1897.

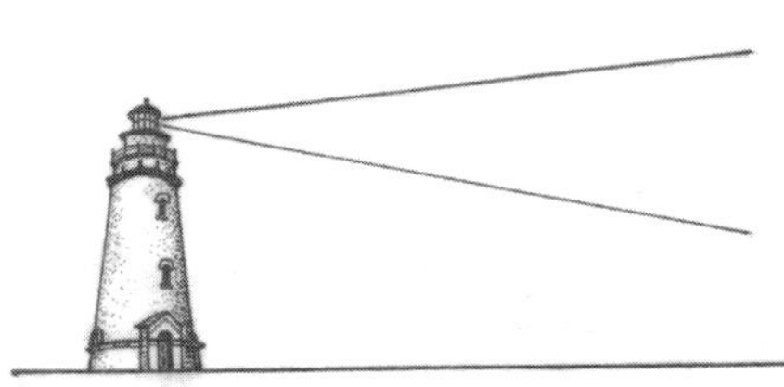

Left to Right:
On bottom step: Margaret J. Thorndyke,
Sarah Williams.
On middle step: Mary J. Evans, Kate Van
Gordon.
On top step: Helene Van Gordon, Gladys
Van Gordon

Temperature Conversion Chart (in degrees)

Fahrenheit	Celsius	Description
225	110	Very cool/very slow
250	130	—
275	140	cool
300	150	—
325	170	very moderate
350	180	moderate
375	190	—
400	200	moderately hot
425	220	hot
450	230	—
475	240	very hot

This chart should be accurate enough for all your cooking needs. Keep in mind the temperatures will vary between different types, brands, and sizes of ovens, in addition to your location's altitude, temperature, humidity, etc. Descriptions and experience were needed when using wood or coal stoves.

The
Early Years

L.-R. Lorin V. Thorndyke, Jr., Capt. L.V. Thorndyke and John Emory Thorndyke

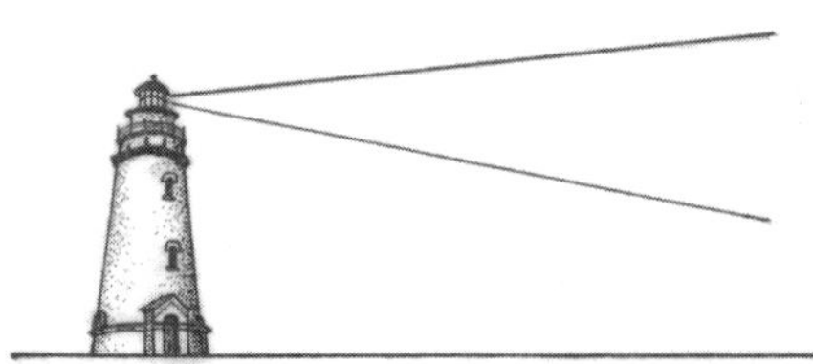

This page and the next give a clearer picture of what was written on the pages in the picture on page 19.

1903	June Bought	
	8 calves 1/2 at head	96.00
1904	sold 9 calves for	172.00
	cleared	76.00
	1/2 of 76 is	35.50

Mag saved	90.00
L.V. saved	6.00
	96.00
Each one to pay	2) 48.00

Notes:

This column is written <u>upside down</u> in the original!

I know the math is not correct, but that's what was written! ....Bev Praver

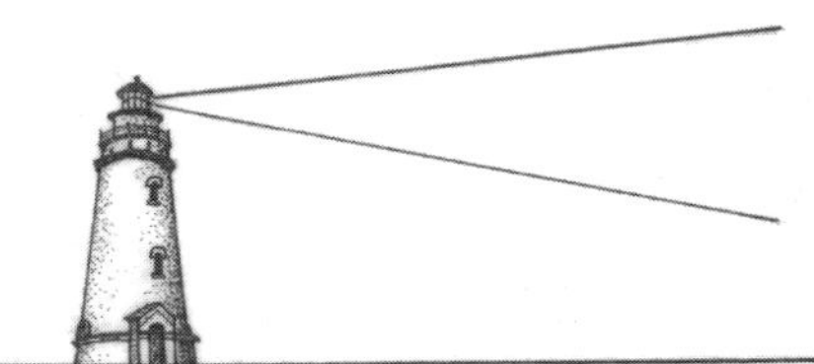

Potato Cake

1 cup butter
2 cups sugar
1 cup mashed potatoes (cold)
1 cup chopped walnuts
? cup grated chocolate
4 eggs
1/2 cup sweet milk
1 teaspoonful cinnamon
1   "   "   "   cloves
1   "   "   "   allspice
a little nutmeg
2 teaspoon fuls baking powder
flour to thicken

It is better if only half the spices are added.

Note: The note about using half the spices was in
the original cookbook.

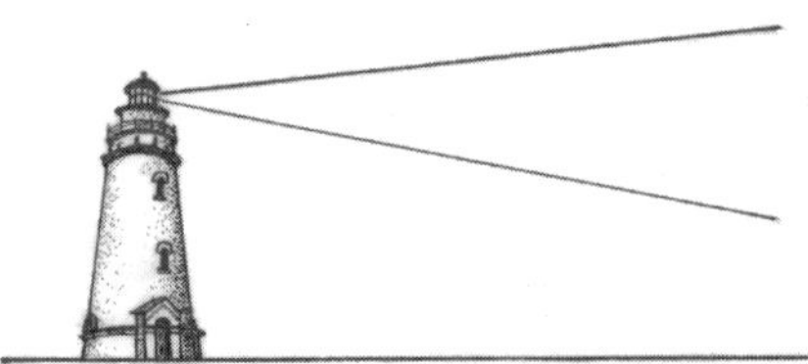

Plain Cake

1/2 cup sugar
2 eggs
1/2 cup butter
2 cups flour
1 1/2 teaspoonful baking powder
and just enough water to stir good

Beat eggs and sugar together then add butter melted, then flower, baking powder, milk, flavor with lemon or vanilla. Bake in a moderate oven.

Dazy Cookies

6 eggs
1/2 pt. lard
1/2 pt. butter
1 tablespoonful Vinegar
1 tablespoonful soda
1 pt. sugar
flower to work stiff
bake in a quick oven

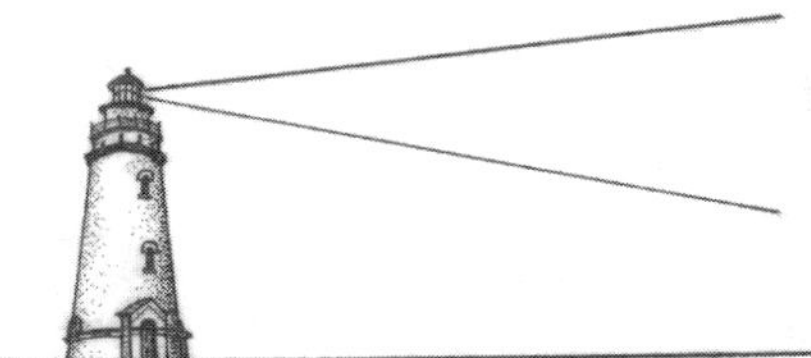

Brown Bread

2 cups fs corn meal
1 "   "   Flour
1 "   " Rye flour
1 qrt " sour milk
2/3 cup of Molasses
1 "   " chopped suet
2 teaspoons of baking power mixed in flour
1 teaspoon Saleratus   Boil 4 hours

Note: Butter can be substituted for the chopped suet. The direction to boil the bread for four hours means to put the bread into 1 lb. coffee cans, place the cans on rings from canning jars in a large canning kettle containing 2 -3 inches of boiling water. Cover pot. Top off water as needed during cooking process.

....Bev Praver

Saleratus | Sal e ra tus |, n.— so called because it is a source of fixed air (carbon dioxide). A white crystalline substance having an alkaline taste and reaction, consisting of sodium bicarbonate. It is largely used in cooking, with sour milk (lactic acid) or cream of tartar, as a substitute for yeast. It is also an ingredient of most baking powders and is used in the preparation of effervescing drinks.

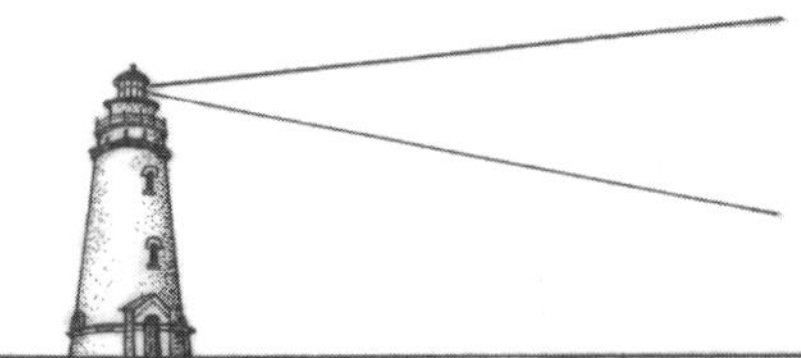

Soft Gingerbread

3 cups flour
1 "   sugar (brown)
2 "   Molasses
1 "   butter
1 "   sour milk
3 eggs - 1 teaspoon soda
Spiceaes ginger cloves
mace & salt
Bake slowly & well

Mollies Receipt

Jelly cake or sponge
2 cups sugar
6 eggs –   1/2 cup milk
5 tablespoo butter melted
3 cups of flour
1 teaspoons baking powder

Mrs. March Muffins

1 pt. flour sifted with 2 heaping teaspoonfuls
Baking Powder- Piece of butter half as large as
an egg- 3 tablespoonfuls sugar- 1 teaspoonful
sweet milk. Bake quickly in hot muffin tins- 2 eggs

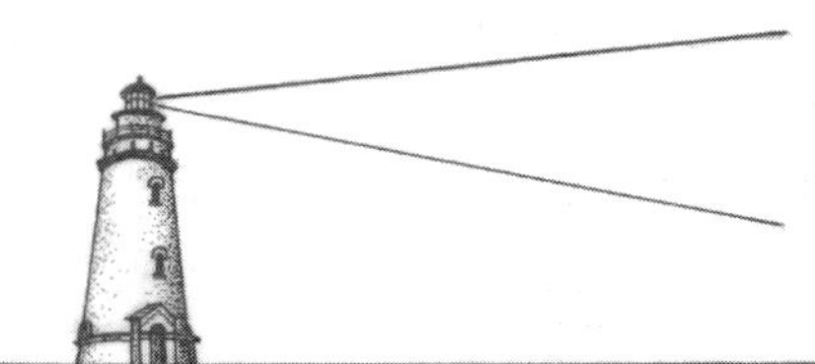

Sponge Cake

1 cup sugar   1/2 cup cold water
1 "   flour.   2 teaspoons of baking powder
one teaspoon lemon   1/2 teaspoon salt
2 eggs
bet the eggs as little as possible
& bet up quickly & bake slowly

Suet Pudding

1 cup of chopped suet
"   "   " Molasses
"   "   " sour milk
"   "   " Raisins
4 "   " flour
1 teaspoon soda – Flaver
with cinnomun Boil for 2 hours

Sauce for Pudding

1 cup sugar   1/2 cup butter
2 teaspoon flour stir butter & sugar together put about 1pt. of boiled water &
sture in the flour. flaver to sute

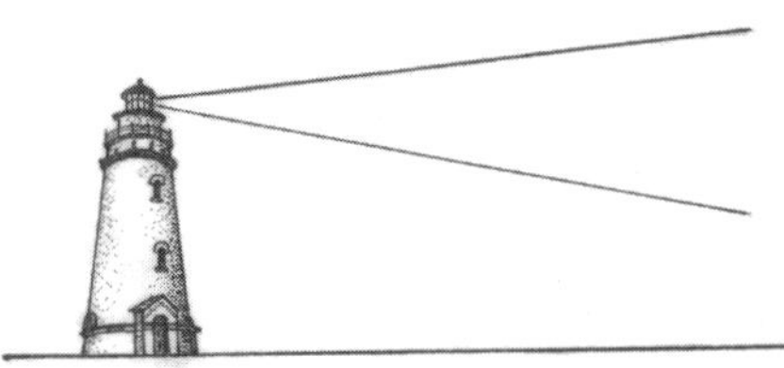

Rolpoly

1 pint of milk   one quart of flower
one half teaspoonfull soda

Add milk and soda
1 teaspoon cream of tarter
butter size of an egg
Cut it into flower

Roll it one inch thick as soft as you can
have it – Spread berries or fruit - over this
sprinkle with Sugar
roll it – up and steam one hour

Rice Puding

a quart of milk
1 cup of rice
1 small cup molasses
1 quarter of a teaspoon salt
bake slowly tow hours or
until the rice looks red like indian meal

Note: "Indian meal" is cornmeal.   ....Bev Praver

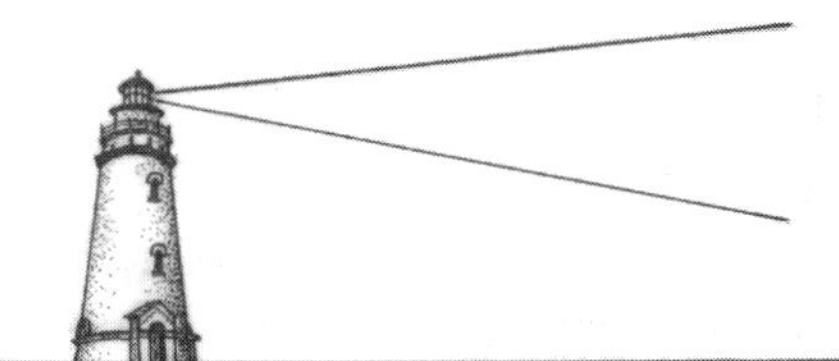

Sour Cream Cookies

One cup sour cream
one and one-half cups sugar
three eggs
two teaspoonfuls cinnamon
two tablespoonfuls chocolate
a little salt
a level teaspoonful of soda,
                                 dissolved in cream
and four cups of flour.
Roll out and bake in a moderately hot oven.

Note - I used 1/8 tsp of salt, 1-1/2 tsp. of vanilla, 3 extra large eggs and approximately 1/4-cup of additional flour to achieve the proper consistency for rolling the dough. I rolled it out to 1/4 inch thick, cut in 3-inch circles and sprinkled with a cinnamon sugar mix before baking in a 375° oven for 12 minutes. I found the texture to be a bit rubbery.

....Bev Praver

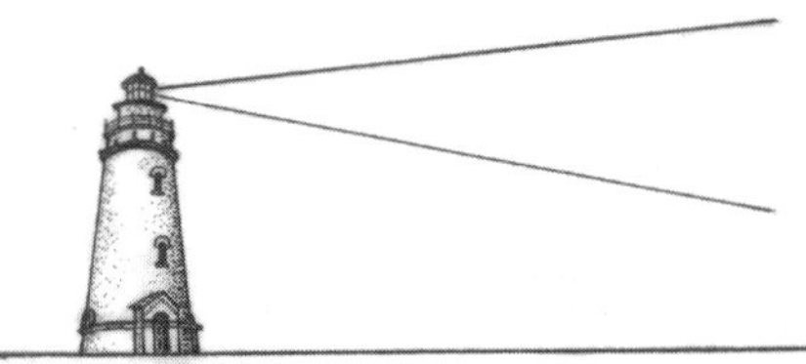

Boiled Salad Dressing

4 eggs   2 tablespoons sugar
1 tablespoon salt   1 "   dry mustard
1 cup sweet milk or cream   1 cup Vinegar
6 tablespoons Salad oil

Beat eggs light – add sugar salt & mustard then oil very sloly

Stirring hot then slowly add milk, lastly vinegar if the latter is strong dilute. cook in double boiler carefully until the consistency of boiled custard. good

Chocolate Filling

1 cup sugar
4 heaping tablespoonfuls grated chocolate
1/2 cup water, boil fifteen or twenty minutes
Add one egg and 1 tablespoonful of cornstarch
Stir, mix the cornstarch in a little water
 beat the egg, add to the cornstarch
stir into the chocolate and boil a few minutes
 stirring all the time
Flavor with a spoonful of vanilla

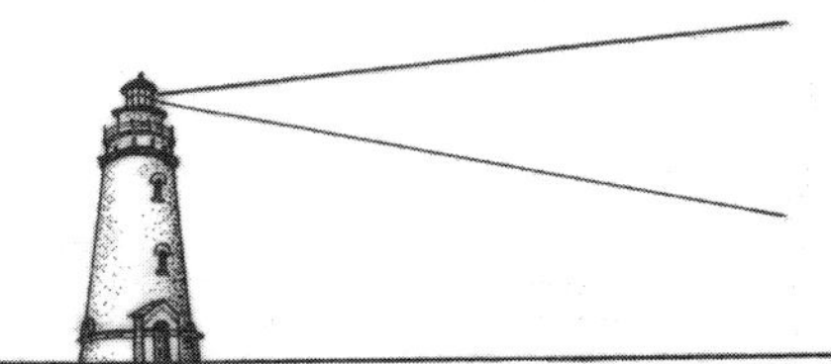

Carrot Pudding

1 cup grated carrots
1 " grated potatoes
1 cup sugar
1   "   flour
1   "   raisins
1/2 "   butter
1/2 teaspoonful cinnamon
1/2 "   "   "   cloves
pinch of salt
  Stir one teaspoonful of soda into the
    potatoes.
Flour the raisins before adding to the mixture
Grease pail well, cover tight and steam 3 hours
      Serve hot with sweet sauce

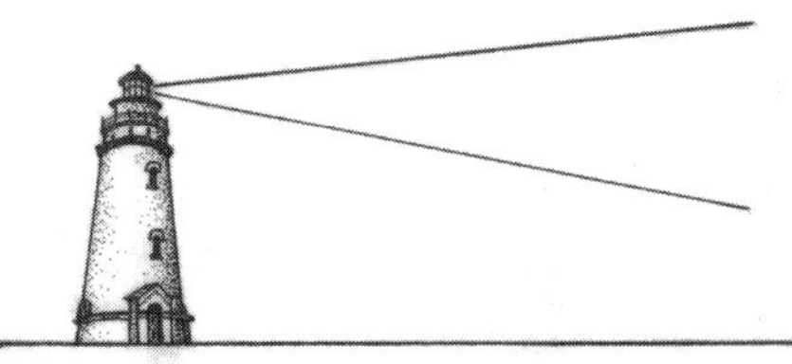

Lady Baltimore Cake

1   cupful sugar
3/4 "   " Crisco®
1/2 "   " cold water
1 tease spoon full Vanilla
2-1/2 cups flour
2-1/2 teaspoons Baking Powder
1/2 teaspoons salt
6 whites of eggs

For Cake – Cream Crisco® & sugar together. Sift together dry ingredients and add alternately with water. Add extract, beat mixture well, then fold in stiffly beaten whites of eggs. Divide into two greased & floured cake tins. Bake in moderate oven twenty five minutes.

Note: Although this recipe is in what we believe to be Elizabeth's side of the cookbook we know it had to have been written after her death. Crisco® did not exist prior to 1911, and Elizabeth died in 1886.

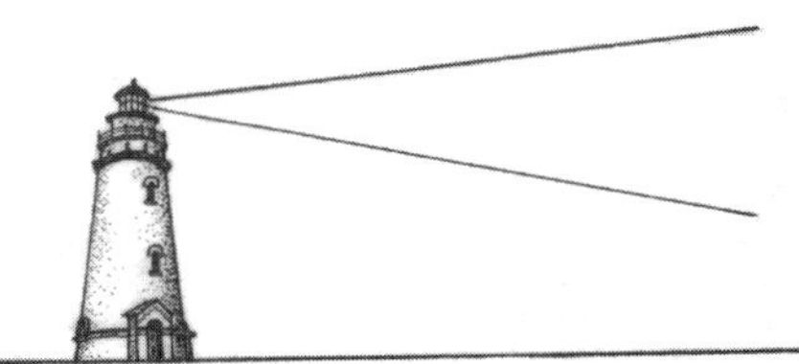

Cream Filling

1 pint of milk & small piece of Butter
put on the stove & let it come
nearly to a boil. Beat one egg &
& add two tablespoonfuls of
sugar and one of flour stir in the
hot milk & cook a little add a
little flavoring cook a little
before putting between the layers

The following recipes are incomplete in one
way or another. Some are missing ingredients
and others are missing cooking directions. See
what you can make of them.

Kateo Cookies

1 cup sugar
a good half cup butter
mix together good then add 1/2 teaspoon soda
in half cup hot water mix stiff & bake.

.....B

Note: Flour seems to missing from this recipe.

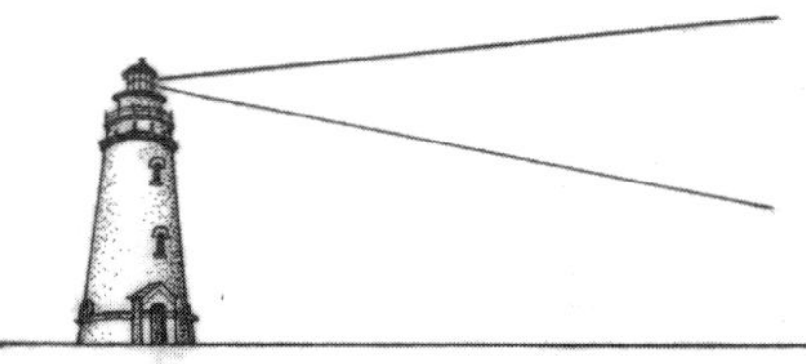

Ginger Snaps

One cup New Orleans Molasses
bring to a boil.
One cup sugar
One egg,
One tablespoonful vinegar
One tablespoonful ginger
One half tablespoonful of cinnamon
Stir together and pore Molasses over
Add one tablespoonful soda in a little hot
water and flower enough to roll

Note: New Orleans molasses was a brand of molasses and was mentioned by Mark Twain in his autobiography in chapter XIII as a sweetener added to castor oil by the local doctors. Molasses from New Orleans is considered to be some of the finest.

A brief history of molasses in America:

In the late 1600s a weathered sloop anchored in Boston Harbor. It rode low in the water because of its heavy cargo. Observers had no way of knowing that this cargo was the first of its kind ever to reach New En-

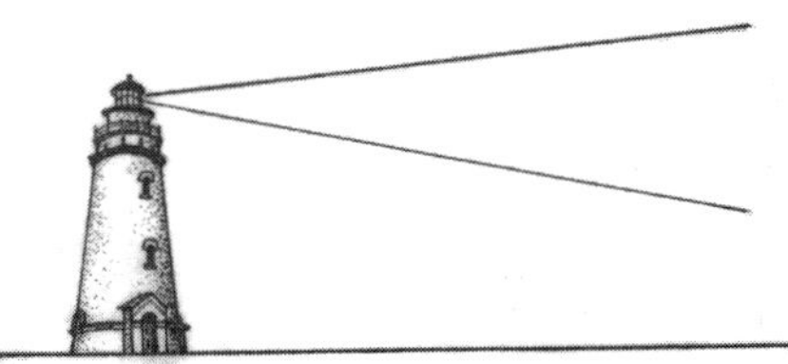

gland and was to change New England's eating and drinking habits forever.

Down in the hold were hogsheads of molasses stowed aboard weeks before in the West Indies. Soon this sweet syrup would be on every table, mixed into hasty pudding, poured over breakfast entrees, used as sweetening in countless recipes and distilled into rum,(much of which went to Africa to be traded for slaves, who were traded in the South for sugar, molasses and money).

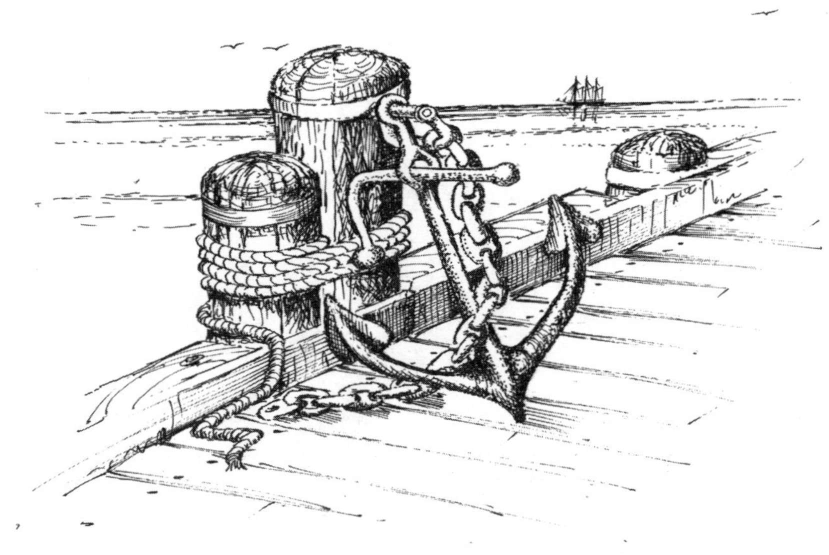

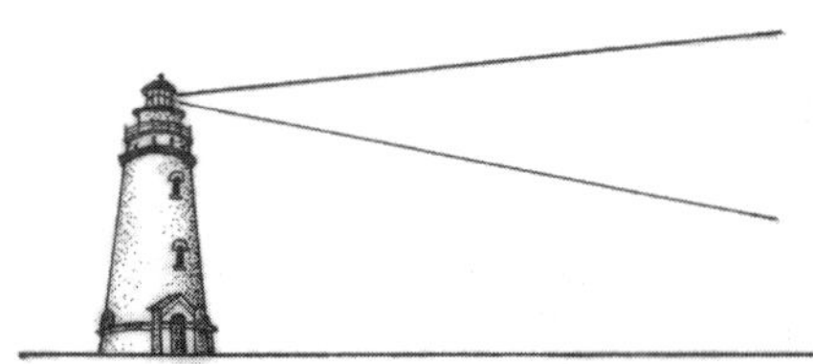

Taft (Soft?) Cake

1 cup of sugar
2   "   " flour
2 teaspoons soda
1   "   cinnamon
1|2   "   cloves and nutmeg
3-1|2 tablespoons chocolate
1 tablespoon cornstarch
stir and add 1-1|2 cups of apple sauce
1|2 cup melted butter

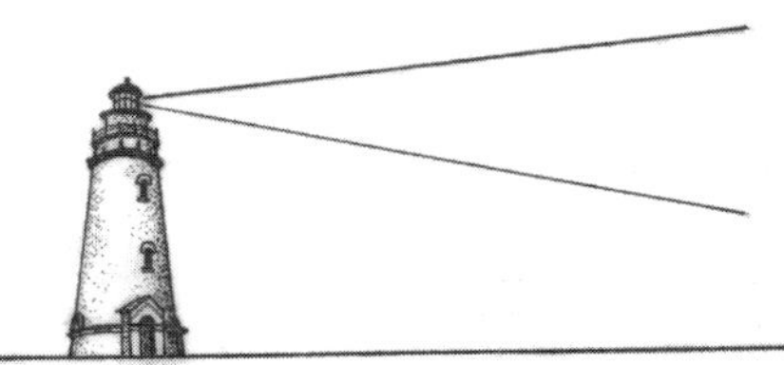

Mrs. M. Winchester
2912 Wheeler St.
  Berkeley, Cal
(This was written at the top of the original page.)

Jam Cake

1 cup sugar   3/4 butter
3 eggs   3 teaspoonfuls sour milk
1 cup blackberry jam
1 teaspoonful each nutmeg, cloves & cinna
    mon
1 teaspoonful soda   2 cups flour

Stella Wood

Note: Neither of these recipes had baking instructions.

Butter Milk Spice Cake

1 cup butter milk   1 cup shugar
1 cup racines chopped   1/4 butter
2 cups flour level
1 tease rounding full Soda
1= nutmeg   1=cloves   1=cinemeon

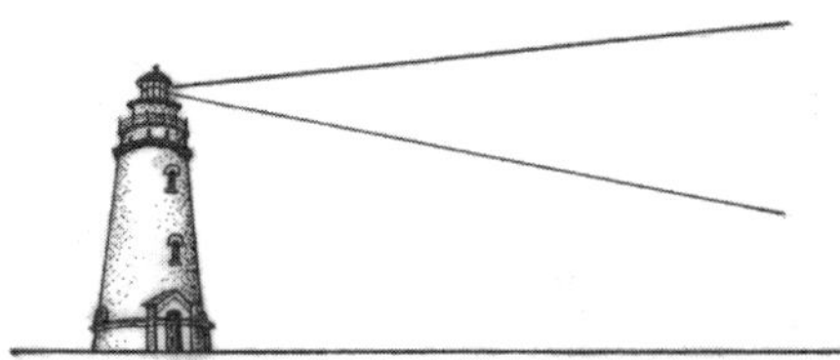

Steamed Brown Bread

2 cups cornmeal
 "   graham flour
 "   sour milk
?? Molasses
? teaspoonful salt
 "   "   of soda

Sponge Gingerbread

1 cup sugar   1 cup sour milk
small teaspoon soda   1 cup Molasses
4 eggs, the yolks & whites beaten seperately
1 cup butter   1 tablespoon of ginger
1 cup of raisins   4 cups flour
   In place of sour milk & soda you can use
sweet milk & Bg powder

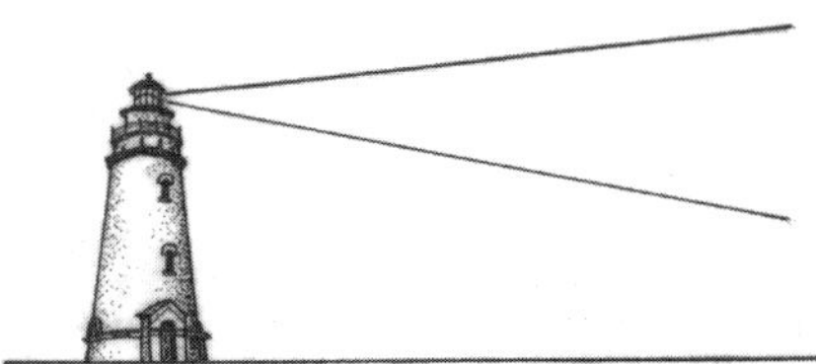

Fudge

Cook 3 cups Sugar
1 cup milk and
1 tablespoon butter
When sugar is melted
add 4 or 5 tablespoon cocoa.
Stir and boil 15 minutes
Take from fire.
Add 1 teaspoon cocoa.
Stir and boil 15 minutes
Take from fire
Add 1 teaspoon vanilla
Stir till creamery pour on
buttered plates. Cut in squares

Note: The following ingredients and cooking direction were written by themselves on a page with no name for the recipe. Does it sound like icing or candy to you?

1   cup sugar
1/2 "   milk
2 tablespoon chocolate
Cook until it strings on a fork

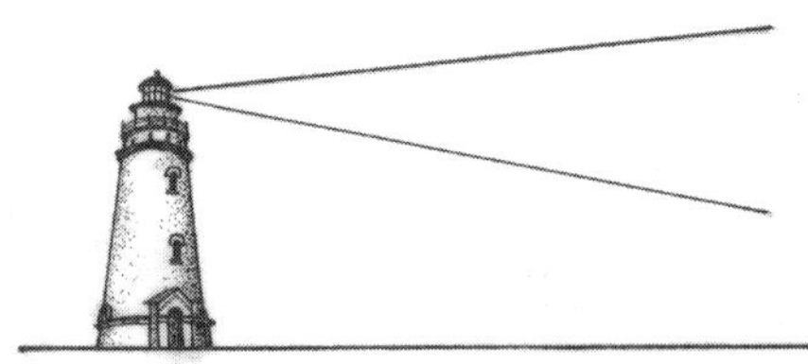

Susie Cookies

2 eggs

1 cup of sugar

1 cup of butter

2 tablespoon fuls of thick sour cream

1 teaspoonful soda

1 teaspoonful of lemon extract or juice of
lemone

flour to roll out stiff

Cream butter and sugar add beaten eggs,
and soda dissolved in cream, extract & flour.

Note: There are no cooking directions for this recipe.

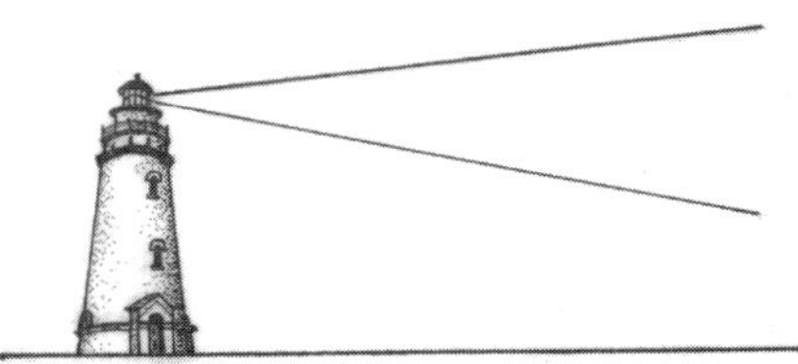

Orange Icing

Boil — 1 cup water with
2 cupful Sugar till it forms
a soft ball when tried in cold water. Then
 pour over well beaten yolks of 4 eggs.
Beat until smooth & thick
Add 1-1/2 teaspoon orange extract &
 spread at once on cake.

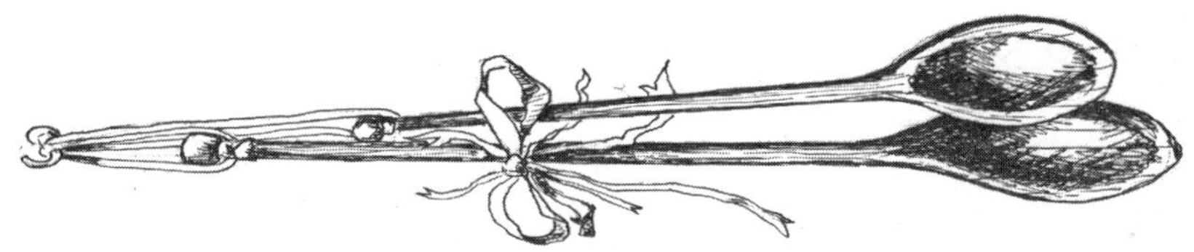

Mollasses Cookies

1/2 cup sugar
1 cup molasses
1/2 cup boiling water
1/2 cup butter or lard
1 teaspoonful ginger
2 teaspoonfuls Soda
Flour enough to roll out.

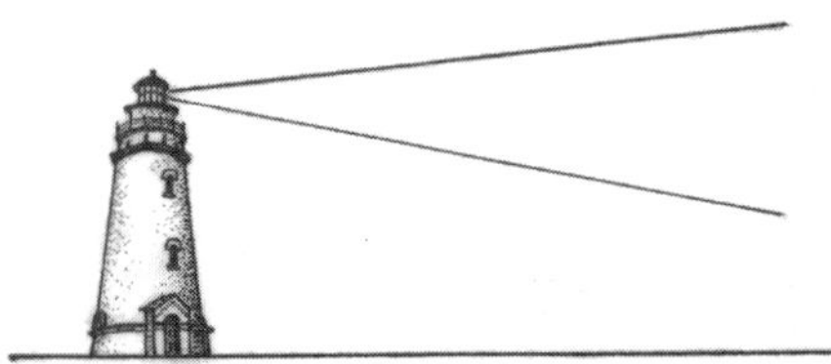

As people do today, the Thorndyke women clipped interesting and useful information from newspapers and magazines and kept the clippings handy for reference. Following are some that they pasted into their cookbooks. I have included some clippings that were torn or difficult to read. You are invited to make your own guess at the missing words.

Newspaper clippings

<u>Reliable Potato Recipes</u>

<u>Moulded Potatoes</u>

Mash half a dozen potatoes to a ....
adding a tablespoon of melted ....
two of rich cream, salt and pep....................
....e; fill custard cups with mixtu............d
bake in a quick oven: These are delicious and can be made even nicer by covering the top of the potatoes with a custard made of an egg, quarter cup of milk and salt (no sugar).

<u>Potato Dice</u>

Cut a half a dozen small potatoes into small dice and after soaking them for half an hour in salted water put them in a kettle in which two cups of lard have been brought to a boil. Cook, stirring occasionly, until all the dice are brown, then serve after draining in a w... hot dish

<u>Potato Hash</u>

Put three sliced cold potatoes into a pan with a lump of butter

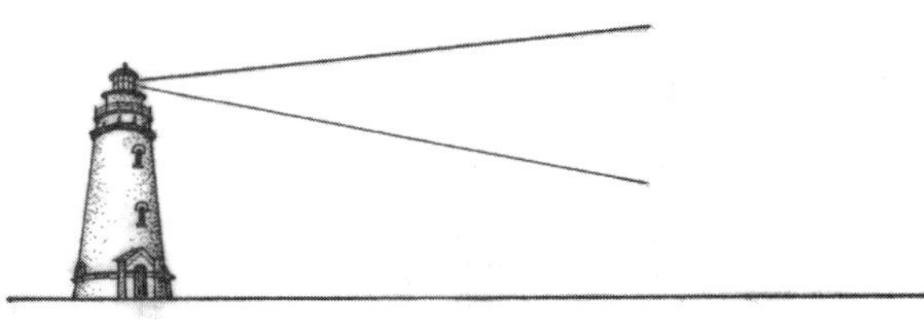

as large as a walnut and when they are light .... add two hard-boiled eggs, ...rd and a sauce made separately, of a cup of milk and a tablespoonful of cornstarch boiled until thickened. Let it all come to a boil, add salt and pepper to taste and, in season, a little parsley.

Old Potatoes Made New

Pare half a dozen potatoes and cut into pieces about as large as a walnut and boil until soft then add a sauce like the one above, let it all boil for just two minutes, taking care that the milk does not scorch, add seasoning and serve. If..... of dried peas be boiled and added the dish seems so natural as to al-most deceive the cook herself.

LEMON JUICE AS A CURE FOR PNEUMONIA

Brooklyn Physician Says It Kills Germs Incident to the Dis-ease.

NEW YORK- February 1 – Just as the statistics of the Health department and more cold weather make the outlook for the campaign against pneumonia and grip far from bright, there comes a prospect of relief from an unexpected source. As a result of careful experiments for more than a year, Dr. G. F. Clark of Brooklyn announces a lemon juice germicide for bacilli of both pneumonia and grip.

With the juice of a lemon Clark has killed germs of pneu-monia in culture tubes, and by the use of this simple remedy in cases where the symptoms of disease are well developed within the last month, he has reduced so materially their virulency that not the slightest doubt exists in his mind as to its effi-cacy. Lemon juice has been used with success for typhoid fever in London, but never before so far as known for pneumo-nia. There were 337 deaths from pneumonia in this city last week, as against 331 for the week before.

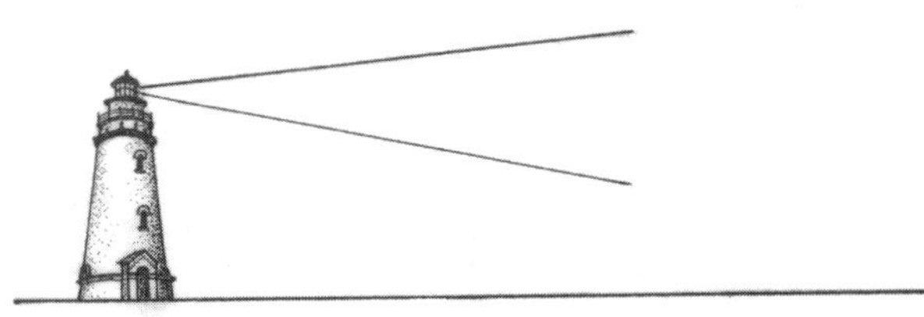

Sour Milk Gingerbread

Sour milk gingerbread, according to a Good Housekeeping recipe, is made as follows; One cup of butter and one cup of sugar creamed, one cup of molasses, one cup of sour milk, two teaspoonfuls of soda dissolved in a little hot water, half a teaspoon of salt, two teaspoonfuls of ginger, one of powdered cinnamon, two beaten eggs, flour to make a mixture as thick as ordinary cake, one cup of raisins, dredged with flour and added the last thing before baking.

QUESTION – Will you please inform me how to get rid of black scale? I read an article in your paper some time ago concerning a remedy and clipped it out, but somehow I lost it. I have several peach trees, two of which are literally covered with the scale; also two orange trees. – C. I., San Pedro

ANSWER – If you are sure the scale on your peach trees is black scale, spray them as soon as the leaves fall with a 7 per cent distillate spray; that is one part of 28 degree distillate to 14 parts of water. If your spray pump is not equipped with a good agitator, dissolve enough whale oil soap in the water to make a strong soap suds before adding the distillate. If possible arrange to have your orange trees fumigated. If not, give them a thorough spraying at once with resin wash, made as follows: Resin, 20 pounds; 88 per cent caustic soda, seven pounds; fish oil, three pints; water, 100 gallons. The resin, caustic soda and fish oil, together with a couple of gallons of water, should be boiled for two hours and then the rest of the water added. Of course you won't need this quantity for two trees, but whatever quantity you make use the ingredients in the above proportion. This is the best black scale spray for citrus trees. However, fairly good results are obtained on black

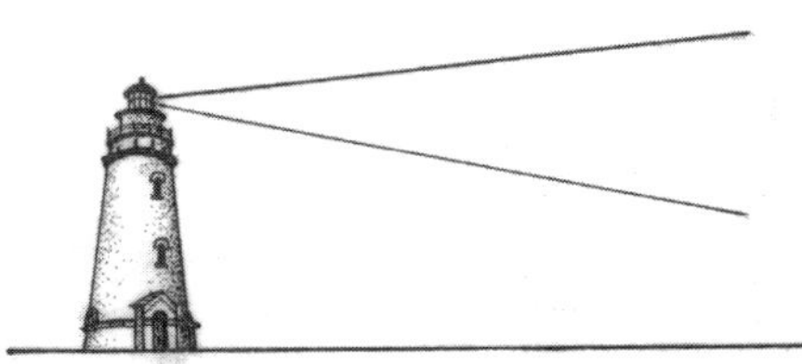

scale with a mixture of one pound of Gold Dust washing powder to five gallons of water. Owing to its being so easy to
prepare, this latter spray may prove the best for you to use as
you only have two trees. Be thorough. More than one spraying
may be necessary –
A. C. Fleury

Note: "Fairbank's Gold Dust Washing Powder - The Many Purpose Cleaner", was produced by the N. K. Fairbanks Soap Company. The business started in 1897 and eventually folded in the 1930s.

recipe from an insert in H-O OATMEAL box:

WHY NOT TRY THIS BREAD?
YOU'LL LIKE IT!

Make your white flour go further, get more nutriment from
each loaf and experience a new delight in bread-baking.
Try the recipes for H-O OATMEAL Bread – printed on the
other side of this slip. H-O Bread is a pleasant change from
"White Flour" Bread; the children will like it, and the fact that
H-O OATMEAL has already been cooked by our special pro-
cess- makes the loaf digestible and tasty.
Be sure to mix ingredients carefully as directed, have a hot
oven, and use good judgment as a first-class baker should.

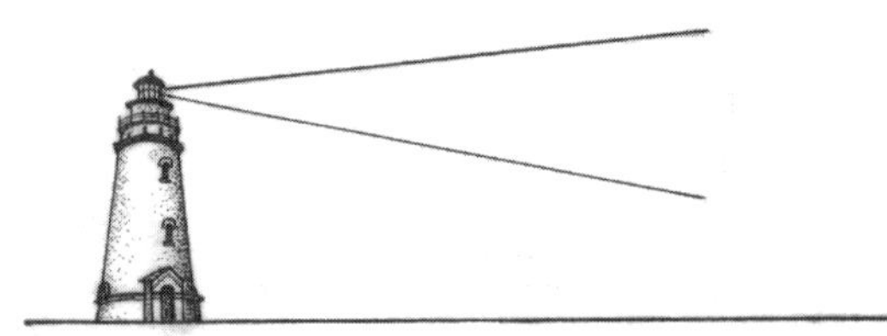

RECIPES FOR "H-O" BREAD

2½ cups H-O OATMEAL. Pour 2½ cups boiling water over same; let stand 1 or 1½ hours. Then add small cake yeast (1c. cake) dissolved in ½ cup luke warm water. Add ½ cup molasses (may be omitted), 1 teaspoonful salt, 2 tablespoonfuls shortening. Stir well. Add 5 cups wheat flour and mix well.
 Let raise; mold into 2 loaves; bake 1 hour.

———————————————————

1 cup H-O OATMEAL – put in dish – pour over 1 cup boiling water – and let stand until cool enough to put in yeast. Add ½ cake compressed yeast (scant) dissolved in cup of luke-warm water, 2 tablespoons shortening; 2 tablespoons brown sugar; 1 tablespoon molasses; ½ teaspoon salt. Enough wheat flour to make it stiff. Mix thoroughly.
Let raise – then mix well – shape into loaves – raise again and bake.
This recipe makes 1 large loaf, or 2 small loaves.

————————————————————-

2 cups of H-O OATMEAL, 5 cups of flour, 2 cups of boiling water, ½ cup molasses, ½ tablespoon salt, 1 tablespoon butter, 1 cake of compressed yeast dissolved in ½ cup of luke-warm water. Add boiling water to oatmeal and let stand 1 hour; add molasses, salt, butter, dissolved yeast cake and flour; let raise until double in bulk, beat thoroughly – use hand to shape – turn into buttered bread pans, let raise again, and bake. 2 loaves or 4 small ones.

———————————————————-

Let 1 cup H-O OATMEAL stand in 2 cups boiling water for 1 hour; add ½ tablespoonful shortening, ½ tablespoon salt, ½ cup molasses, ½ cake yeast dissolved in ½ cup warm water and a little soda, 5 cups wheat flour.
Mix well and bake 45 minutes. Makes 2 loaves.

The H-O Company, Buffalo, N.Y.
Makers of H-O, Force and Presto

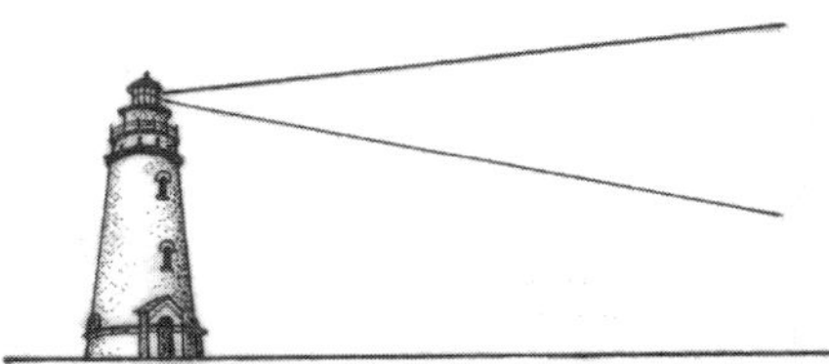

In 1913 the United States imported more than 38,000,000 tons of grass and clover seed, 13,000,000 of which came from Germany. In 1915 the importations were not heavy, but over three-fourths of them came from France.

Fresh or canned rhubarb is useful for cleaning aluminum cooking utensils. One or two stalks, either fresh or canned, cut in small pieces are added to each quart of water and boiled in the discolored kettle until it is clean.

Spain devotes 3,500,000 acres to olives.

Note: Aluminum cookware was first produced by the Pittsburg Reduction Company, later called Aluminum Company of America (ALCOA), in 1892.

TO RELIEVE CATTARHAL DEAFNESS AND HEAD NOISES
If you have cattarhal deafness or head noises go to your druggist and get 1 ounce of Parmint (double strength) and add to it $\frac{1}{4}$ pint of hot water and 4 ounces of granulated sugar. Take one teaspoonful four times a day.

This will bring quick relief from the distressing head noises. Clogged nostrils should open, breathing become easy and the mucus stop dropping into the throat.

It is easy to prepare, costs little and is pleasant to take. Anyone who has catarrhal deafness or head noises should give this prescription a trial.

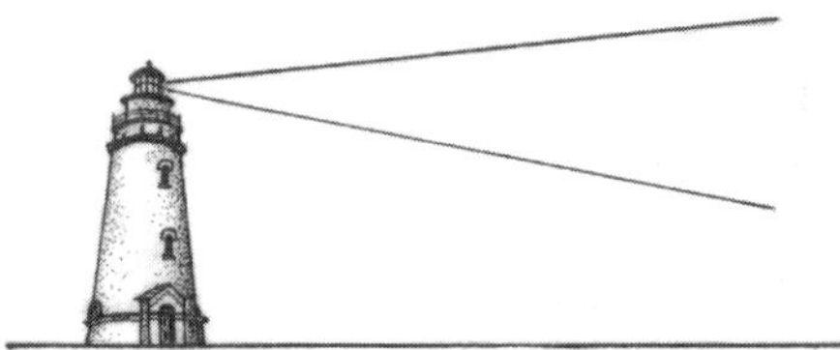

Note: The next two recipes are cut from facing pages of the same magazine or newspaper.

**Appetizing and wholesome as well as economical.
Will keep for 2 or 3 weeks**

EGGLESS, MILKLESS, BUTTERLESS CAKE

1 cup brown sugar
1-$\frac{1}{4}$ cups water
1 cup seeded raisins
2 ounces citron, cut fine
1/3 cup shortening

1 teaspoon nutmeg
1 teaspoon cinnamon
$\frac{1}{2}$ teaspoon salt
2 cups flour

5 teaspoons Royal Baking Powder

DIRECTIONS: – Boil sugar, water, fruit, shortening, salt and spices together in saucepan 3 minutes. When cool, add flour and baking powder which have been sifted together. Mix well, bake in loaf pan about 45 minutes.

(the old method (Fruit Cake) called for two eggs.)

**Royal Baking Powder is made from
adds none but health**

No Alum

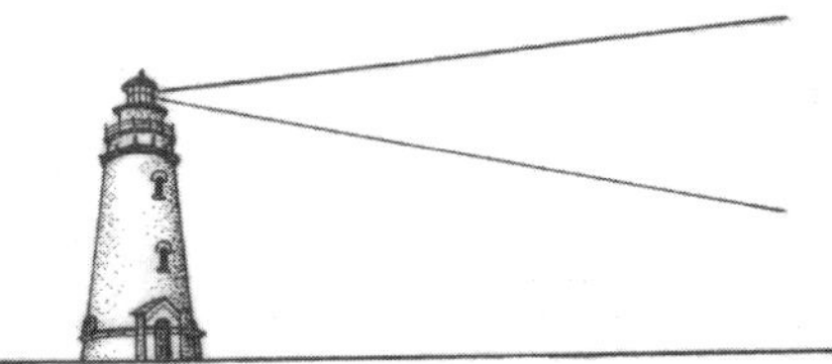

A good cake to adopt for a regular standard dessert; delicious and will please everybody

CHOCOLATE LAYER CAKE

2 eggs   2 cups flour
1-½ cups sugar   4 teaspoons Royal baking Powder
1 cup milk   ¼ teaspoon salt
                    1 teaspoon vanilla

DIRECTIONS: - Beat egg yolks until thick: add sugar gradually and beat well. Add vanilla, milk and stiffly beaten whites of eggs; add flour, baking powder and salt, which have been sifted together. Bake in three greased cake pans about 15 minutes in a hot oven.

CHOCOLATE ICING

1-½ cups granulated sugar   3 tablespoons cocoa
¾ cup cold water   1 teaspoon vanilla
        2 teaspoons Royal Baking Powder

DIRECTIONS: - Mix sugar, water, baking powder, and cocoa in a saucepan and boil without stirring until mixture makes a soft ball when tested in cold water. Remove from fire and when bubbling has stopped, pour on wet platter. Cool, add vanilla and work up with knife until thick enough to spread between layers and top of cake.
(the old method called for 3 eggs)

Cream of Tartar, derived from Grapes and ful qualities of the food.

No Phosphate

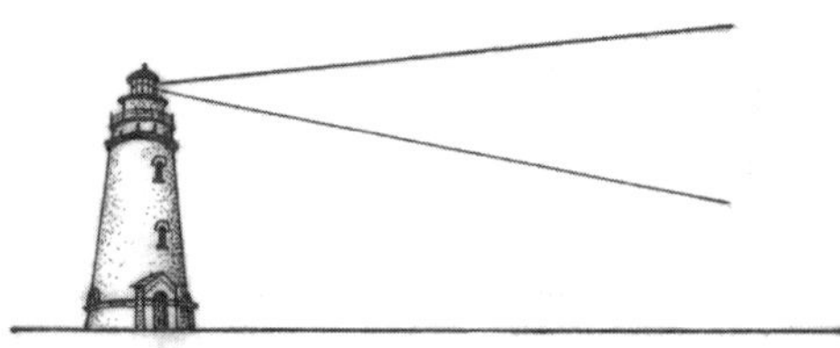

Our Prize
Winning Recipe

Sent in by Mrs. Laura Harrington, 1050 Pismo Street,
San Luis Obispo, Calif.

We sincerely thank all the people who forwarded their
recipes.

Favorite
Pineapple Lemon Pie

1-1/4 cups of rich milk
2 egg yolks
1/4 teaspoon salt
1/4 cup lemon juice
1 tablespoon butter
1 teaspoon grated lemon

1 cup sugar
3 tablespoons of cornstarch
1 cup drained grated pineapple

Scald milk, add sugar, salt & cornstarch which have been well blended. Cook 15 minutes on top of double boiler (or until thick and transparent) stirring constantly. Pour small amount of mixture over the beaten egg yolks, then add the egg mixture to the milk mixture in double boiler and cook for about three minutes, stirring constantly. Just before removing from the fire add the lemon juice, lemon rind, butter and grated pineapple; beat with a heavy spoon. Turn into a baked pie shell, cover with a meringue made from the whites; beat whites until foamy, add $\frac{1}{4}$ teaspoon cream of tartar, beat until thick, then add four tablespoons of powdered sugar—one at a time and beat until heavy. Cover pie with meringue and bake in a slow oven about 15 minutes.

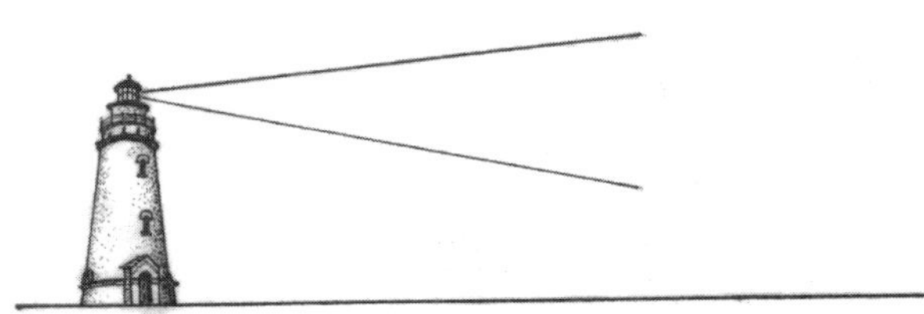

DEE-LICIOUS LEMON PIE

1-1/2 cups sugar
5 tablespoons cornstarch
Dash of salt
6 tablespoons lemon juice
2 tablespoons butter or margarine

4 eggs beaten separately
Grated rind of 1 lemon
1-1/2 cups boiling water

Mix the sugar and cornstarch together very thoroughly. Add the salt and boiling water, then cook together, stirring constantly, over hot water 8 minutes, When nearly done add the butter or margarine. Beat the egg yolks enough to blend, add the grated rind and lemon juice. Combine with the cornstarch mixture and cook for two minutes more. Set aside to cool. Pile into a baked cooled pastry shell. Cover the top with meringue made from egg whites, using $\frac{1}{2}$ cup of sugar (2 tablespoons to each egg white). Bake until meringue is browned, in a moderately slow (325 degree F.) oven about twenty minutes.

Variation: Two of the egg whites may be stiffly beaten and folded into the filling, if desired, making a meringue of the remaining egg whites — and four tablespoons of sugar.

Note: Margarine was invented in France in 1870. Production began in this country around 1873.

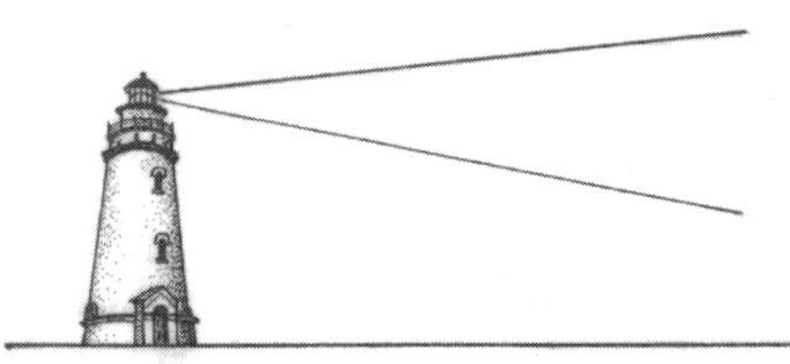

The following recipes are from Margaret's section of the original cookbook. Very few of the recipes in this section are complete. It was presumed that one knew how to bake a cake. When one cooked on a coal or wood stove, much depended on one's knowledge of one's own stove. So when Margaret wrote down a recipe for her own use she didn't bother with cooking instructions. She knew how to cook!

Corn Meal Puffs

Scald a full cup of milk add one tablespoon of butter & one fourth teaspoon of salt then grandly (gradually) stir in one half of cup of cornmeal cook a few minutes Stiring constantly then cool beat tow (two) eggs lightly add one fourth cup of flour & tow (two) teaspoon of beaking (baking) powder Sifted together mix thoroughly turn into hot buttered muffin panes & bake fifteen to twenty minutes in a hot oven this recipe makes twelve delicios (delicious) puffs.

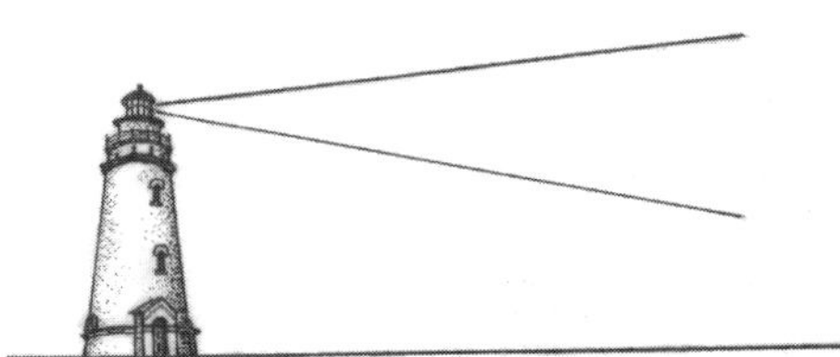

Brown Bread

One & one half cups of cornmeal one & one half cups of flour one cup molasses one pint of sour milk tow (two) teaspoon soda one teaspoon salt Steam three hours thren (then) dry in oven.

Stewed Prunes^{Wood}

(Wood is the last name of a Thorndyke family friend.)

Pound of prunes
half pint of water
quarter cup shugar
juice of 1 Lemon

Soak prunes in warm water for 15 minutes then wash & stew in covered pan for tow(two) hours add water as needed when done add the Lemon juice.

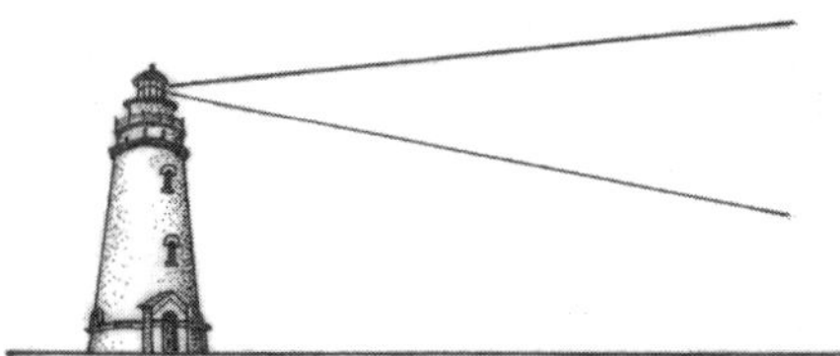

Oatmeal Cookies

1 cup molasses or Karo®
2 cups oatmeal (rolled oats)
2 cups flour
1 cup shortening
1/2 teaspoon soda
1/2 teaspoon baking powder
1 teaspoon cinnamon
1/2 teaspoon salt
4 tablespoon sweet milk

Mix and sift flour, baking powder, soda, salt and cinnamon and add to rolled oats. Then add melted shortening, milk and molasses. Mix well and drop by teaspoons on greased pan and bake in quick oven about 15 minutes or until nice brown.

Note: Karo® didn't exist before 1902.

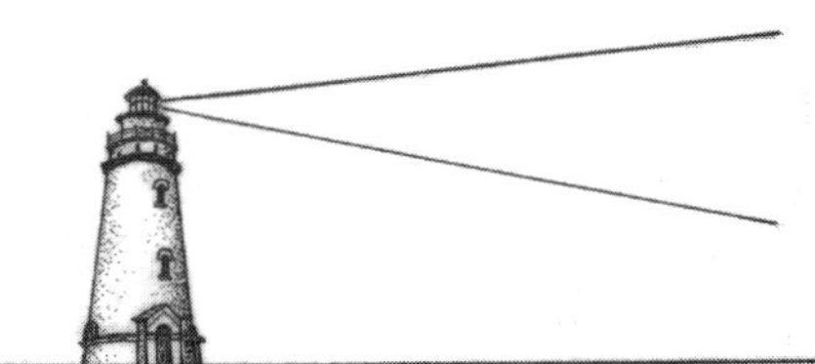

Granmother Cookies

1/2 cupful of Butter
1 cupful of sugar
1 egg
4 tablespoonfuls of hot milk
1 teaspoonful cream of tartar
1/2 cupful of Raisins
4 cupfuls of Flour

Cream the butter with sugar, add the egg well beaten and the soda in desolved milk. Sift the cream of tartar in with the flour with baking powder roll & sprinkle with sugar dip raisins in milk bake in moderate oven 12' 15' minutes. (12-15 minutes)

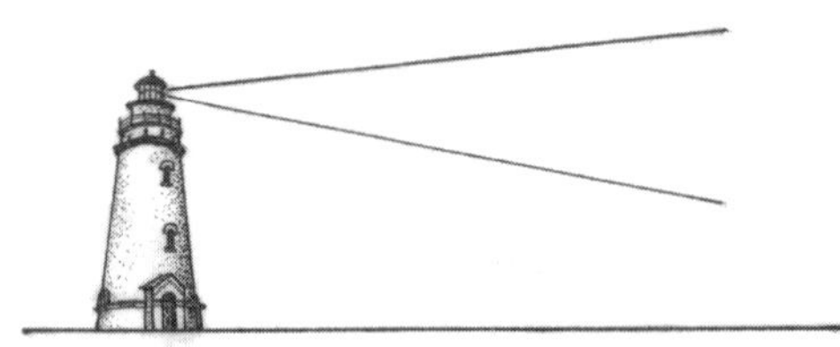

Mrs. Bosticks Boiled Icing

2/3 cup of sugar   2/3 of milk   Flavors

Boil till it threads and whip until cool enough for cake.

Lady Baltimore Cake

1 cupful sugar
3/4 cupful Crisco®
1/2 cupful cold water
Note: There is no more to this recipe on this page.

Boiled Frosting

Boil together 1 cup sugar 1/4 cup water. Beat the white of one egg until stiff. When the syrup will make a soft ball on cold water, pour it over the egg white and beat until it will spread on the cake. Chocolate, nuts, raisins or any flavoring may be added.

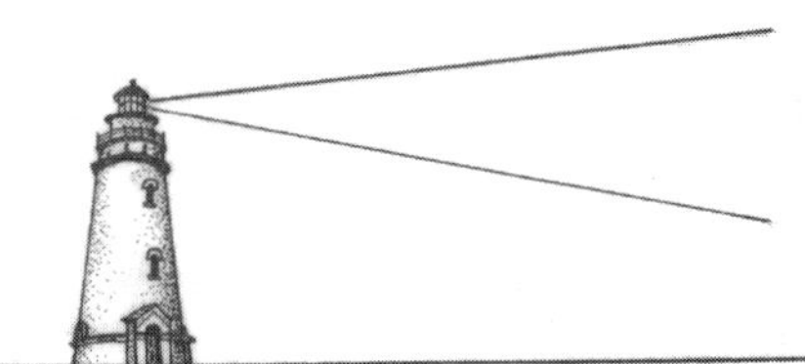

Emergency Cake

Sift together one heavy cup of flour, one scant cup sugar, 1 heaping teaspoon baking powder. Melt 1/3 cup butter then break 2 eggs into the cup and fill the cup with milk. Pour into the dry ingredients and stir thoroughly. Flavor as desired. Can be baked in layers, loaf cake or cup cakes.

Mrs. W. J. Christiansen

Note: I flavored this with 1 tsp. vanilla and baked it in a greased and floured loaf pan at 350° for 45 minutes and found it very tasty.   ....Bev Praver

Frost Drops

One & one half cups sugar tow (two) eggs one & one half cups hot water one teaspoons soda one teaspoon salt one cup raisins one teaspoon soda one teaspoon salt one cup raisins one teaspoon cinnamon stir stiff

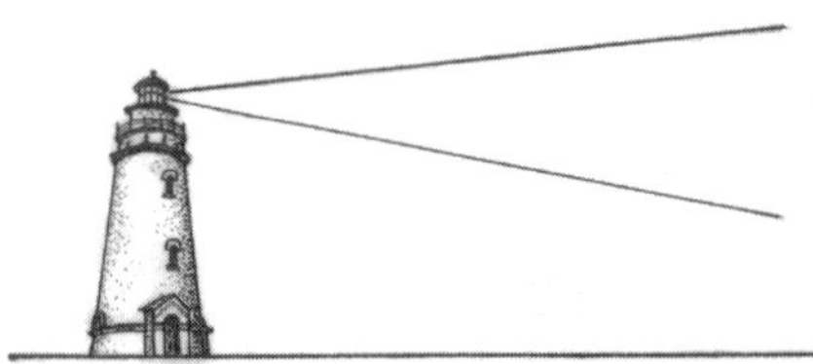

Plum Pudding *it good*

1 cup		sweet milk
1 "		molasses
1 "		rasanes, chopped
1 "		curants
1	teaspoon	cloves
1	"	soda

salt to taste

make quite thick (probably with flour)

makes four B Powder cans full

Steam 2 hours

add citron & walnuts to taste.

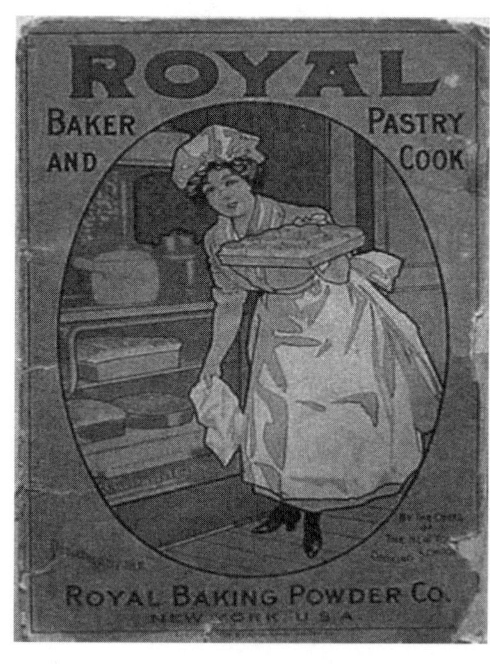

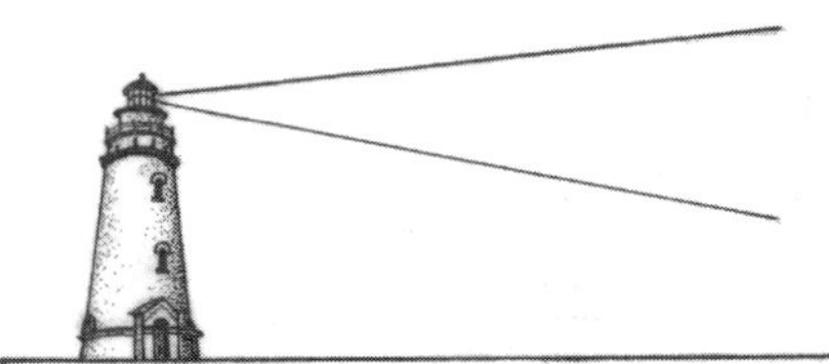

The following recipes are incomplete in one way or another. Use your knowledge and imagination to give them a try.

Salad Dressing

1 egg	2 tablespoonfuls sugar
little salt & mustard	2/3 cup vinegar
pepper	

Note: No directions

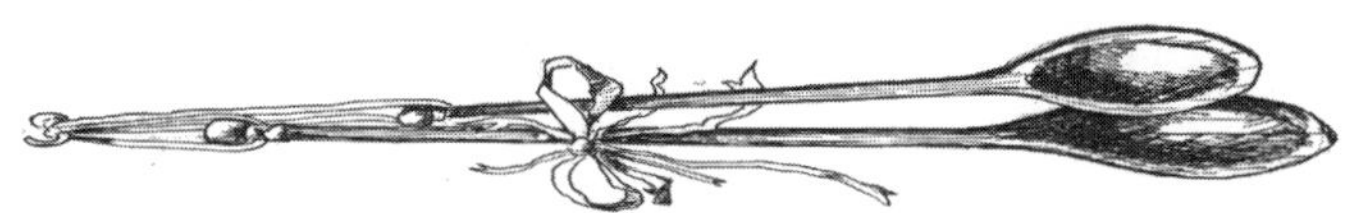

Note: The following was handwritten on the last page of the original cookbook. I presume it is a home remedy, perhaps for a poltice. - Bev Praver

1 teaspoonful ground B (Bone?)
.... "   Alum
.... " Boraric acid
.... " fluid extract of Hawaiian el
     or witch hazel
...........p of hot water

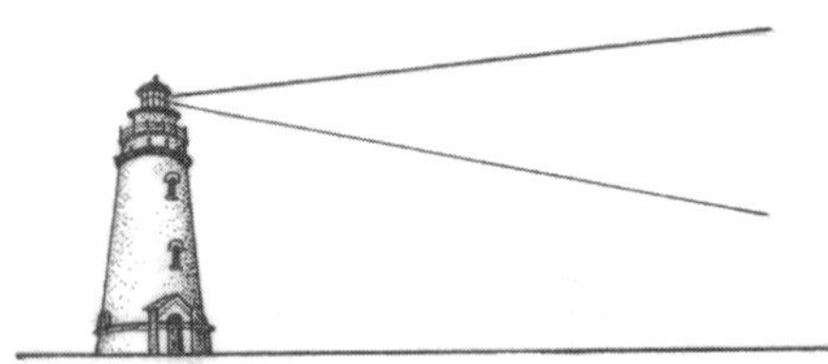

Queen of Puding

Cream the butter & Shugar
Half cup butter cup shugar
Cup & half bread crumbs
Quart of milk
3 eggs 2 whites for frosting
bake one houre
half cup of proons
Note: no directions!

Note: No title on the following recipe.

Beat 2 eggs very lightly. Add 1 cup of sugar and beat till lemon color. Stir in 1 cup of flour sifted with 1-1/2 teaspoonfuls of baking powder and 1/2 teaspoonful of salt. Add quickly 1/2 cup of hot milk and 1 tablespoon of melted butter and any desired flavoring. Bake in moderate oven. Makes a delicious layer cake if baked in sheets.

This may appear very thin batter, but do not add more flour.

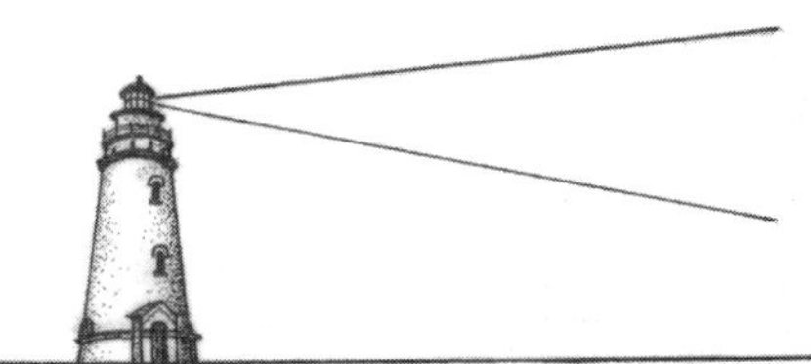

Bran or Health Muffins

1 cup of Bran
1 cup of graham flour
1 teaspoon salt
1 tablespoon Brown Sugar
4 teaspoon Royal Baking Powder
1 cup milk
3 tablespoons shortening

Note: No baking directions are given.

Note: "Whole-wheat" flour was also referred to as "graham" flour in the USA. It was invented in the mid-1800s by Sylvester Graham. Prior to that, bran was thrown out in the milling process!

Water Wafers ^{Wood}

(Wood is the last name of a family friend.)

quart sifted flour half pint of cold water teaspoonful of salt. Mix thoroughly. Roul out thin & cut into small cakes put into a pan to bake in a hot oven.

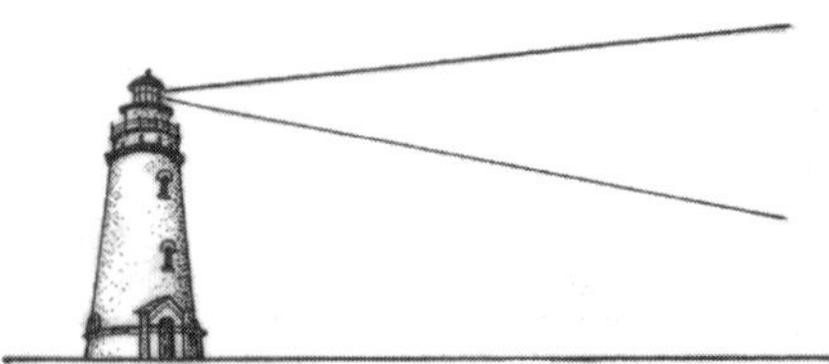

Cream Layer Cake

1 cup sugar
1 cup milk
2 cups of flour
4 teaspoons Royal baking powder
1 egg   2 table butter
1 teaspoon flavoring
2 butter layer cake
Cream filling & icing on top

Bread Pudding

La Caramel = Mix
One pint of soft Breadcrumbs with 1/2 cup-
                    ful seeded racines
2 tablespoons of sugar & 2 eggs
stir in 1 cupful of milk
Bake in a well buttered pudding dish until
brown then boil 1/2 cupfuls brown sugar
with 1/2 cupful of milk
4 tablespoonfuls of Chocolate
Stir until smooth and spread hot over the
pudding

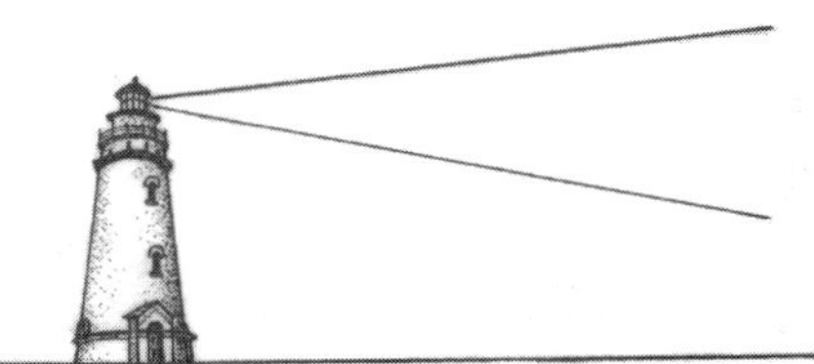

Apple Sauce Cake

1 cup shugar   1 cup butter
            cream together
1 cup applesauce   1 teaspoon soda
1 teaspoon cinnamon   1   "   cloves
1   "   alspice   a little nutmeg
2 cups of flower   choppe raisins
            Bake in loaf

Ermas Spice Cake   good

1 cup of butter
add 2 eggs   1 cup racines
3/4 cup molasses   1 cup sour milk
1 teaspoon soda   2/2 cup flower
& spice to taste

*Note: The flour amount is probably 2 1/2 cups.
No cooking directions given.*

Erma was the wife of John Emory Thorndyke.

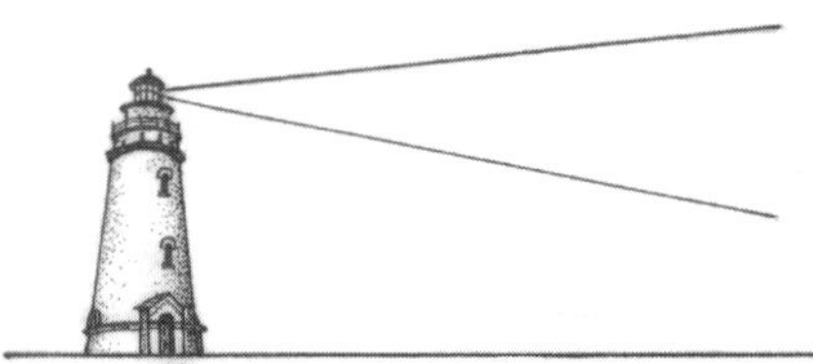

2 cups flower
1 cup shugar
 half of butter
1 table of cornstarch
3 table of chocolate
2 teasp of soda
salt & spices
half of nuts and racines
1/2 cup of apple sauce
half of butter
teaspoon Vineala

Sour Milk Doughnuts

2 cupfuls flour
Scant teaspoon soda
Grating nutmeg
Half ladle of butter
1/2 cup sugar

One egg
1/2 cup of sour milk

Note: No directions

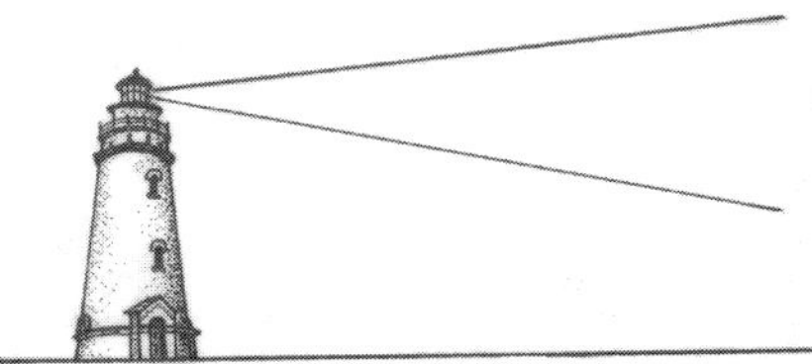

One Egg Cake   *Vivian W.*

2 cups flour (scant)
"   "   sugar sifted together
with two teaspoon B.P.
1 egg 3 tablespoonsful of melted butter in a
cup, fill the cup with milk and stir all together.

Notes: There are no cooking instructions for this recipe.
Vivian Webb is the daughter of Maud Rogers
Thorndyke's half sister, Lois Shaug Webb. Vivian had
a twin sister, Lillian.

Lightening Cake

1 scant cup sugar   1-1/2 cup of flour
1-1/2 teaspoon baking powder
Mix this thoroughly together. Then take same
cup and break two eggs into the cup and finish
filling the cup up with milk. Empty this into the
flour and stirr well. Then add two tablespoon full
of melted butter and stirr well and add flavoring
to suit the taste.

This makes a three layer cake but the same
recipt will make a good loaf cake if you use 2 cup
of flour instead of 1-1/2 .

Florence Langworthy's cake

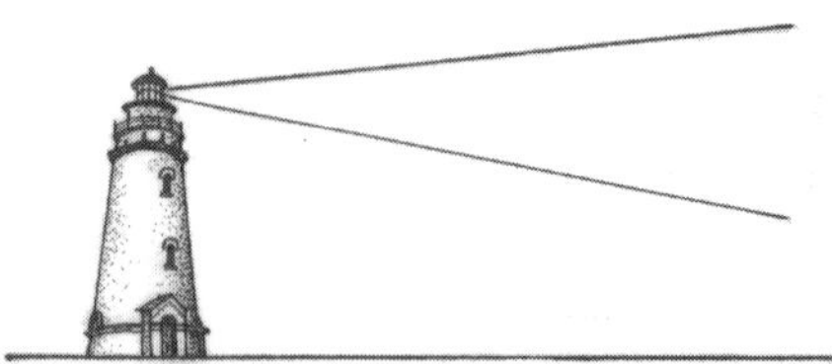

Ginger Snaps   *Lois W.*

1 cup of sugar

1/2 cup butter   two eggs   1 cup molasses

1 tablespoon of cinnamon

2 tablespoon of ginger   1 teaspoon of soda

flour to make very stiff

(mix smoothe and bake quick)

Note: Lois Shaug Webb is a half sister to Erma Rogers Thorndyke and Maud Rogers Thorndyke.

Lemon Pie

1 pint boiling water   8 tablespoon sugar

2 tablespoon cornstarch   juice of one lemon

yolkes of 2 eggs

beat whites of two eggs with 2 tablespoons

sugar for top of each pie.

One Egg Cake

1 cup sugar   butter size of egg (creamed)

1 egg beat separately   1 cup of milk

2 cups of flour   2 teaspoon of flavoring

2 teaspoon of baking powder

Note: No directions

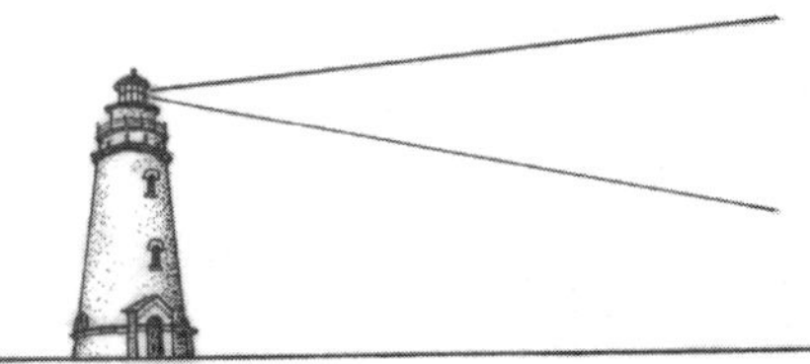

Spice Cake

1/2 cup butter   1 cup sugar
2 eggs   1/2 cup milk
1 tablespoon molasses
1 teaspoon cinnamon
1/2 "   nutmeg
1/2 "   cloves
1 cup raisins
2 tablespoon baking powder
flour to thicken

Note: No cooking instructions again.

Roll Jelly Cake

4 eggs   1 cup of sugar
1 teaspoon of baking powder
flavor to taste

Bake in quick oven, turn out on a cloth, spread with jelly. Roll by keeping cloth between cake and hands. One half recepts can be used.

Note: There appears to be a lack of flour in this recipe!

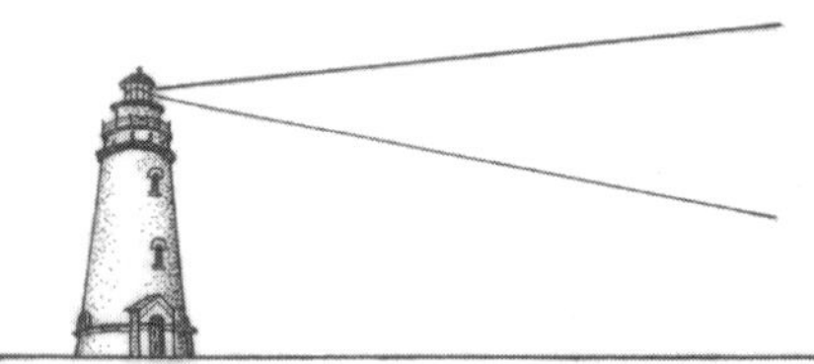

Ginger Bread

1 cup of molasses	1 — — Sagar
1 cup of sour milk	1 teaspoon soda
1 of 2 – ginger	2 eggs
spices to taste	1 cup of Raisins
flour to make a stiff batter	

Everyday Cake *Lillie Evans*

Beat 2 eggs very lightly. Add 1 cup of sugar and beat till lemon color. Stir in 1 cup of flour sifted with 1-1/2 teaspoonfuls of baking powder and 1/2 teaspoonful of salt. Add quickly 1/2 cup of hot milk and 1 tablespoon of melted butter and any desired flavoring. Bake in moderate oven.

Makes a delicious layer cake if baked in sheets.

This may appear very thin batter, but do not add more flour.

Note: Lillie Evans is the daughter-in-law of Mary Jarmon Evans, who is a sister of Elizabeth and Margaret.

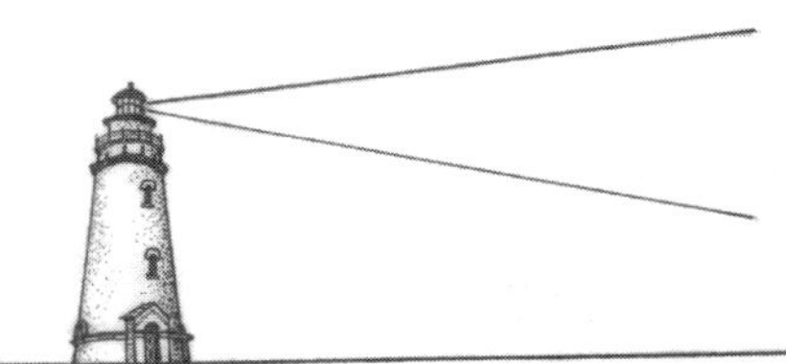

Coffee Pudding

1 quart bread crumbs or cracker crumbs
moisten with coffee
until soft. use 3 eggs
spices, cinnamon, cloves
raisens, currants, citron
& 1 level teaspoon of soda

Note: No directions!

Peculiars

1 pint of flour, sifted with 1 teaspoonful baking powder, a little salt, one egg; mix with one
pint sweet milk, beat well to a batter, and bake
quick in buttered gem pans already hot.

*Note: Gem Pans are miniature muffin pans in which
the diameter of each indentation is 1-1/4 to 2 inches.*
....Bev Praver

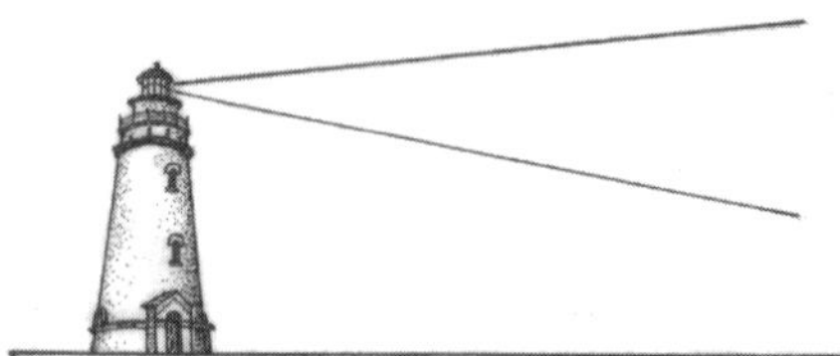

Mince Meat *Erma*

2 lb. fresh lean meat boiled & when cold
chop fine

Boil 4 Or 5 lbs. so as to make 2 lbs. after
being boiled and chopped

2 lbs. beef suet chopped fine

5 lbs. apples   2 lbs. currants

3 lbs. rainins seeded & chopped

3/4 lbs. citron   2 tablespoons cinnamon

1 tablespoons mace and alspice

1   "   cloves   1 tablespoon salt

2 1/2 lbs. Brown sugar   1 teaspoon nutmeg

1 qt. Sherry wine   1 pt. Brandy

If you can't (use ?) wine, you can use cider or you can leave it out.

This is Mrs. Murray's receipt. Ma always used it.

Note: Erma was the wife of John Emory Thorndyke. I believe the instruction to boil 4 or 5 lbs. of meat was written as an explanation of how to get the 2 lbs. of lean meat. ....Bev Praver

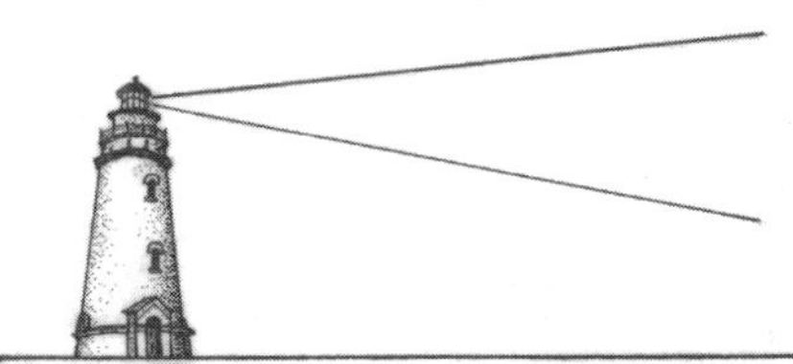

Plain Layer Cake

1 cup of sugar
3 eggs
1 cup of flour before sifting
butter size of egg
6 teaspoons of milk   Baking Powder
any flavoring desired

8 qarts. Strained Catsup

8 quarts strained tomatoes
1   tablespoon Cinnamon
1   "   Cloves
1 teaspoon full R. Pepper
5 tablespoon   mustard   1 tablespoon salt
1   "   mace   1 pt vinegar
1-1/4 sugar

<u>this is quite hot</u>

Lorin V. Thorndyke, Jr.
and
Maud Rogers Thorndyke

The

Second

Generation

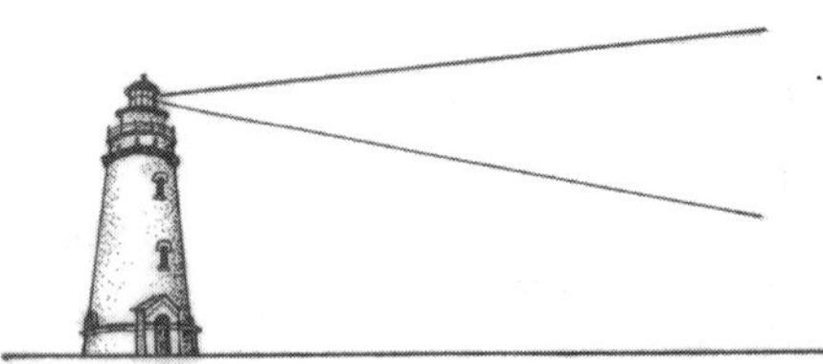

Maud Rogers Thorndyke assembled a cook-book, using a small ledger book to write in, and pasted in the recipes she'd clipped from magazines and newspapers, as well. The book begins with a handwritten recipe for beer.

Lom's Beer

1 gal. water put on stove, let it boil, then put in hops and boil 10 minutes, then add can of malt and boil 15 minutes, then add 5 cups of sugar boil 15 minutes, then take from fire and put in crock and fill it with boiling water, let it cool then add yeast, 1-1/2 cakes and small package of gelletine (sic).   *5 gal. crock*

48 or 50 pint bot.

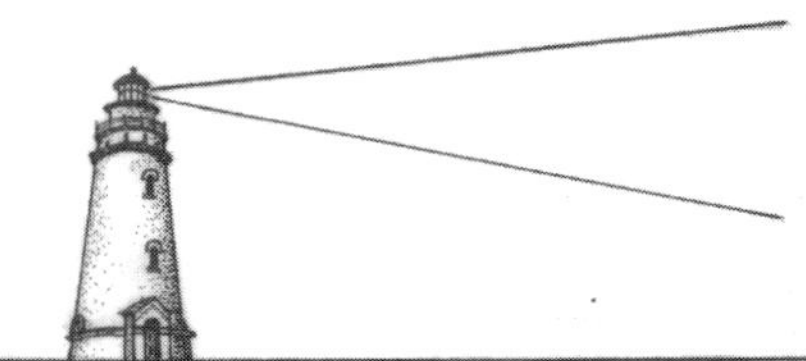

The next section of Maud's book was for cakes. These were all clipped from magazines or newspapers.

As the following recipes demonstrate, even when Maud was clipping recipes, printing exact baking instructions wasn't always considered neccessary. It was assumed that a competent housewive would know how to cook anything!

Holiday Cake

3/4 cup butter

2 cups sugar

1 cup milk

2-1/2 cups flour

3/4 teaspoon salt

2 teaspoons baking powder

Whites of 4 eggs

1 tablespoon grated lemon rind

Cream butter and sugar and mix dry ingredients. Add beaten egg whites, flour and milk and beat hard. Take out one-third of this mixture and add:

1-1/2 teaspoon cinnamon

1/2 cup citron

1 teaspoon allspice

1 cup raisins

Bake this mixture in one layer; bake other mixture in two layers.

(Continued on page 78)

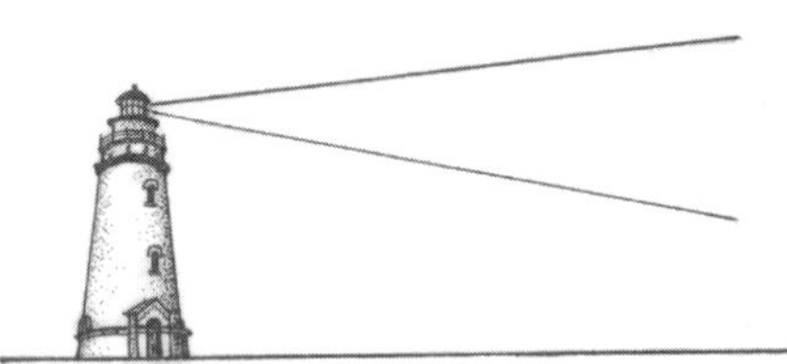

Use the spice layer in the center, with this filling between layers:

1 cup shelled walnuts   2 bottles vanilla
1 pound confectioner's sugar

Make an icing of confectioner's sugar and orange juice for the outside of the cake. Decorate with nuts and dates, if desired.

Marshmalllow Cake

1/4 cup butter   1 cup sugar
1/2 cup sweet milk   2 cups flour
2 teaspoons Watkins® Baking Powder
2 teaspoons Watkins® Lemon Extract
Whites four eggs beaten stiff and folded in.

Chocolate Cake

1/2 cup Watkins® Cocoa   1 cup sweet milk
1/2 cup white sugar   yolk of 1 egg

Boil well together and let cool.

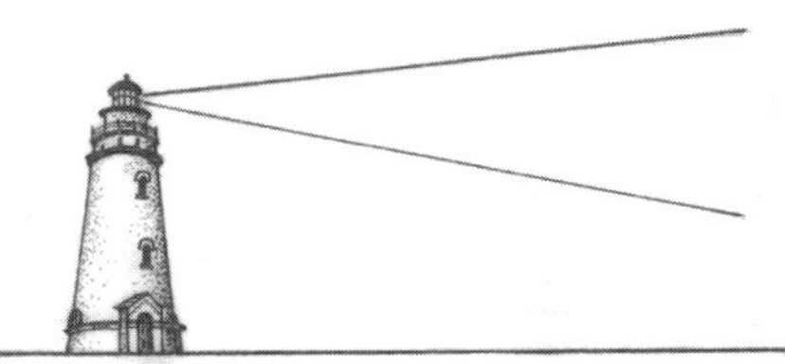

Next combine:

1 cup sugar

2 eggs

1/2 cup butter

*1/2 cup sour milk into which 1 teaspoon
        soda has been dissolved.*

*Mix both parts together and add 2 cups flour.
Bake in moderate oven in layers. Ice with chocolate icing and nuts.*

White Nut Cake

3/4 cup butter   *2-1/2 cups flour*
1-1/2 cups sugar   *Whites of 8 eggs*
1 teaspoon Watkins®Vanilla   *1/2 cup milk*
1/2 teaspoon cream of tartar
2 teaspoons Watkins®Baking Powder
1 cup walnut meats, cut in pieces

*Method: Stir butter until creamy, add sugar
gradually, mixing well, sift dry ingredients together and add nutmeats and flavoring and mix
well. Add whites of eggs beaten very stiff, fold-
ing in carefully. Bake in two greased loaf tins 35
to 45 minutes in a moderate oven.*

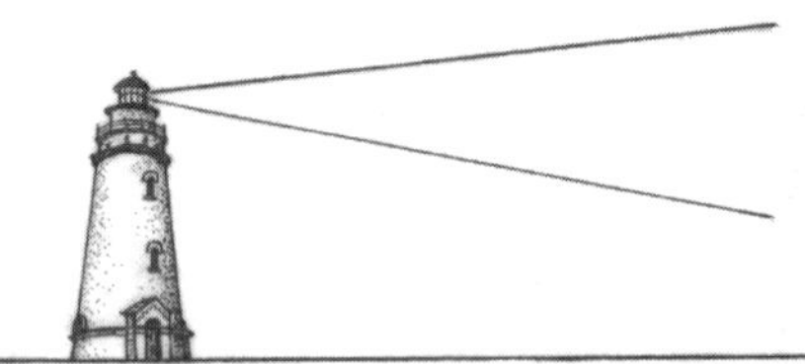

Three Cakes Made From One Recipe
But With Three Kinds of Frosting

Cake

Cream one-half cup of butter, beat in the grated rind of one orange and one cup of sugar, the beaten yolks of four eggs, and, alternately, one cup of milk and three cups of flour sifted with four teaspoonfuls and one-half of Watkins® Baking Powder. Put into three cake pans five inches square; bake twnty-five minutes in an oven at 450 degrees Fah.

Black Chocolate Cake

Melt four ounces of chocolate and one-half cup of butter in one cup of boiling water, beating until thoroughly mixed. Add two cups of sugar, one-half teaspoonful of salt, two cups of flour, and one teaspoonful and one-half of soda, sifted together; add one-half cup of thick sour milk and beat; lastly, add two eggs, beaten without separating. Pour into well-greased and floured layer-cake pans and bake twenty minutes in an oven at 400 degrees Fah. When put into pans this mixture may seem too thin to promise success, but the result is a very moist and light cake. Fill and ice with.....(the words aren't legible here)

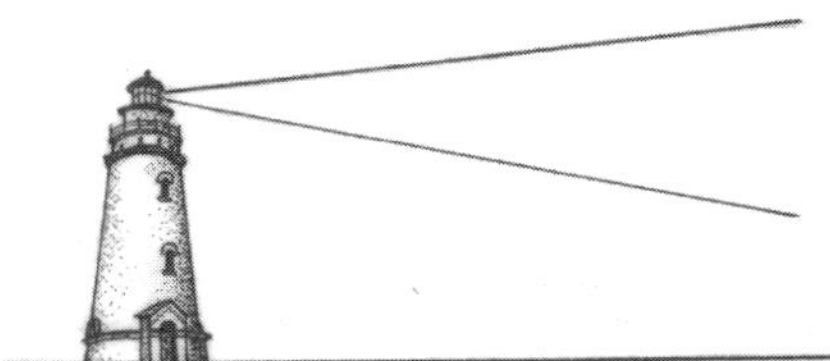

White Cake

1/2 cup of shortening   1-1/2 cups sugar
3 cups pastry flour (Globe A1 ®)
3 teaspoons baking powder
1 teaspoon salt   1 cup water
1 teaspoon lemon juice
1 teaspoon vanilla or lemon extract
4 eggs (Nulaid ®)

Cream shortening and sugar thoroughly. Sift together flour, baking powder and salt. Add lemon juice and vanilla, mix well. Stir in stiffly beaten egg whites. Pour into two oiled and floured layer pans. Bake in oven 350 degrees F. for fifteen minutes, increase to 400 degrees F. for five minutes, then back to 340 degrees F. for five minutes. Remove to wire racks and cool before spreading with icing.

Note: The earliest mention I could find of Nulaid® brand eggs is 1960. Globe A1 flour dates from at least 1943. ... Bev Praver

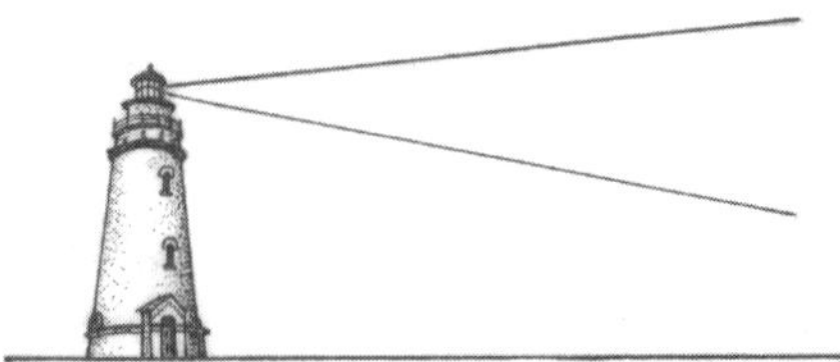

Caramel Sponge Cake

1-1/2 cups sugar
1 teaspoon Watkin's®vanilla
1-3/4 cups sifted pastry flour
4 eggs
3 level teaspoons Watkin's®Baking Powder
1/2 cup boiling water
1/4 teaspoon salt

Put 1 cup of the sugar in a pan and place the pan on the stove. Heat , stirring meanwhile, until the sugar is all melted and of a light brown color, but do not let burn. Add the boiling water and stir until all lumps are dissolved. This makes about 1 cup of syrup. Beat the 4 egg whites until stiff. Add beaten yolks and the remaining half cup of sugar. Mix salt, baking powder and flour and add to the egg mixture alternately with the hot syrup. Add vanilla. Bake like any sponge cake in a moderate oven and frost with caramel frosting.

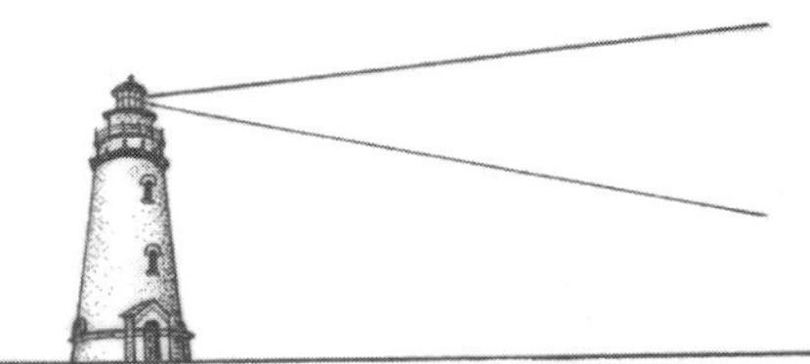

Watkins®
Strawberry Shortcake

2-1/2 cups flour	1/2 teaspoon salt
5 teaspoons Watkins® Baking Powder	
1/2 cup shortening	Scant cup of milk
Butter	Strawberries
1-1/2 cups sugar	whipped cream

Sift together flour, baking powder and salt; work in shortening and then use milk as needed to mix a soft dough. Spread the dough in two well-greased pans and bake about 15 minutes. Turn one cake on a large plate, spread with butter, cover with strawberries mixed with sugar; set the second cake above the berries, spread with butter and cover with the rest of the berries. Serve with or without cream.

Note: Watkin's® started as the J.R. Watkins Medical Company in 1868 selling natural remedies and began selling vanilla extract, black pepper and cinnamon in 1895.

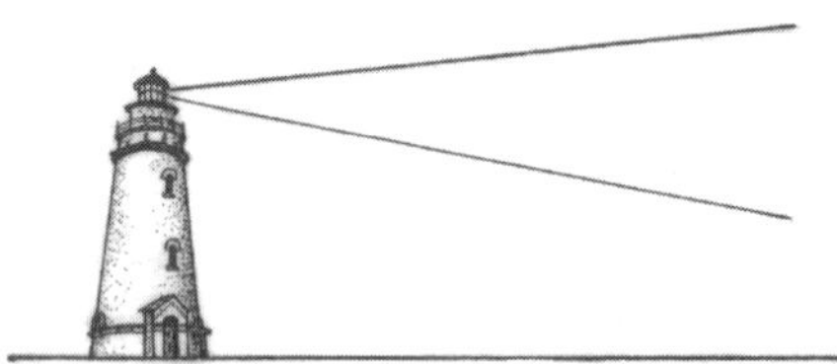

Cocoa Fudge Cake

1/2 cupful butter   1 cupful sugar
1 cupful chopped nut meats (if desired)
1 cupful flour (very scant)   3 eggs
4 tablespoonfuls Watkins®Cocoa
1 teaspoonful Watkins®Baking Powder
1 teaspoonful Watkins®Vanilla

Melt the butter, beat the eggs and add the cocoa to them, then the sugar, vanilla, flour sifted with baking powder and the nut meats, if used; stir the melted butter in last, beat well, spread in shallow pans, bake in moderate oven. Put together with cocoa icing, or marshmallow icing, as desired.

Water Melon Cake

2 cups white sugar   1 cup butter
1 cup sweet milk   Whites four eggs
1 teaspoon Watkins®Vanilla and Coum.
3 teaspoons Watkins®Quality Baking Powder. Flour enough to stiffen. Divide dough into halves. Color one red with red sugar. Add 1/2 cup raisins dredged in flour to the other half.

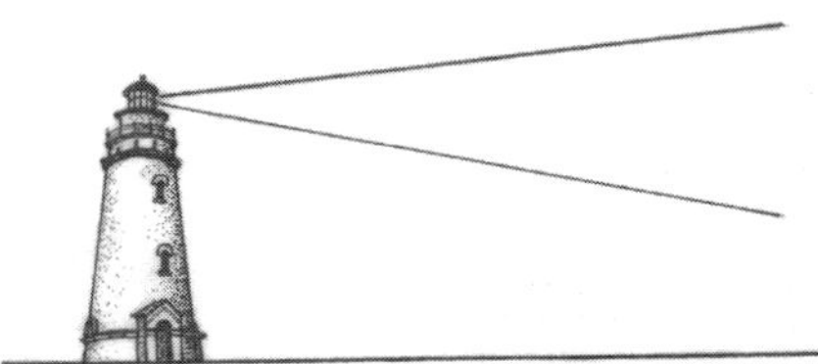

Note: Coum. is an abbreviation of Coumarin. It is the concrete essence of the tonka bean, the fruit of Dipterix (formerly Coumarouna), which is a white crystalline substance, with a vanilla-like odor, used in flavoring. Coumarin in also made artificially.

Also, once again, there are no baking instructions included. Maud knew how to bake a cake so she probably didn't feel the need to clip the instructions as the book was only meant for her own use.

Cream Puffs

1 cup hot water   1/2 cup butter

Boil together. Add 1 cup white flour while boiling. Stir to a paste and when cold stir in 3 eggs not beaten. Stir 5 minutes, put on buttered tins. Bake 30 minutes.

Filling for Cream Puffs

1 cup milk   1/2 cup sugar
1 egg   3 teaspoons flour
1 teaspoon Watkins®Vanilla and Lemon
                    extract mixed together.

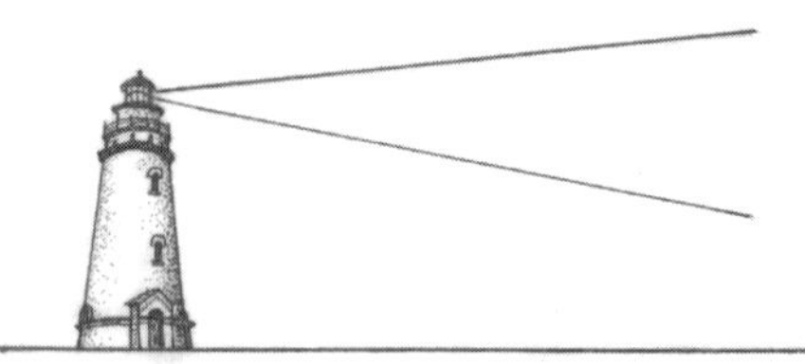

Cocoa Cake Without Eggs

2 cups brown sugar   1/2 cup lard
1/2 cup Watkins®Cocoa   2-1/2 cups flour
1 cup sour milk or buttermilk

Last of all add 1/2 cup hot water to which 1 level teaspoon soda has been added. This makes 3 big layers and is improved by adding 1 teaspoon Watkins® Vanilla

Cocoanut Cake

1 cup sugar   1 cup butter
3 cups flour   1 cup milk
1/2 teaspoon salt   4 eggs
2 teaspoons Watkins®Vanilla
3 teaspoons Watkins®Baking Powder

Cream butter and sugar together, sift flour, baking powder and salt and add alternately with the beaten yolks of eggs and milk. Beat thoroughly, then add stiffly beaten whites of eggs and flavoring and mix gently. Grease 3 layer tins, dust with

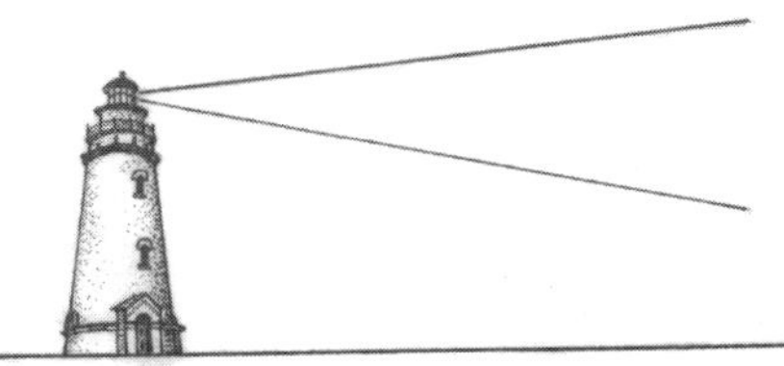

flour and divide mixture. Bake in moderate oven 20 minutes.

Note: I don't know why this is called Cocoa-nut. ....Bev Praver

Fruit Cake

1 cup shortening   1-1/2 cups brown sugar
4 eggs   3 cups flour
1 teaspoon baking powder   2 teaspoons salt
2 teaspoons cinnamon   1 teaspoon allspice
1 teaspoon ground cloves   1 cup cider
1 cup chopped citron   1 cup raisins
2 cups candied fruits, chopped   3 cups nuts
1 cup chopped figs   1 cup chopped dates

Mix shortening, sugar and egg yolks together well. Sift together spices, salt, baking powder and two cups of the flour and add alternately with the cider. Mix fruits and nuts with remaining flour and add. Finally fold in egg whites, beaten stiff, and bake in a very slow oven for about four hours.

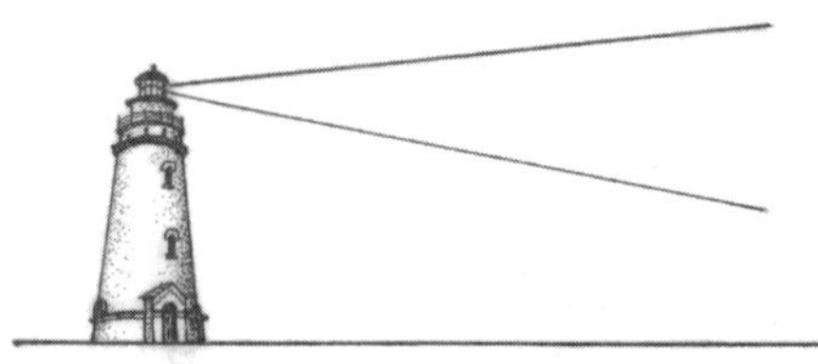

Chocolate Sponge

4 eggs (*Nulaid*®)
4 tablespoons granulated sugar
3/4 cup ground chocolate (*Ghirardelli's*®)
1 cup milk (*Dairy Delivery*)
2 tablespoons cracker crumbs, sifted
Pinch salt

Beat yolks of eggs until very light. Add gradually, beating all the time with Dover egg beater, the sugar and chocolate. When all is added, beat in gradually the milk and cracker meal. Beat egg whites very stiff and beat into the custard mixture. Pour into a well buttered ring mold or casserole. Place in a pan containing hot water to reach two-thirds of the mold. Bake in oven 330 degree F. for twenty-five minutes.

Note: The Dairy Delivery company in Millbrae California was acquired by the Borden company in 1929. In the first half of the twentieth century, milk was delivered to homes in much of the United States.

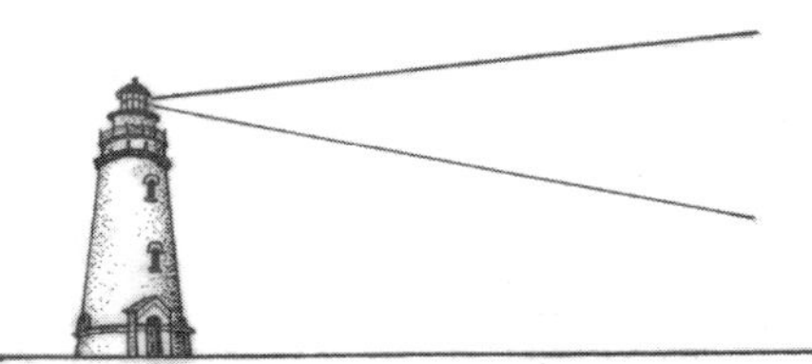

The egg beater was one of two technological innovations which was purchased in sufficient numbers to make a substantial impact on American cooking (the other was the cast-iron stove). In the Sears 1897 catalog, a "Dover" egg beater sold for 9¢. You may remember the egg beater that your mother or grandmother used.

Dover Egg Beater

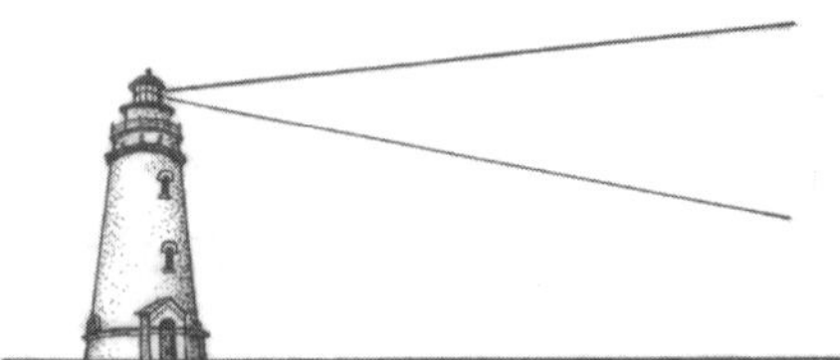

Brown Stone Front Cake

(First Part)

3/4 cup ground chocolate (Ghirardelli's®)

1/2 cup brown sugar

1 egg yolk beaten (Nulaid®)

1/2 cup milk (Dairy Delivery)

Mix ingredients and cook slowly until thick;
   cool.

(Second Part)

1/2 cup butter or substitute

1 cup brown sugar   2 eggs (Nulaid®)

1/2 cup milk (Dairy Delivery)

2 cups flour (Globe A1®)

2 teaspoons baking powder

1/4 teaspoon soda   1 teaspoon vanilla

Cream butter and sugar thoroughly; add well beaten eggs, sifted dry ingredients and milk alternately, then cooled chocolate mixture and vanilla. Beat batter until smooth. Bake in three greased layer cake pans in a moderate oven (about 350 degrees F.) 15-20 minutes. Cool and put together with 7 minute icing or a white boiled icing.

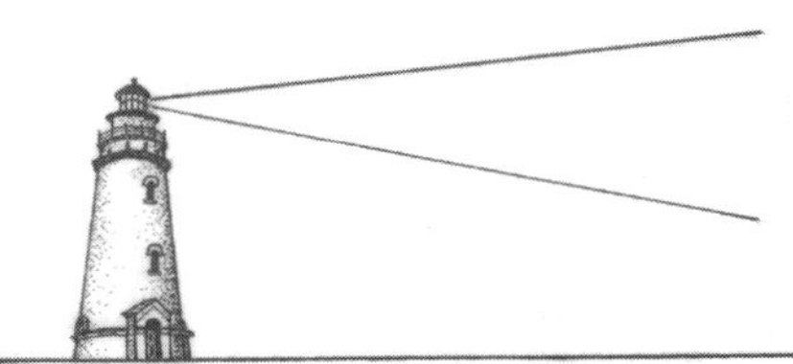

Note: The earliest reference I could find to Brown Stone Front Cake was in a 1913 cookbook referenced on the internet.   ....Bev Praver

Note: Domingo Ghirardelli began making chocvlate in California in 1852. Today the company is owned by Lindt and Sprungli Chocolate of Switzerland.

Here is another recipe for Brown Stone Front Cake that Maud clipped and saved.

Brown Stone Front Cake

1/2 cup butter	1/2 cup hot water
1-1/2 cups sugar	1/2 cup sweet milk
3/4 cup Watkins®Cocoa	2 eggs
1 teaspoon Watkins®Vanilla	2 cups flour
1 teaspoon soda	

Cream butter and sugar. Dissolve cocoa in hot water and add the eggs beaten. Add milk and flavoring. Dissolve soda in hot water and add flour. This makes a splendid cake and is a rich mahogany color.

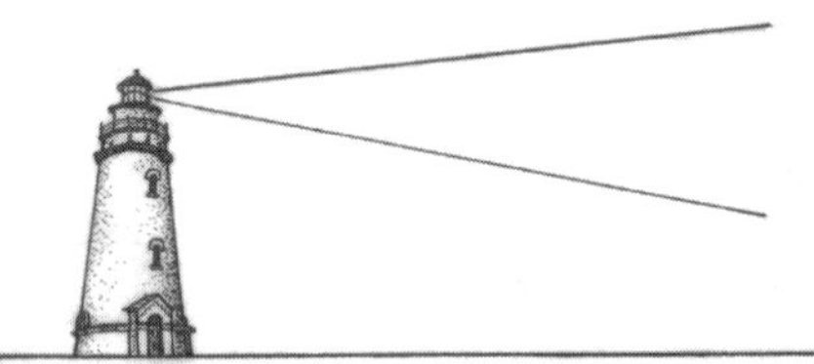

Marble Cocoa Cake

2 cups flour sifted 3 times
3 egg whites   2/3 cup sweet milk
1/2 cup butter   1 cup sugar
1/2 teaspoon Watkins®Vanilla
3 teaspoons Watkins®Baking Powder

Cream butter and sugar. Sift flour and add baking powder, then sift again. Add milk and flour alternately to creamed mixture, add flavoring and the beaten whites of eggs. Separate the batter and to one half add 3 teaspoons of Watkins®Cocoa, 1/2 teaspoon each of Watkins® Nutmeg, Cinnamon and Allspice and 1/4 teaspoon soda. Beat well and drop into a pan with horn in middle, first white then dark batter. Bake 45 minutes in moderate oven. Ice with confectioner's icing made by beating 1 1/2 cups confectioner's sugar and 3 tablespoons cream and 1/2 teaspoon Watkins® Lemon or Pineapple extract.

Note: I presume the pan with horn in the middle is a pan used for angel food cakes. They use their own special pan which Greg Patent in "Baking in America" states

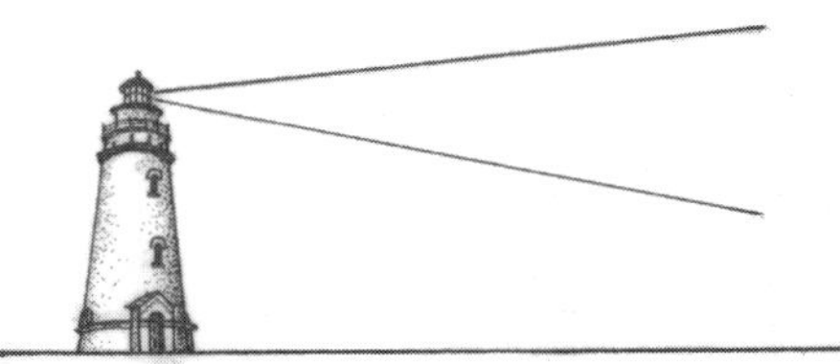

was invented in the late 1800s. He says the first tube pans were, in fact, square and the "central tube assured the even distribution of heat to the batter, resulting in cakes that cooked more quickly."

Sponge Cake

4 eggs   1 Lemon
1 cup sugar   1 tsp. baking powder
1 cup Globe A1® flour

Separate eggs, beat yolks in mixing bowl, add lemon juice and sufficient water to make one half cup. Beat in sugar, then flour and baking powder. Finally fold in stiffly beaten egg whites. Bake in moderate oven.

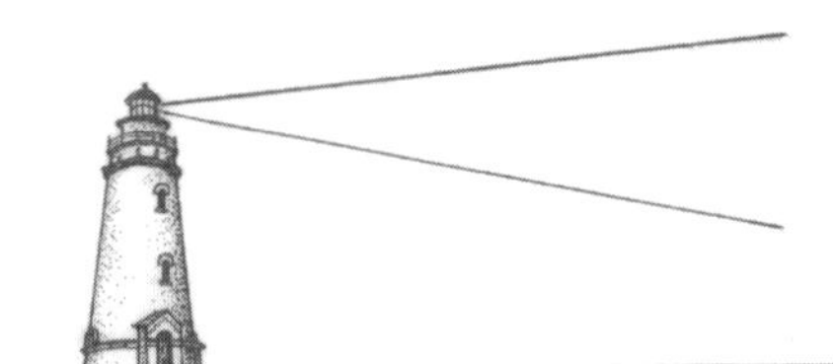

Cream Cake

1 cup sugar   1 cup Watkins®Lemon
         Dessert

1/2 cup sweet milk 1/2 cup sweet cream

1 well-beaten egg 1/8 teaspoon salt

1-7/8 cups sifted flour

2 teaspoons Watkins®Baking Powder

Add milk and cream to sugar and stir well, then add the well-beaten egg. Sift flour, Dessert, Baking Powder and salt several times and add to above mixture. A half a cup of nutmeats may be added.

Sauce

Mix Watkins®Dessert according to proportions of recipe on the container, adding again as much milk as the recipe calls for and 1/4 more sugar. Used over bread pudding, rice pudding, etc., it gives new and delightful taste and flavor.

Note: Watkins®Dessert mixes are still available on the internet.

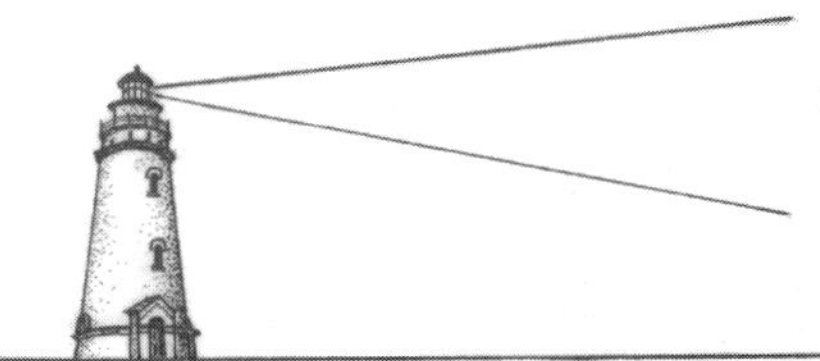

Lady Baltimore Cake

(All measurements level. Sift flour once before measuring)

1-1/2 cups sugar   3 eggs

4 teaspoons baking powder

3/4 cup butter or substitute

1 teaspoon almond flavoring

1/2 teaspoon vanilla flavoring

1 cup milk or warm water

1/2 teaspoon salt, if butter substitute is used

3 cups Swans Down Cake Flour®

Sift flour once, measure, add the other dry ingredients, and sift four times. Cream shortening, add the sugar gradually, the egg yolks unbeaten. Add the milk and dry ingredients alternately, beating hard after each addition, then add the flavoring and fold in the stiffly beaten egg whites. Bake in three layers at a temperature of 350 degrees F. for thirty minutes. Put together with Lady Baltimore filling and white icing. This makes a very large cake. For a smaller cake use half of the recipe.

Note: Maud did not clip a recipe for the Lady Baltimore filling. Following is a recipe for the filling:

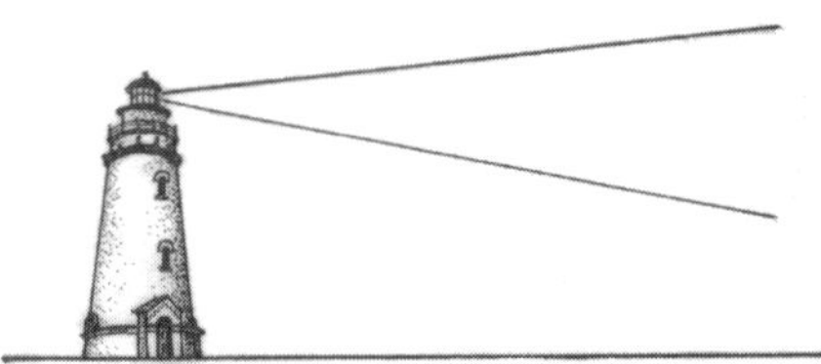

Lady Baltimore Filling and Frosting

2 egg whites
dash salt
1-1/2 teaspoons light corn syrup
1 teaspoon vanilla
1/2 cup dried apricots, chopped
1/2 cup raisins
1/2 cup pecans, chopped

1/3 cup water
1-1/2 cups sugar

Combine egg whites, sugar, salt, water and syrup in top of double boiler. Beat 1 minute. Place over rapidly boiling water. Beat constantly on high heat 7 minutes or until frosting stands in peaks. Remove from boiling water. Transfer to large bowl; add vanilla. Beat 1 minute. For Filling: Add fruits and nuts to 1/3 of the frosting.

Note: Lady Baltimore cake was first mentioned by novelist Owen Wister in his 1906 novel, Lady Baltimore . Legend has it that a young woman gave Wister such a cake, which he later chronicled in his novel. The fruit in the filling varies according to taste.

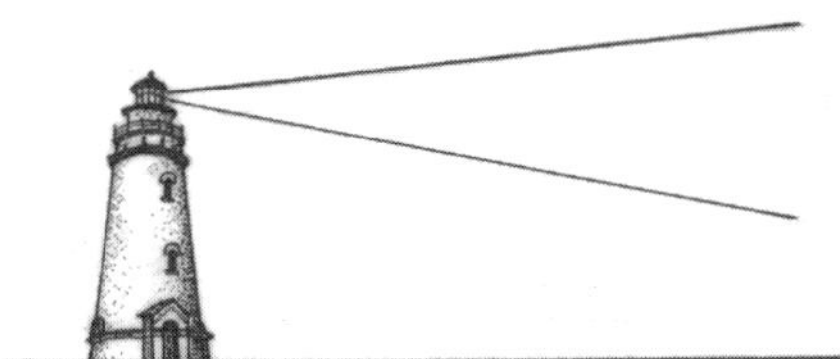

Cocoa Cream Cake

3/4 cup butter	3 eggs
2-1/2 cups flour	1 cup sugar
2 tablespoons Watkins®Cocoa	1 cup milk
3-1/2 teaspoons Watkins®Baking Powder	
1 teaspoon Watkins®Vanilla	

Cream butter, blend in sugar and cocoa. Stir in the eggs one by one without previous beating. Sift baking powder with the flour and add alternately with milk to other mixture; then add extract. Bake in 2 or 3 layers and put together with the following frosting:

White of one egg
2 teaspoons cold water
3/4 cup confectioner's sugar
1/2 teaspoon Watkins®Vanilla

Beat white of egg until stiff; add water and sugar. Beat thoroughly, then add flavoring. Spread between layers and on top of cake.

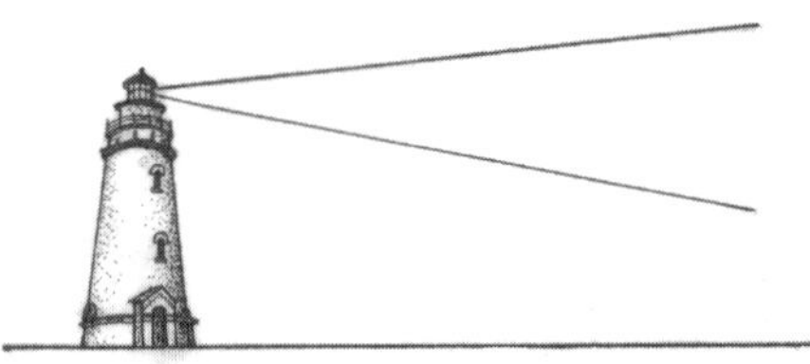

Upside-Down Cake

1-1/2 cups Globe A1® flour
1/2 teaspoon salt   1 cup sugar
2 teaspoons baking powder
1/4 cup shortening   1/4 cup butter
1/2 cup milk (Dairy Delivery)
1/4 cup brown sugar   2 eggs (Nulaid®)
1 small can grated pineapple
1 cup chopped nuts   1 teaspoon vanilla

Melt the butter in a heavy frying pan and stir in the brown sugar. Spread evenly and cover with the grated pineapple. Over this sprinkle the chopped nuts, then pour in the cake batter, made as follows: Cream the shortening and sugar, add the well-beaten eggs, fold in the flour which has been sifted with the salt and baking powder, adding it a little at a time alternately with the milk. Last add the vanilla. Bake in a moderate oven (350 degrees) for forty-five minutes. Turn out on a large plate and top with whipped cream.

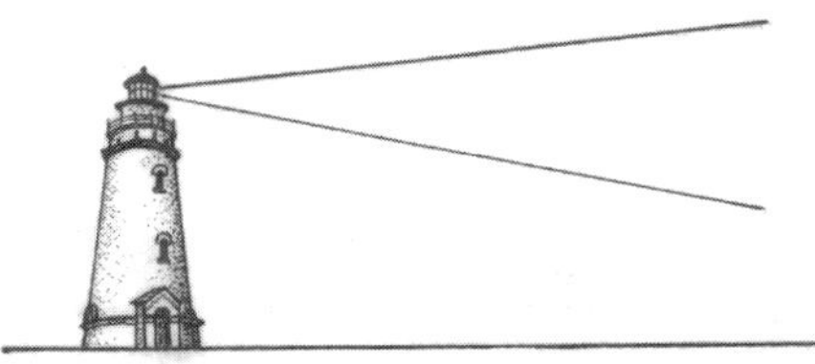

Dromedary®Date Torte

1/2 cup flour   1/2 cup sugar
1/8 teaspoon salt   1/2 teaspoon vanilla
1 teaspoon baking powder
1 cup chopped nutmeats   2 eggs
1 package Dromedary®Dates, sliced

Sift the dry ingredients. Beat the eggs; beat in the sugar gradually; add the vanilla, nuts and dates. Stir in the dry ingredients. Bake in a shallow pan which has been lined with paper and oiled in a moderate oven (300° F. – 325° F.) for about 1 hour. Cut in squares when cool. Serve with whipped cream or a small ball of vanilla ice cream.

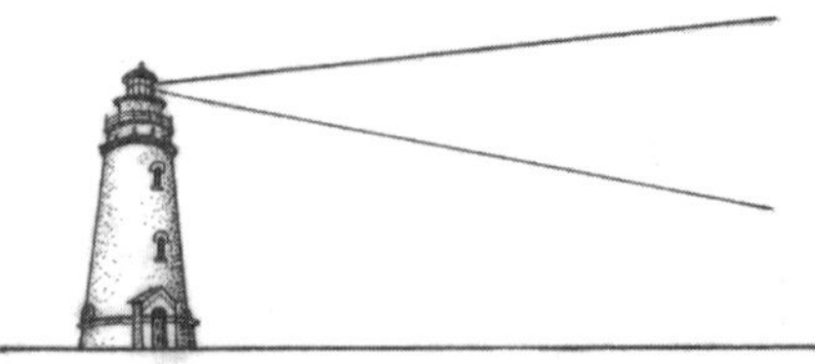

Applesauce Fruit Cake Without Milk

1 cupful brown sugar
1-1/2 cups apple sauce
1 teaspoonful Watkins®Cinnamon
2-1/2 cupfuls flour
1 teaspoonful Watkins®Nutmeg
1/2 cupful shortening
1 lb. raisins
2 teaspoonfuls baking soda
1 teaspoonful Watkins®Cloves
1/2 teaspoonful salt
3 tablespoonfuls vinegar

Cream shortening and sugar thoroughly together, add apple sauce, flour, raisins, spices, salt, and soda mixed with vinegar. Mix and pour into greased and floured cake tin and bake in moderate oven one and a half hours. Sufficient for one cake.

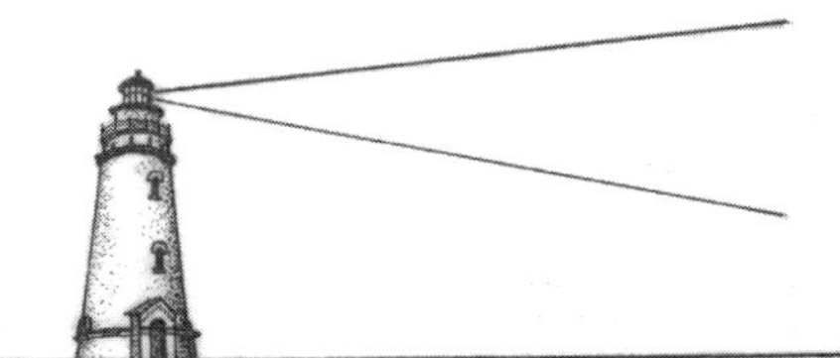

Raisin Pound Cake

1 cup butter
5 eggs
1/2 teaspoonful Watkins® Baking Powder
1 cup sugar
2 cups sifted flour
1 teaspoon each Watkins® Lemon
*   and Vanilla flavoring*
1 cup seeded or seedless raisins

Cream the butter until waxy; add sugar gradually, beating until mixture is very creamy and white. Beat eggs until very light; sift flour and baking powder after measuring. Add about 1/2 cup of flour, stir into mixture, then add a portion of the eggs. Continue to add these ingredients alternately, beating batter between each addition until smooth. Reserve about 2 tablespoons of flour to which add fruit, then carefully fold into mixture with flavoring. Pour into an ungreased papered loaf pan and bake in a very moderate oven about 1 hour if a brick shaped pan is used, or 45 minutes if in a square pan.

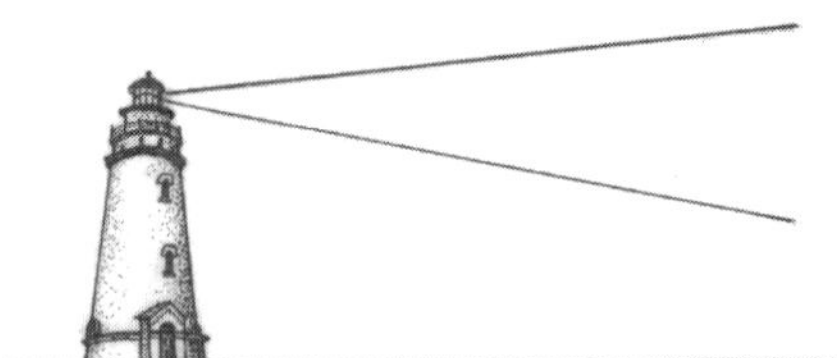

Nut Cake

1 cup butter	2 cups sugar
1 tsp. nutmeg	1 tsp. cinnamon
1 tsp. allspice	1 tsp. vanilla
1-1/2 cups chopped walnuts	
1 cup warm water	
3 cups Globe A1® flour	4 eggs
4 tsp. baking powder	1/4 tsp. salt

Cream butter and sugar. Add egg yolks, spices, nuts and water. Sift in flour, baking powder and salt. Fold in last the stiffly beaten egg whites. Bake in layers or loaf.

White Cake

1/2 cup butter	1 cup sugar
1/2 cup milk	1/2 cup cornstarch
1 cup Globe A1® flour	1 tsp. baking powder
Flavoring	3 egg whites

Cream butter and sugar. Add cornstarch mixed with milk, then flour and baking powder and flavoring. Fold in stiffly beaten egg whites. Bake in loaf or two layers.

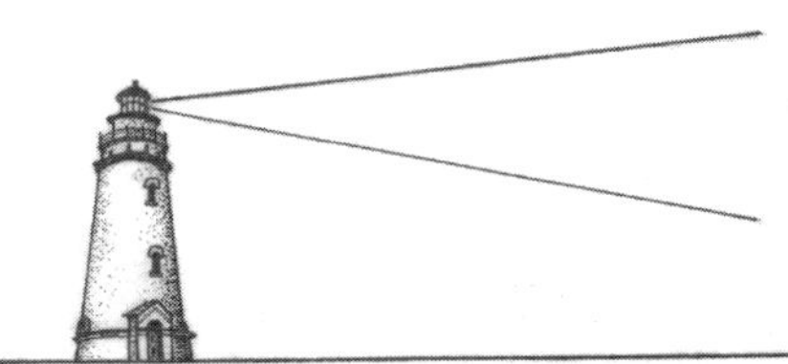

Breakfast Berry Cake of Fresh Berries

Sift a quart of flour with six teaspoonfuls of Watkins Ò Baking Powder, one teaspoonful of salt. Rub into the mixture four tablespoonfuls of butter, and work into a very soft dough with a pint of rich milk. Roll lightly or pat out in two sheets; with one of these line a baking pan, fill with berries of any kind, sprinkle over them one-half a cup of sugar, blanket with the second sheet, press down gently (the first sheet should rise slightly at the sides of the pan), bake, cut in squares, and direct the family to split these open and spread generously with sugar and butter, or with maple syrup and butter, and eat them while hot.

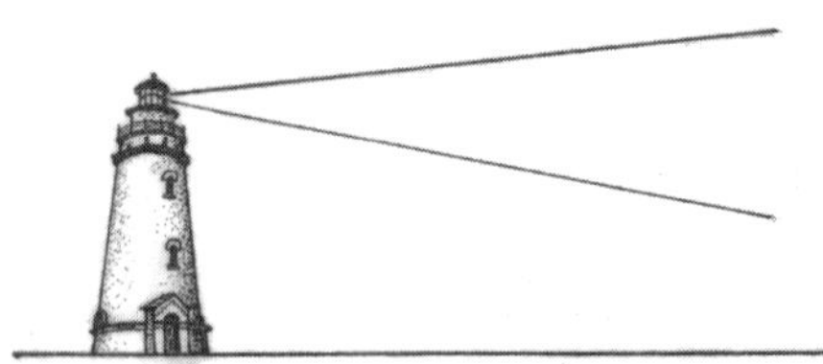

The next section of Maude's book has recipes for pies of many varieties.

Chocolate Butterscotch Pie

Butter size of an egg, one cup brown sugar. Put in skillet and brown. Add 1-1/2 cups of milk, yolks of 2 eggs, 2 level tablespoons of Watkins®Chocolate Dessert and 1 teaspoon of Watkins®Vanilla. Place beaten whites of eggs on top, after pouring in rich pie crust.

Butterscotch Pie

1 cup brown sugar	2 eggs
2 tablespoons flour	1 cup water
2 tablespoons butter	
1 teaspoon Watkins®Van.,Van.& Coum.	

Mix sugar, flour, yolks of eggs to paste, add gradually water, butter and Watkins®Vanilla, Van. and Coumarin.

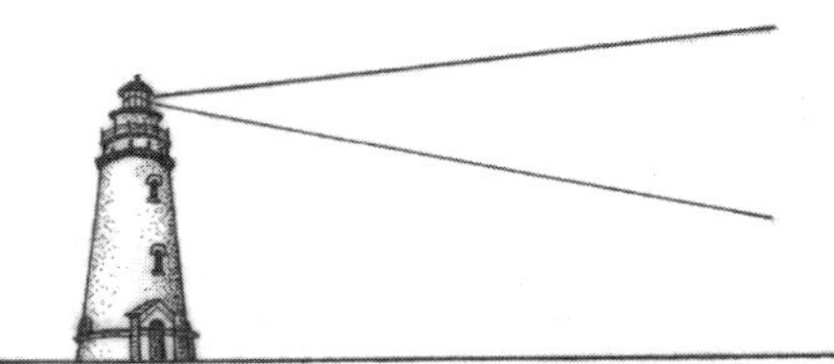

Watkins®Coconut Rice Pie

1 cup rice

2 tablespoons butter

1 cup raisins

1 teaspoon Watkins®Vanilla

2 tablespoons Watkins®Coconut Dessert

1 cup sugar

3 eggs

Boil rice, add Watkins®Coconut Dessert (moistened with a little cold water or milk), sugar and butter. Then let cool and add eggs, raisins and Vanilla.

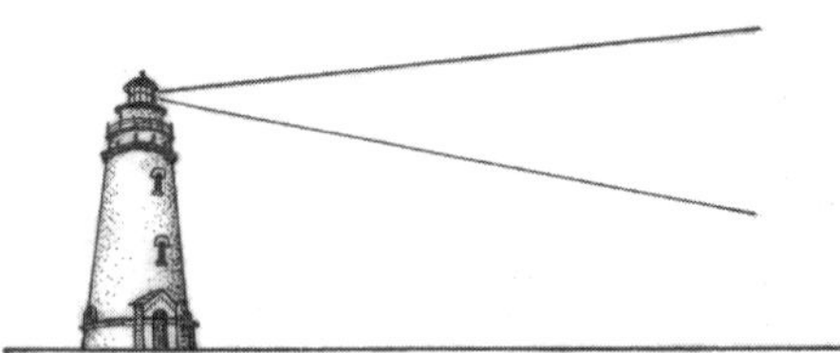

Boston Cream Pie

1/3 cup butter   1 cup sugar
2 eggs beaten light   1/2 cup milk
1 teaspoon Watkins®Vanilla
1-1/2 cups flour
3 teaspoons Watkins®Baking Powder

Cream butter and sugar, add eggs and milk. Then gradually add the flour and baking powder sifted with a pinch of salt. Lastly add the Vanilla. Bake in two layer cake pans.

Cream Filling For Boston Cream Pie

1/2 cup water and 1/2 cup milk, add 1/2 cup sugar and bring to a boil. Dissolve 3 heaping tablespoons Watkins®Coconut Dessert in 1/2 cup cold milk. Combine and boil until thick, about 3 minutes. When cool add 1 teaspoon vanilla (Watkins®) and spread between layers. Cover top with confectioner's sugar.

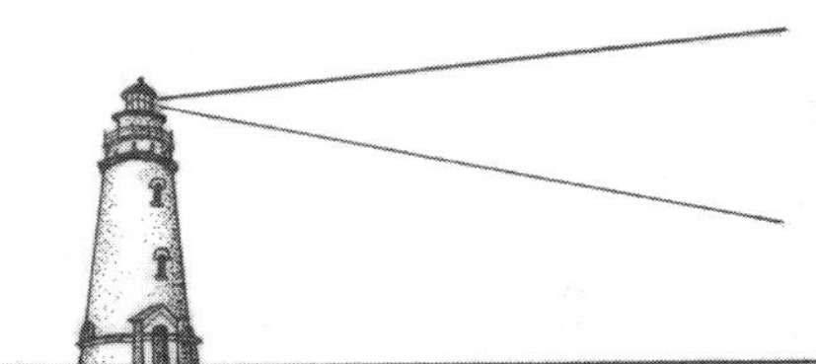

Lemon Meringue Pie

1-1/2 cupfuls sugar   Pastry
1-1/2 cupfuls boiling water
5 tablespoonsful cornstarch
1/3 teaspoonful salt
1 tablespoon shortening   2 eggs (Nulaid®)
5 tablespoons lemon juice
Grate rind of three-fourths of a lemon.

Thoroughly mix together the cornstarch salt and sugar and add to the boiling water, stirring constantly. When thick, transfer to a double boiler and cook for at least ten minutes. Add the shortening and slowly stir this into the egg yolks, slightly beaten. Then add the lemon juice and rind. In the meantime, the pastry should have been prepared and baked on an inverted pie plate. When this crust is almost brown enough, it should be put in the pie plate, the cooled filling poured in and the whole covered with a meringue made by beating the egg whites stiff, adding a few drops of lemon extract or juice and two tablespoonfuls of powdered sugar. Bake in a moderate oven (350 degrees F.) about ten minutes longer.

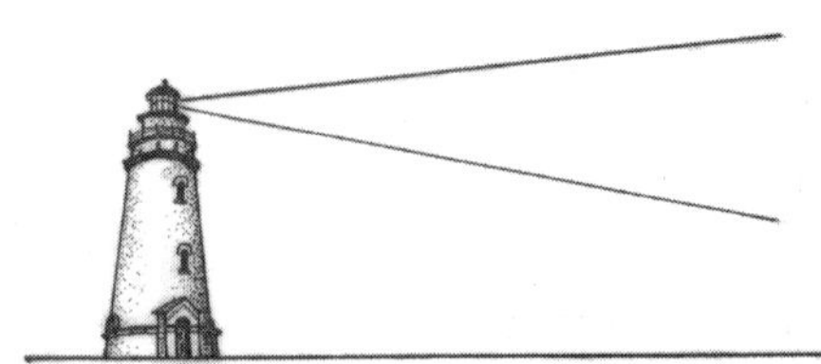

Cocoa Pie

1/2 cup Watkins®Cocoa

1 1/2 cups sugar

1/4 cup cornstarch

2 teaspoons Watkins®Vanilla

3/4 teaspoon salt

3 eggs

2 cups milk

Mix and sift cocoa, sugar, cornstarch and salt. Add unbeaten egg yolks with milk and stir well. Cook in double boiler until thick, stirring constantly. Remove from fire, add vanilla and pour into baked pie crust. Cover with meringue made by beating egg whites until stiff, adding 1/2 teaspoon Watkins®Baking Powder and 6 tablespoons sugar. Brown in oven.

Custard Pie

2 eggs

1 cup milk

1 large tablespoon flour

1 large tablespoon Watkins®Vanilla

1 large tablespoon melted butter

1/2 cup sugar

Note: No directions were given, only ingredients.

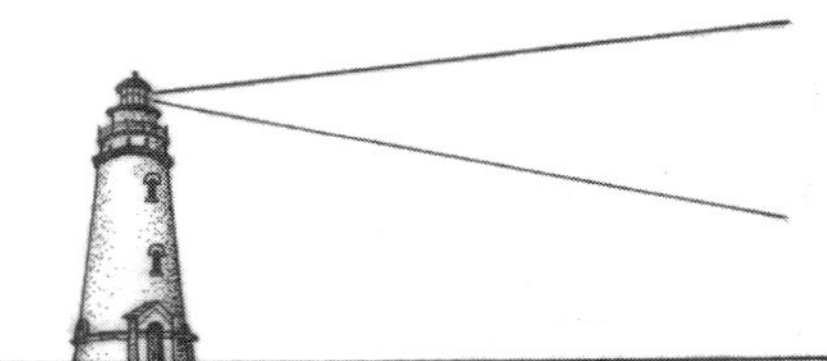

Walnut Pie

4 tablespoons Globe A1® flour

1 cup brown sugar

1/4 teaspoon salt

1/2 cup chopped walnut meats

2 (Nulaid®) eggs

2 tablespoons butter

2 cups milk (Dairy Delivery)

6 tablespoons granulated sugar

1/4 teaspoon vanilla

Scald the milk and add it slowly to the mixture of the flour, salt and half the brown sugar. Cook in a double boiler for twenty minutes, stirring until thickened. Add the egg yolks beaten with the rest of the brown sugar, and cook a few minutes longer. Add the butter, remove from fire and cool. Pour into a baked pie shell, cover with the nuts and top with a meringue made as follows: Beat the eggs whites very stiff, add four tablespoons of sugar and beat well; add two tablespoons of sugar and the vanilla and beat again. Place in a slow oven (300 degrees) for fifteen minutes to set the meringue.

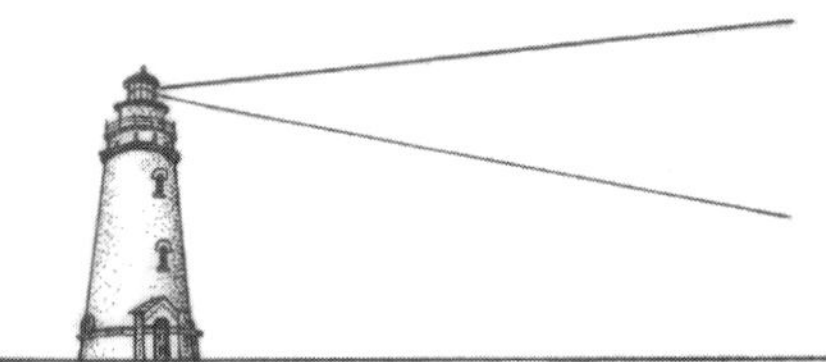

Butterscotch Pie

1 cup brown sugar   1 cup water
3 tablespoons flour (Globe A1®)
1 egg (Nulaid®)   3 tablespoons butter

Place sugar in a saucepan over the fire and stir until melted and a rich brown color. Add a cup of water and continue cooking until the sugar is dissolved. Blend the butter with the flour and stir into the brown liquid. Cook until thick, then quickly beat in the egg which has been well beaten. Pour into baked pie shell.

Chocolate Cream Pie

1/3 cup of cornstarch   1/2 cup sugar
2 cups milk, scalded (Dairy Delivery)
3/4 cup Ghirardelli's® ground chocolate
3 egg yolks (Nulaid®)   1 teaspoon vanilla
3/4 teaspoon cinnamon

Sift together cornstarch and sugar and add to hot milk. Stir and cook until smooth. Add chocolate, stir well to mix thoroughly. Add slightly beaten egg yolks and allow to cook for a few min-

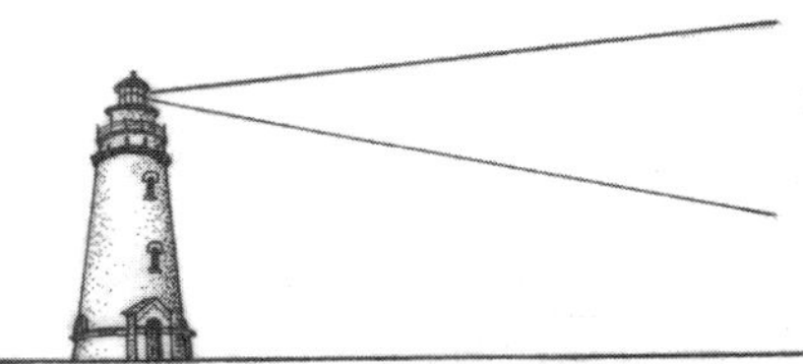

utes longer., stir gently. When thick, remove from stove, add cinnamon and vanilla. Fill pastry shells with chocolate mixture and top with meringue. Bake in oven 275 degrees F. about 15 minutes to cook and brown meringue.

Cookies were very popular as a dessert, as a snack or as a reward for good behavior. Here are some of the cookie recipes Maud collected.

Three-Part Cookies

First Part

4-1/2 cups cake flour or 3 cups bread flour
1 cup shortening
Cut the shortening into the flour as for pie crust and add one-half teaspoon salt.

Second Part

2 eggs beaten   1 cup sugar
Beat the sugar into the eggs.

(continued on page 112)

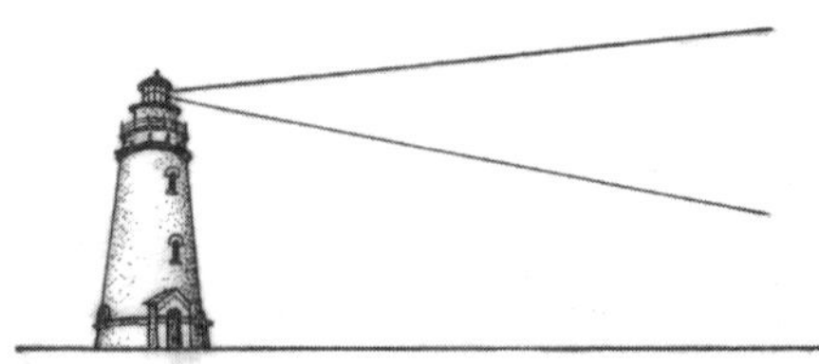

Third Part

4 tablespoons sweet milk   1 teaspoon soda
1 teaspoon vanilla   nutmeg , if desired

Add the egg and sugar mixture to No. 1, then add mixture No. 3 to No. 1. It will not be necessary to add any more flour for rolling. The cookies may be rolled and baked immediately. If you want to keep them soft, put them in a covered receptacle. Bake 14 minutes at 425 degrees F. Makes 53 large cookies.

Brownies

1 cup brown sugar   1/2 cup flour
1 teaspoon Watkins®Vanilla   1 egg
2 tablespoons Watkins®Cocoa
1/4 cup melted butter   1 cup chopped nuts

Mix and spread with knife in small pan. Bake in very moderate oven 20 minutes. Turn out of pan as soon as taken from oven and cut in strips about 1 x 4 inches. Roll in powdered sugar.

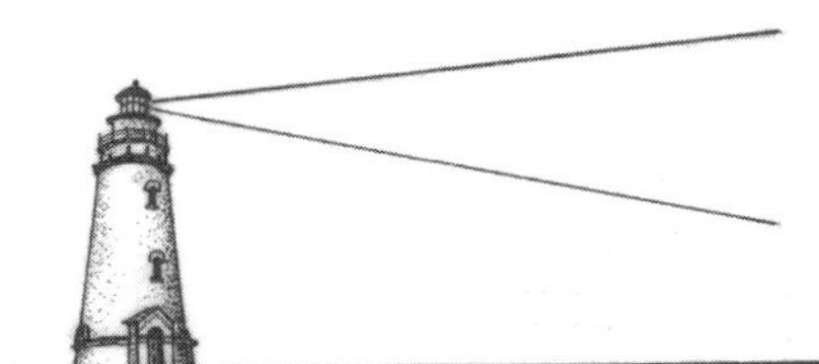

Chocolate Potato Drop Cookies

1/3 cup butter or butter substitute
1 cup sugar   2 eggs (separated)
1/2 teaspoon salt   1 cup flour
2 squares bitter chocolate (melted)
1 cup mashed potatoes   1/3 cup raisins
1/2 cup chopped nuts
3 teaspoons baking powder

Sift flour and baking powder. Cream the fat and beat in the sugar, then the egg yolks and chocolate; add the mashed potatoes, then the nuts and raisins rolled in the flour and baking powder mixture, and last the beaten whites of the eggs. Drop in small portions onto the aluminum cookie sheet and bake in moderate oven, 350 degrees F.

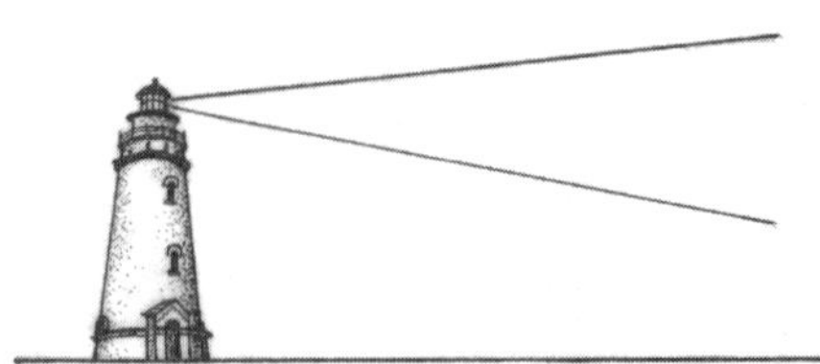

Butterscotch Cookies

1/2 cup butter or substitute
2 cups brown sugar
2 eggs
1/2 tablespoon vanilla
1/2 tablespoon cream of tartar
1/2 teaspoon soda
3-1/2 cups cake flour

Mix in order given. Chill, roll thin, cut with cookie cutter, and place on cookie sheet. Bake in hot oven, 425 degrees F.

Old Fashioned Cookies

2 cups sugar   2 eggs
1 cup butter   1 teaspoon baking soda
1 cup sour cream   or   1/2 cup buttermilk
2 teaspoons Watkins®Vanilla or Lemon Extract
2 teaspoons Watkins®Baking Powder

Note: No flour is listed in the ingredients. Maud did not paste the directions in with this recipe.

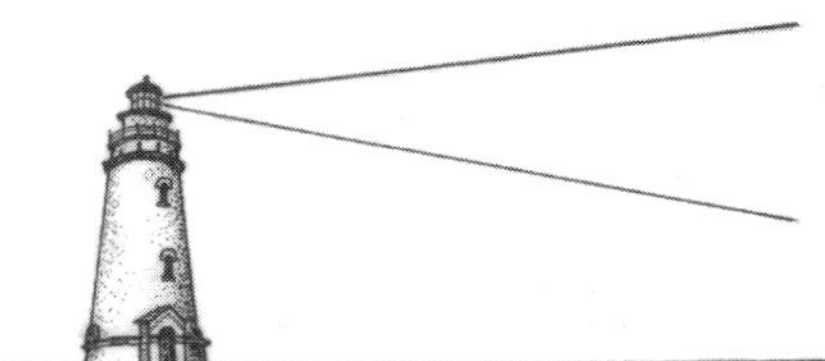

Chocolate Ice Box Cookies

1/2 cup shortening   1-1/2 cups white sugar
8 tablespoons ground chocolate
            (Ghirardelli's®)
1 egg (Nulaid®)
2 tablespoons boiling water
1/4 cup milk (Dairy Delivery)
2-1/2 cups flour (Globe A1®)
1/2 teaspoon salt   1 teaspoon vanilla
2 teaspoons baking powder

Cream shortening and sugar. Add well beaten egg, melted chocolate and milk. Then add flour, salt and baking powder sifted together. Add vanilla. Shape into rolls two inches in diameter and place in refigerator six hours. Slice thin, bake at 375 degrees F. for twelve minutes.

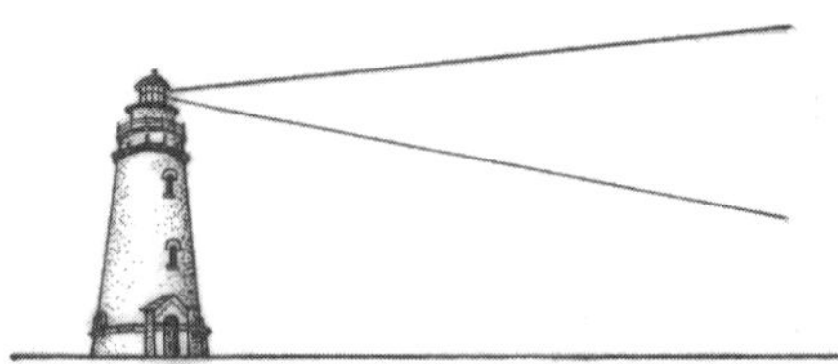

Sour Milk Cookies

2 tablespoons butter	2 cups sugar
2 eggs	1 cup sour cream
1/2 teaspoon soda	4 cups flour

Cream butter, add sugar and stir, add eggs, mix well and add the rest of the ingredients, the soda with the sour cream, toss on floured board, roll out thin and cut in rounds. Bake in hot oven ten minutes.

Note: I used 1/2 cup of butter, 2 tsp. vanilla and an additional 1-1/2 cups of flour to make the consistency dense enough to roll out. I sprinkled them with cinnamon sugar and baked them on a greased cookie sheet for 10 minutes at 375 degrees F. They were very good and strongly resembled the ones my grandmother used to make.

....Bev Praver

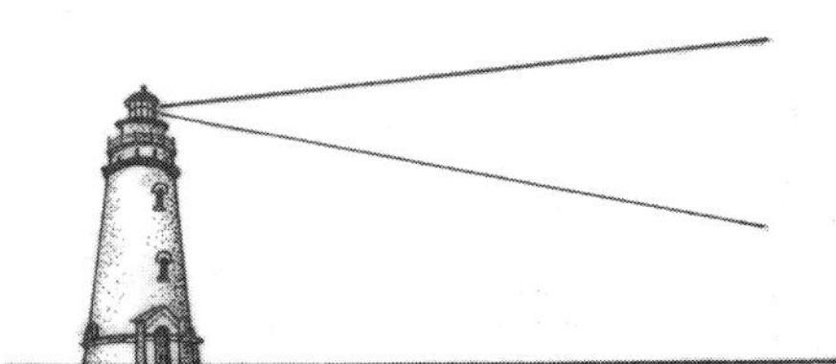

Fudge Cookies

Shave two ounces of chocolate in a cup and set in a pan of hot water to melt. Sift together two-thirds of a cup of flour, 1 teaspoon of cinnamon, 1 teaspoon of baking powder, one-fourth teaspoon of salt: - sift two or three times. Beat two eggs until very light then beat in 1 cup of sugar, one-fourth at a time. Stir in lightly 1 teaspoon of vanilla, the melted chocolate, three-fourth cup of finely cut walnut meats and lastly the dry ingredients. Drop on greased pans, not more than a teaspoonful at a time and bake in a moderate oven.

Nut Patties

1 egg beaten	5 tablespoons flour
1 cup English Walnuts	1 cup sugar

Beat egg and sugar until very light; into this stir the nuts, then add the flour. Drop on tins with teaspoon, make about size of macaroons and bake in a medium hot oven about 10 minutes.

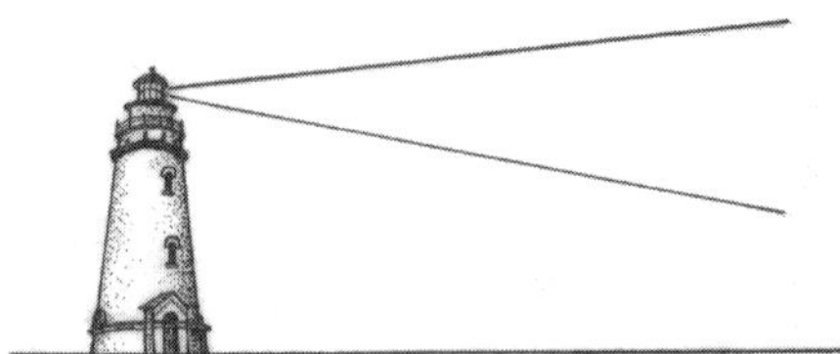

Chocolate Walnut Wafers

3 eggs (Nulaid®)
1/4 cup ground chocolate (Ghirardelli's®)
1-1/4 cups flour
1/4 teaspoon salt
1 tablespoon molasses
1/4 cup butter, melted
1 cup chopped walnuts
1/2 teaspoon vanilla
2 cups brown sugar
1/2 teaspoon soda

Beat eggs light; add sugar gradually and continue beating. Add chocolate, flour, soda and salt, sifted together twice and remaining ingredients. Drop from a tablespoon on a greased sheet. Bake in a rather hot oven (about 375 degrees F.). Will make about 6 dozen wafers.

Cocoa Marshmallow Roll

Mix 1/2 cup sugar with 2 tablespoons Watkins®Cocoa. Then add 2 eggs and beat until very light. Stir in 1 tablespoon of melted butter, then 1/2 cup of pastry flour sifted with 3/4 tea-

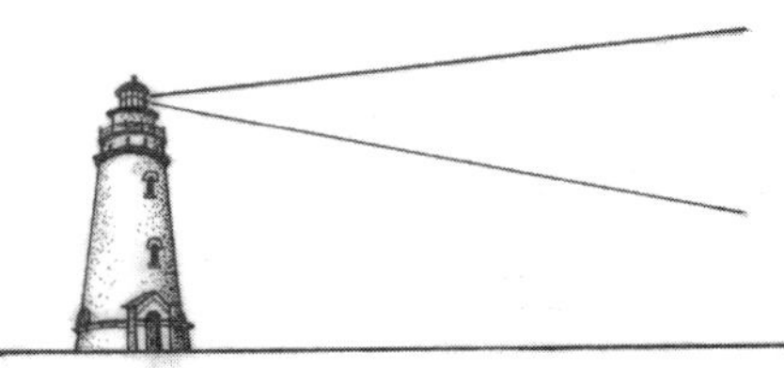

spoon of Watkins® Baking Powder. Pour into a greased shallow pan and bake in a moderate oven for 12 to 15 minutes. Turn out on a piece of brown paper sprinkled with powdered sugar. Spread with marshmallow whip or cream and roll up like a jelly roll. Wrap the paper or cloth around it and let stand until cold. Ice with chocolate frosting.

Sally Anne Cookies

1 cup white sugar	1 cup brown sugar
4-1/2 cups flour	1 teaspoon soda
3 well-beaten eggs	1/2 cup lard
2 teaspoons Watkins® Cinnamon	
1 teaspoon Watkins® Baking Powder	
1 cup butter	1 cup chopped nuts

In the evening mix the dough and form into rolls and let stand overnight. In the morning slice thin and bake.

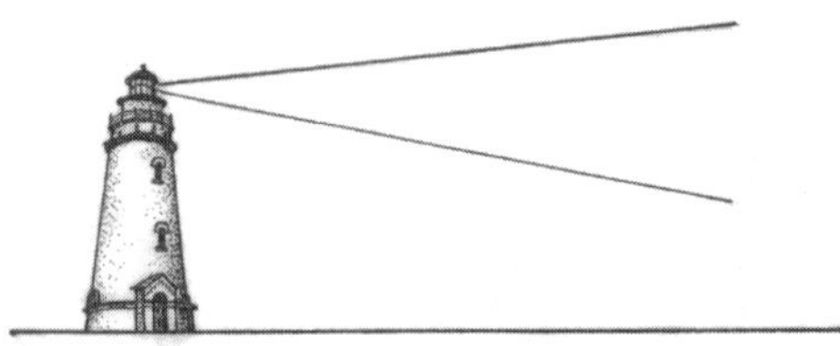

Date Hermits To Serve 4 Dozen

3 eggs   1-1/2 cups chopped dates
1 cup sugar   1 cup flour
1 cup broken nutmeats   3/4 teaspoon salt
1 teaspoon baking powder
1 cup powdered sugar   1 teaspoon vanilla

Beat eggs and add the sugar. Beat for 1 minute. Add the flour, baking powder, salt, vanilla, dates and nuts. When well mixed pour into a shallow pan, which has been fitted with waxed paper. Bake in a moderately slow oven for 30 minutes. Remove from oven and turn out upside down on a paper. Tear off the waxed paper and use a sharp knife and cut the mixture into 1-1/2 inch squares. Roll in the powdered sugar at once and let cool on waxed paper.

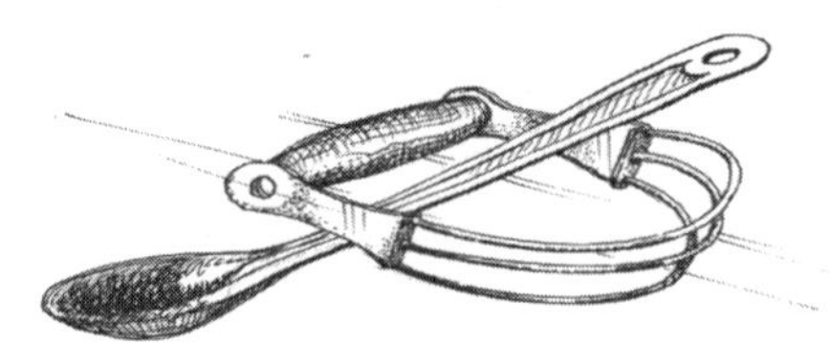

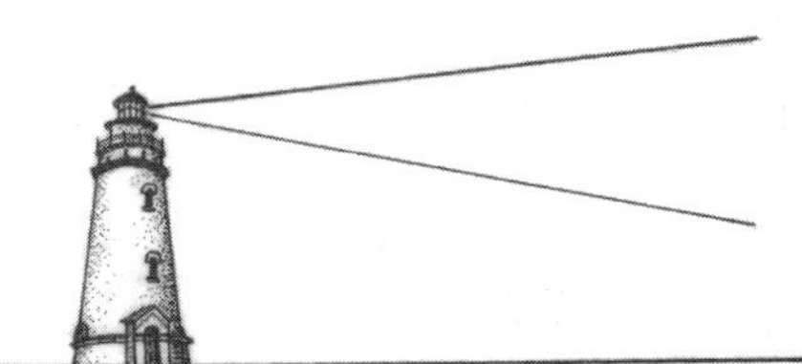

Hermits

3/4 cup shortening
1-1/2 cups brown sugar
3 eggs well-beaten
3/4 teaspoonful soda
2-1/2 cups pastry flour
1/2 teaspoonful cinnamon
1/2 teaspoonful nutmeg
1 cup chopped walnut meats

Cream the shortening and sugar and add the well-beaten eggs. Sift 2 cups of flour with the soda and spices and add to mixture. Add raisins and nuts mixed with rest of flour. Drop by teaspoonfuls on greased baking sheets about 2 inches apart. Bake in a hot oven of 400 deg. F. for 10 minutes.

Note: Although raisins are called for in the directions of this recipe they are not listed in the ingredients on the original. They may be an optional ingredient.

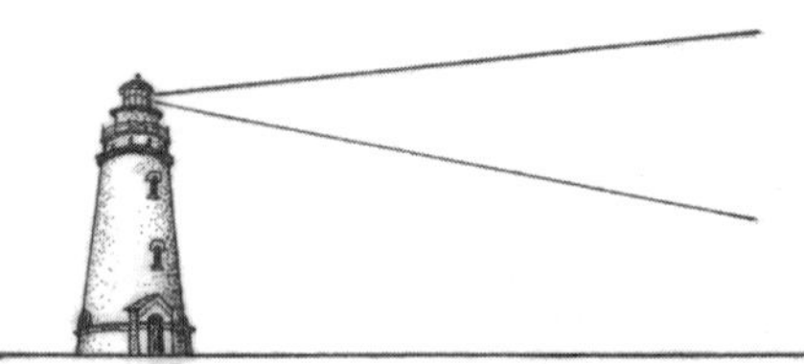

Cocoa Cookies

1/2 cup shortening   1 cup sugar
1/2 cup Watkins®Cocoa   2 eggs
1/3 cup milk   4 cups flour
4 teaspoons Watkins®Baking Powder

Cream the sugar and the shortening together; add the milk slowly, then the eggs well beaten and the cocoa; sift the flour and baking powder together and add to make a stiff dough. Roll out one quarter inch thick and cut. Bake in a hot oven 12 to 15 minutes. Decorate with white icing.

Drop Cookies(No.1)

1 cup of sugar, 1 cup of shortening, 1/2 teaspoon ginger, 1/2 teaspoon cloves, 2 teaspoons soda, dissolved in a cup of boiling water, 1 cup raisins.

Note: There's no flour listed in this recipe! Maud must have missed some of it when she clipped it.

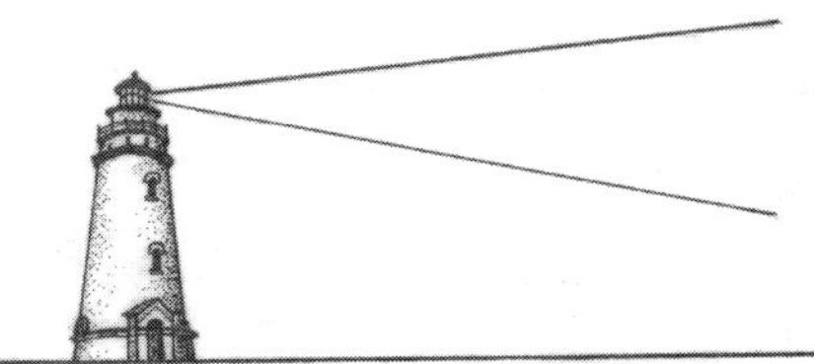

White Cookies

2 cupfuls sugar   2 eggs
1 teaspoonful baking soda   Flour
1 cupful shortening   1 teaspoonful salt
1/2 cupful thick sour milk
1 teaspoonful Watkins®Vanilla Extract
1 teaspoonful Watkins®Lemon Extract

Cream shortening and sugar together, add eggs well beaten, soda mixed with sour milk, salt, extracts, and about 5 cupfuls of flour. Roll very thin, cut with cookie cutter, lay on greased tins, bake in moderately hot oven five minutes. To keep any length of time, when cold, place in covered tins and set in cool place, and they will be as crisp as when first baked. Sufficient for 90 cookies.

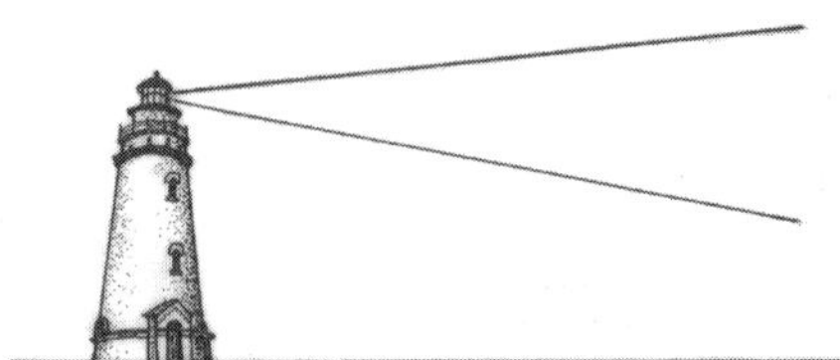

Soft Molasses Cookies

3/4 cup butter   1 cup sugar
1 egg   1 cup molasses
1 teaspoon soda   3/4 cup hot water
4 cups flour   1 teaspoon cinnamon
1/4 teaspoon ginger   1 teaspoon salt

Cream butter, add sugar, well beaten egg, molasses and hot water, then the mixed and sifted ingredients. Drop from a spoon in a warm buttered pan; bake 8 minutes in moderate oven. Or take only enough water to make a dough that may be rolled and cut with a cookie cutter.

Drop Cookies (No.2)

1/2 cup of butter, 1 cup of sugar. 2/3 cup of top milk, 1 egg, 2-1/2cups of flour, 2 teaspoons baking powder. Drop with a spoon and put a raisin or a walnut kernel in the center. Bake quickly until light brown.

Note: Top milk is the cream that rose to the top before milk was homogenized.

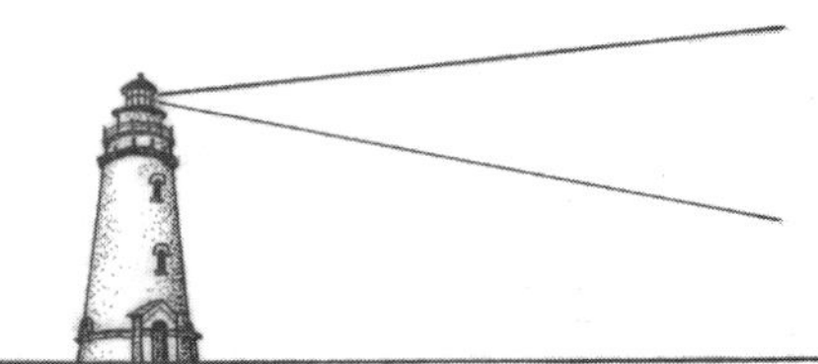

Sour Cream Cookies

1 cup brown sugar

1/4 cup Golden State®butter

1 Golden State®egg, beaten

1/2 cup Golden State®sour cream

2 cups flour

1/2 teaspoon soda

1/2 teaspoon each nutmeg and cinnamon

1 teaspoon combination baking powder

1 cup chopped nutmeats

Sift the flour once, measure, and sift again with soda, salt, spices, and baking powder. Cream butter and sugar together, add beaten egg and nutmeats. Add dry ingredients alterenately with cream. Mix well. Drop by teaspoonfuls onto greased cookie sheets. Bake in a moderately hot oven, 375 degrees F. about 15 minutes.

Note: Shortly after 1900 many of the small creameries in Humboldt county, California, consolidated into larger creameries. The Central Creamery, located on north Main Street in Ferndale, became the mother plant of the Golden State Creamery, one of the largest in the state.

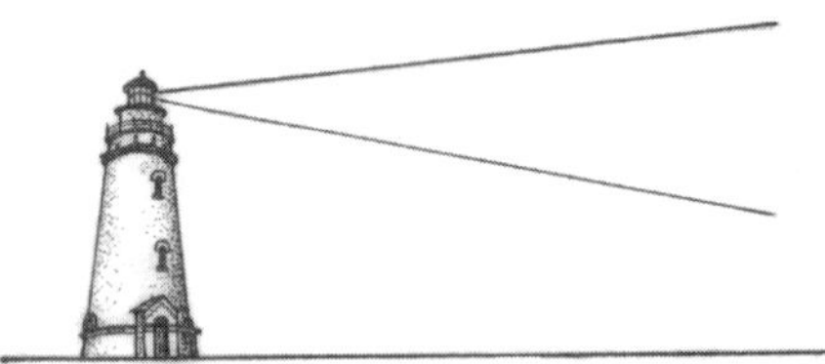

Soft Molasses Cookies
Second recipe

1/2 cup shortening   1/2 cup brown sugar
1 egg, well-beaten   1/2 cup molasses
1 teaspoonful cinnamon
1 teaspoonful ginger   1/2 cup hot milk
1/4 teaspoonful soda
1/2 teaspoonful salt   2 cups flour
1-1/2 teaspoonfuls baking powder

Cream shortening, add sugar, and cream thoroughly. Add the well-beaten egg, molasses, spices, and soda, which has been mixed together with the hot milk. Add the flour which has been sifted with the salt and baking powder. Stir well, and drop by teaspoonfuls on a well greased cookie sheet. Bake in a moderate oven of 300 deg. F. for 10 minutes. Makes about 3 dozen cookies.

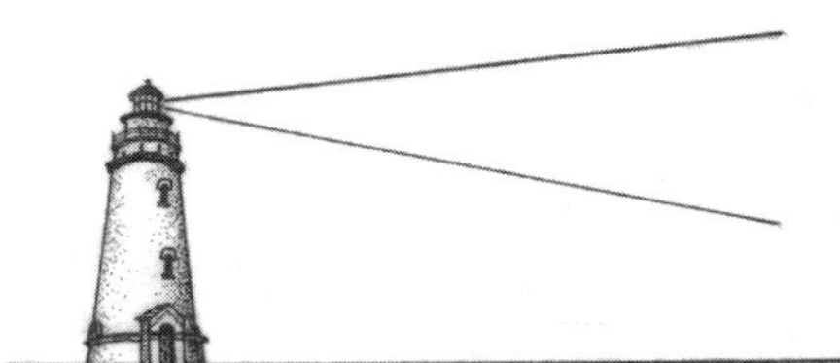

Tarts

One cup milk; 1 cup sugar; mix 3 tablespoons Watkins®Coconut Dessert in 1/2 cup milk, 1 egg beaten yolk and white. Boil the above mixture until thick. Line muffin tins with pie pastry; bake. When cold fill with above mixture. Spread each with black raspberry jam and cover with whipped cream.

Dromedary®Date Bars

3/4 cup flour	1 cup brown sugar
1/2 teaspoon baking powder	2 eggs
1/2 teaspoon salt	1/2 cup chopped nuts
1/2 package sliced Dromedary®Dates	

Sift the dry ingredients. Beat the eggs; beat in the sugar gradually. Add the dates and nuts. Stir in the dry ingredients. Spread the mixture over a shallow pan lined with paper and oiled. Bake in a moderate oven (350 °F.) for 30 minutes. When cool cut into strips. Recipe will make 18 bars.

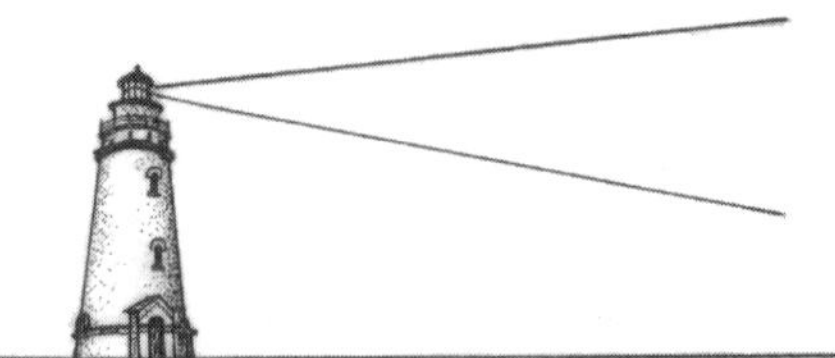

Butterscotch Sticks

1/4 cup shortening   1 egg, unbeaten
2/3 cup light brown sugar
1 tablespoonful baking powder
1/4 cup pecan meats   1 cup bread flour
1/2 teaspoonful vanilla

Melt the butter, add the sugar and when well blended remove from the heat and cool until luke-warm. Add the egg unbeaten and beat mixture well. Then add the flour which has been sifted with the baking powder, add the nutmeats and vanilla. Spread mixture in a shallow pan about 6 inches square, lined with wax paper. Bake in a slow oven of 300 deg. F. about 30 minutes. Cut into sticks.

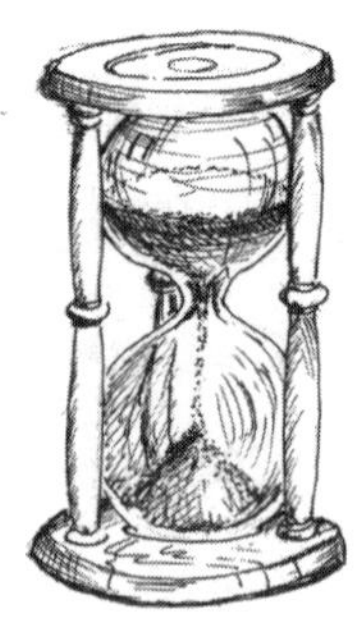

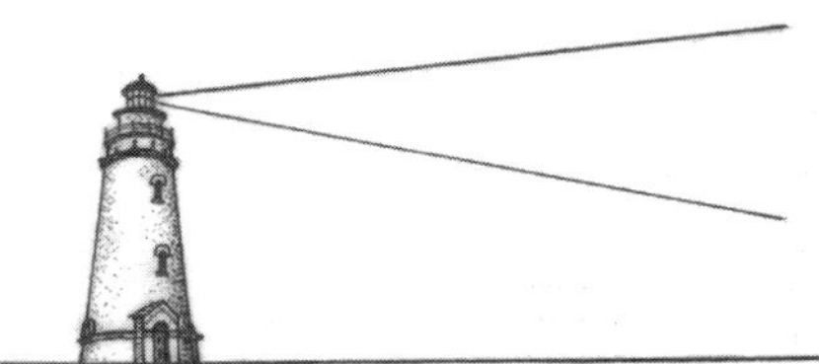

The last section of Maud's book has recipes for doughnuts, candies and puddings.

Watkins® Doughnuts

2-3/4 cups sifted flour   1 egg
1/2 tablespoon shortening   1/2 cup milk
2 teaspoons Watkins® Baking Powder
1/2 teaspoon salt   2/3 cup sugar
1/2 teaspoon Watkins® Nutmeg

Sift together flour, baking powder, salt and nutmeg and work in shortening. Beat the egg, beat in sugar and milk and stir into the dry ingredients. Take out a little at a time on a floured board, roll into a sheet, cut out with a doughnut cutter and fry in deep fat. The fat is at the right temperature when it browns a crumb of bread in 60 seconds.

Chocolate Roll Fudge

2 cups sugar   1 tablespoon corn syrup
1/3 cup ground chocolate (Ghirardelli's®)
1 cup milk (Dairy Delivery)
1/8 teaspoon salt   1 tablespoon butter
1 teaspoon vanilla

(Continued on page 130)

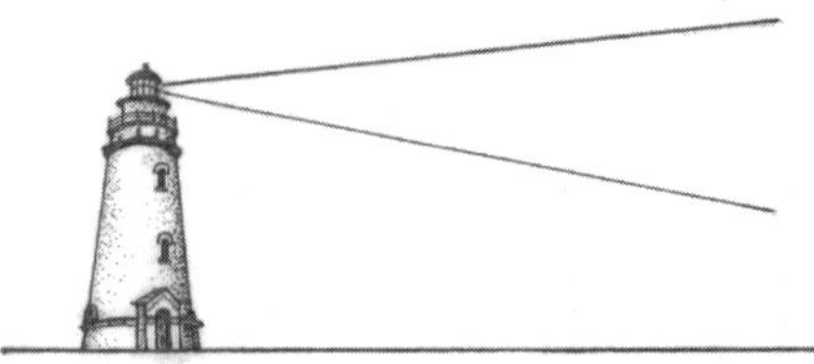

Chopped nuts, raisins, figs or dates

Heat sugar, chocolate, corn syrup and milk over a low flame until sugar is completely dissolved. Boil gently to soft ball stage, or 236 degrees F. and cool. When fudge is lukewarm add butter and vanilla and beat until creamy. Then knead on a plate for 5 or 6 minutes. Divide into four parts and pat out into rolls 4 or 5 inches long. Chopped nuts, raisins, figs or dates may be kneaded into fudge or rolls covered with chopped nuts or coconut.

Cocoa Fudge

1 cup Watkins® Cocoa   2 cups milk
4 cups white sugar   1 cup chopped nuts
3 tablespoons butter   1 teaspoon Watkins®
                                      Vanilla

Sift cocoa and sugar together; add milk and stir well. Place over fire, bring to boiling point and boil gently until a little dropped in cold water forms a soft ball. Do not stir during the boiling process. Remove from fire, add butter and let cool. Then add vanilla and chopped nuts and beat until creamy. Pour into buttered pan and mark into squares before it hardens.

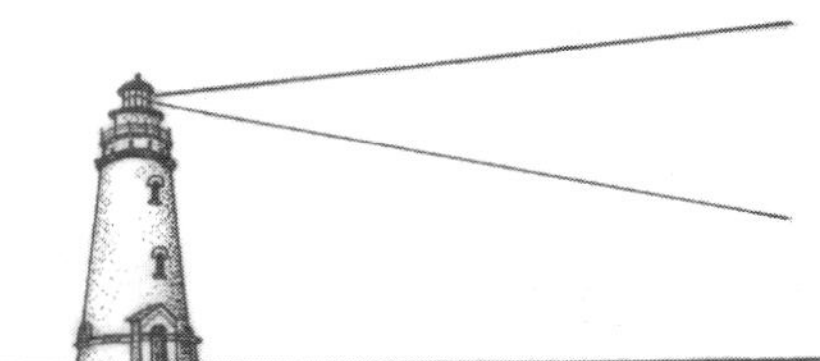

Steamed Chocolate Pudding

2 eggs   2 tablespoons Watkins®Cocoa

2-1/2 tablespoons butter   1/2 cup milk

2 scant cups flour   1/2 cup sugar

2 scant teaspoons Watkins®Baking Powder

1 teaspoon Watkins®Vanilla

Cream butter and sugar, add eggs one at a time, and beat well. Add cocoa mixed with flour and baking powder and 1/2 cup milk alternately. Lastly add melted butter. Put in mold and steam 3 hours. Serve with hard sauce.

Chocolate Pudding Steamed Balls

3 eggs (Nulaid®)   1 cup sugar

1/3 cup Star® Olive Oil   1/2 teaspoon salt

1/2 cup(Ghirardelli's®) ground chocolate

2 tablespoons boiling water

1/4 cup milk (Dairy Delivery)

1 teaspoon vanilla

1 1/2 cups flour (Globe A1®)

2 teaspoons baking powder

Beat eggs. Add sugar gradually, beating well to thoroughly dissolve. Add oil, chocolate (which

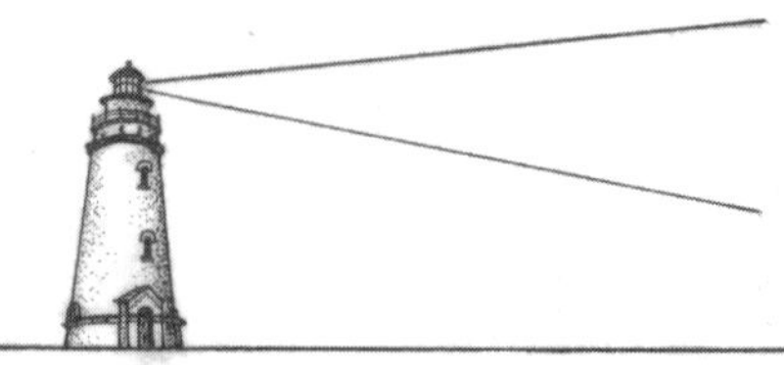

has been stirred smooth in the boiling water), milk and vanilla.; beat until smooth. Sift together flour, baking powder and salt and add to first mixture. Pour in oiled and floured muffin tins. Bake in oven 400 degrees F. about 20 minutes with pan standing in larger pan of hot water. Serve hot with hard sauce or marshmallow sauce.

Variation 1. This pudding may be varied by the addition of 1/2 cup nutmeats.

Variation 2. One-fourth cup of strawberry jam or orange marmalade may be substituted for the milk for variety.

Variation 3. This batter may be poured into an oiled and floured ring mold then placed in a pan of hot water and steamed as above. The center of the mold may be filled with jam or whipped cream.

Note: In 1898 Angelo Giurlani, an Italian immigrant, settled in San Francisco and began importing Mediterranean products and the Star® brand was introduced to the western states.

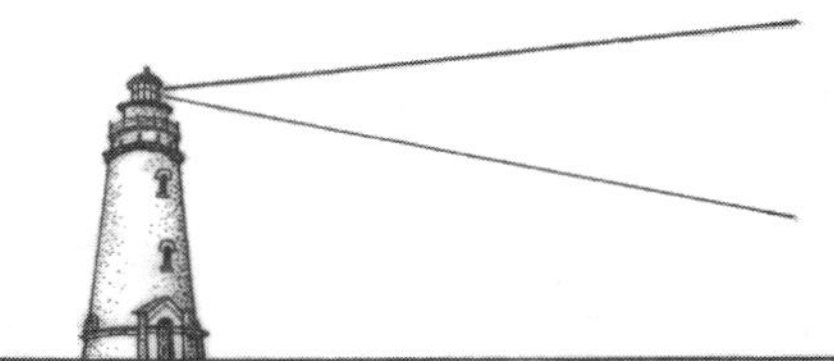

These last two recipes were handwritten on a loose page:

Chocolate Frosting

12 marshmallows
1 small can Hershey's® syrup

Melt in double boiler, fold in 1/2 pint whipped cream.

Note: No name given to this recipe by Maud.

2 boxes strawberries   1 cup sugar
1 cup crushed berries
3 tablespoons cornstarch

Boil until clear. Cool, put in pie shell over sliced berries. Top with whipped cream and strawberries.

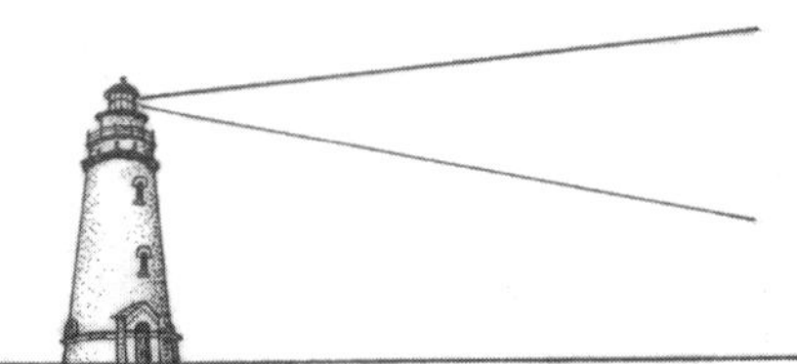

Donna Jean Thorndyke Schneider spent a lot of time with her grandfather, Lorin V. Thorndyke, Jr., as she was growing up. She made a list for us of the many things that he mentioned to her about the foods he ate while growing up. Donna is the source of most recipes credited to the Thorndyke Family.

Dried Codfish.................in cakes and gravies

Dried Beef...................in gravies and stews

Corned Beef.......in stew, cabbage and hash

Oysters.........................in stew, scalloped and raw

Clams..................in chowder, on half shell & fried

Steelhead (trout)..........................fried and baked

Baked Heart and Liver...........fried with onions

Abalone..........................fried, in chowder, in cakes

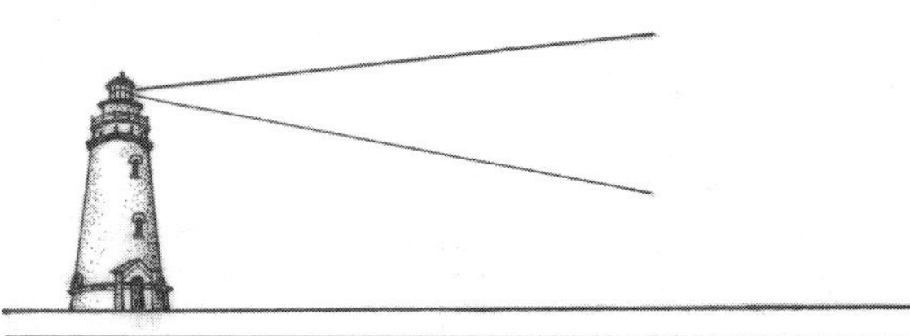

Salt Pork...fried and in beans

Tongue...in sandwiches

Sausage Patties...........stored in lard until needed

Dried Corn.............scalloped, chowder, succotash

Dried Apples...........................stewed, pies, fritters

Sauerkraut............................corned beef, spareribs,
salad, side dish

Potatoes.................fried, boiled, soup, creamed

Carrots.......................stews, soup, creamed, salad

Rice soup was a favorite; leftover the next
day, it became rice pudding

Cornmeal mush.................................fried, sugared

Scrapple

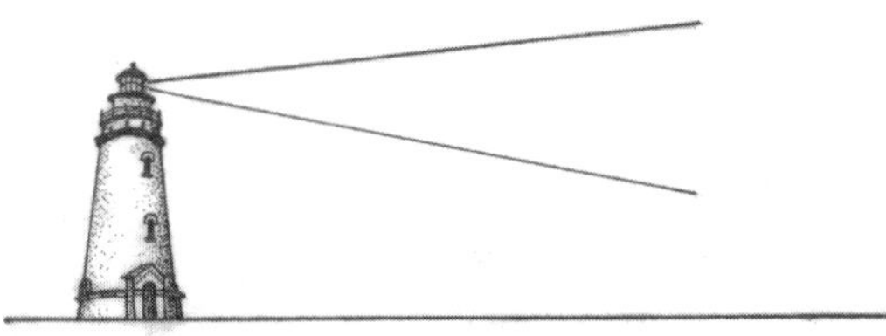

Candied squash..baked

Rhubarb..stewed, pie

Fried bread dough called "pa-lee-lees"

Eggs were stored in water-grass for months at
a time

Graveyard stew....a late-night favorite after a
watch

Watercress used as wilted-lettuce salad

Sometimes made yeast of hops and cornmeal

Note: Graveyard stew is sometimes known as milk toast. Donna Jean says that Graveyard stew was one of her grandfather's favorites, as a bowl of bread with milk poured over it. It was undoubtedly much better with homemade bread and milk fresh from the cow.

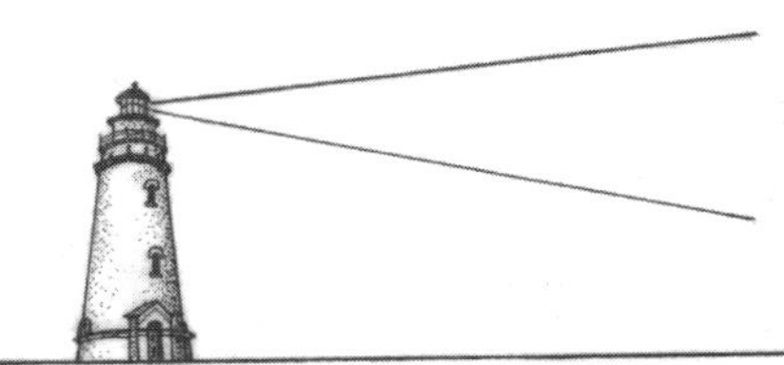

On the following pages I present as many reci-pes as I can for these favorites of Lorin V. Thorndyke, Jr. Some are from "Crumbs from Everybody's Table" an old cookbook used by Mar-garet Thorndyke, his stepmother and aunt, some are from current family members and some are from me.

....Bev Praver

Codfish Cakes

3 lbs. boneless dried cod
3 lbs. white potatoes
1 tablespoon parsley
1 stick butter
2 large eggs

Boil codfish for 1-1/2 hours. Change the water and boil in fresh water for 1 hour more. Drain and cool. Peel potatoes, boil until tender, then mash. Shred codfish and add to potatoes with other in-gredients. Shape into cakes and fry in hot oil.

Note: This is a simple recipe and is likely similar to what Lorin Jr.'s mother, aunt or wife might have made.

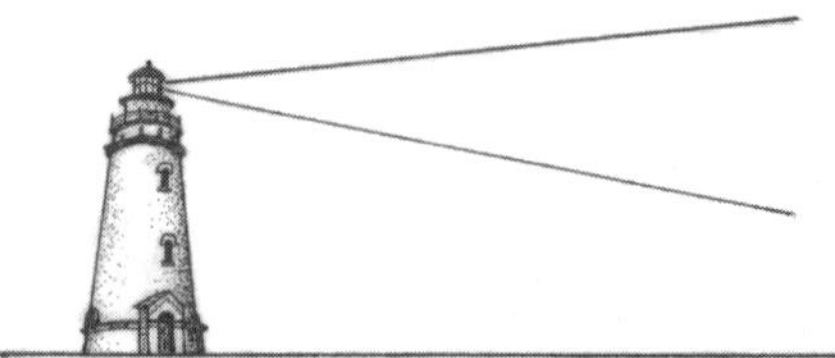

Dried Beef Gravy

1/4 lb. dried beef
3 tablespoons flour

2 tablespoons butter
3 cups milk

Melt butter in skillet. Tear dried beef into small pieces and stir into the butter. Brown meat lightly and stir in flour. When flour is dissolved, add milk and stir constantly over low heat until thick.

Dried Beef Stew

1/2 cup olive oil   pinch of dried oregano
2 medium onions, halved and thickly sliced
2 medium green bell peppers, seeded and cut
                                    into thin strips
2-1/2 lbs of salt-dried beef, desalted and
                              cooked until tender
1 cup of liquid reserved from cooking beef
1 cup chopped tomatoes
2 cloves of garlic, minced
salt and pepper to taste

Heat oil over low heat in a large saucepan. Add onions, bell peppers and garlic. Stir until tender, about 5 minutes. Add tomatoes and oregano.

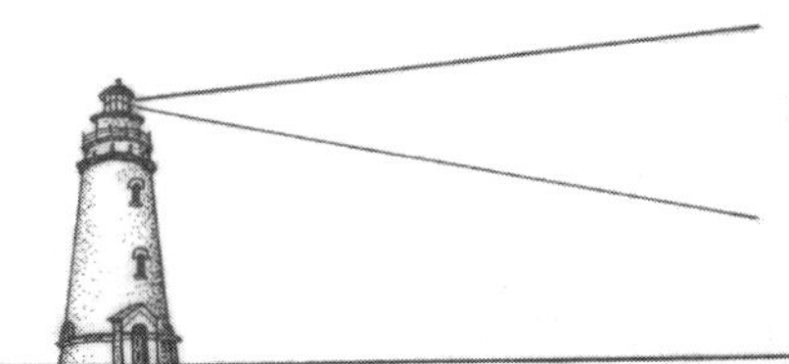

Cook another 10 minutes and then set aside.

Cut the cooked beef into 2-inch chunks and shred it. Return the tomato mixture to the stove over low heat. Add the beef and reserved liquid, and simmer, uncovered for 25 - 30 minutes.

Correct the seasonings and serve hot with white rice or boiled potatoes.

Note: I presume that if you were able to find dried beef in large pieces that you would desalt it by soaking it overnight in water. You might try using fresh beef in place of the dried in this recipe.   ....Bev Praver

Oyster Stew

1 pint shucked oysters, with liquor
1 quart milk
1/4 cup (1/2 stick) margarine or butter
  salt and pepper to taste

In 4-quart pan, cook oysters, with liquor, over low heat until edges of oysters just begin to curl. Add milk, margarine or butter, salt and pepper. Heat slowly until hot; do not boil.

Makes about 6 cups.

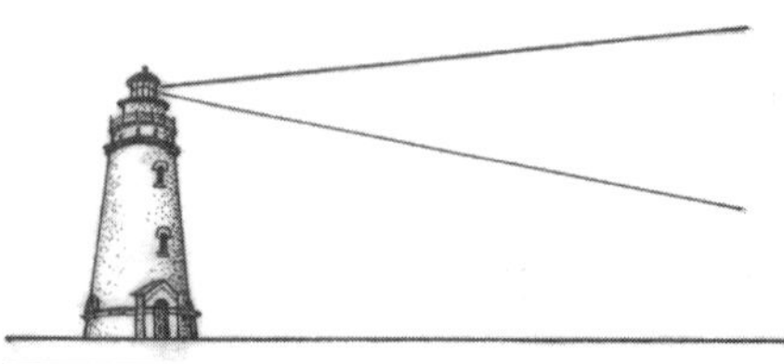

Corned beef was not something you bought at the grocery store in the early days of the twentieth century. Following are directions for making your own:

To Corn Beef

One hundred pounds of beef, eight pounds of salt, four pounds of brown sugar, one-quarter pound of saltpeter, one-quarter pound of black pepper. Pulverize (everything but the beef) and mix well. Put a layer of the mixture on the bottom of the barrel, then a layer of beef, then mixture, and so on until beef is all used, then place a weight on it. In three or four days it will make its own brine. Keep covered under the brine and it will keep until it is consumed.

Note: This recipe is from "Crumbs from Everybody's Table". It was a community cookbook compiled by Mrs. Arina Porter and Mrs. Eva Ball for the ladies of St. Paul's guild in Salinas in 1907.

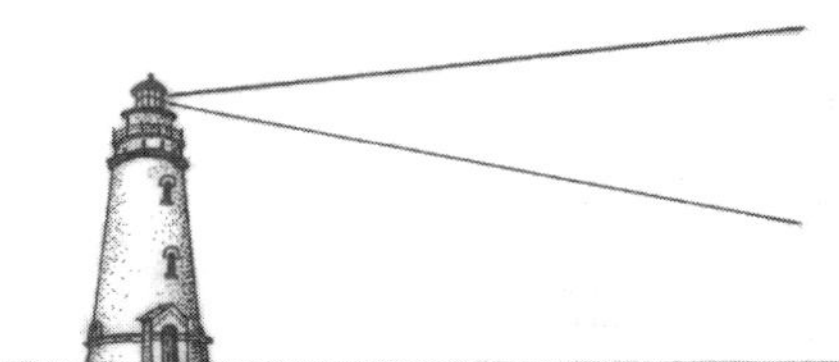

Scalloped Oysters

1/2 cup butter
2 cups (2 slices) of soft bread crumbs
1/4 cup grated Parmesan cheese
1/4 teaspoon salt   dash of mace, if desired
1 pint of fresh shucked oysters, drained
1/4 cup of milk or cream

Heat oven to 375°F. In 8-or 9-inch square pan, melt the margarine in pan in oven. Stir in bread crumbs, cheese, salt and mace. Remove about half of crumbs, arrange remaining crumbs evenly in pan. Place oysters over crumbs, pour milk over top. Sprinkle with remaining crumbs. Bake at 375°F. for 20 to 25 minutes or until lightly browned. Makes 4 servings

Raw Oysters

The flavor of the oyster is so delicate that they are best served well chilled, or have them shucked at the table and served with just a squeeze of lemon juice, and a grinding of black pepper.

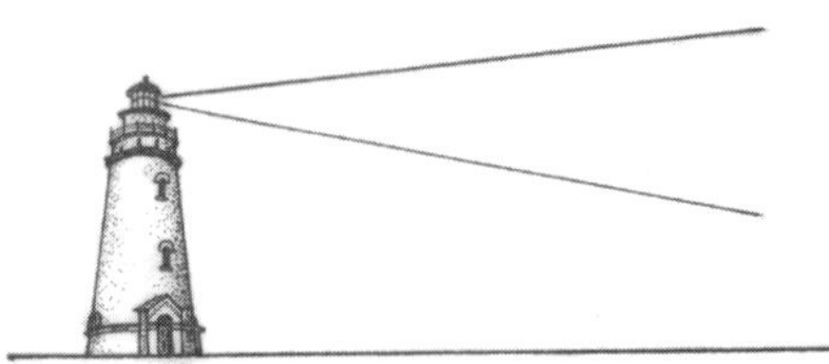

Oysters On The Half-shell

When serving oysters as part of the dinner, allow 6-8 oysters per person. Always buy fresh oysters.

6-8 oysters per person
crushed or cracked ice
black pepper or cayenne pepper
lemons, cut in quarters

Open the shell and drain the water from the shell without disturbing the oyster. Remove the top half of the shell and place the bottom half of the shell with the oyster in it on a plate of crushed ice. Sprinkle with lemon juice, salt, cayenne or black pepper and serve with buttered crackers.

Clams on the Half Shell

Littleneck or cherrystone clams with lemon and cocktail sauce. Make sure to use very fresh clams. Cover with ice until the shells can be opened. Open just before eating

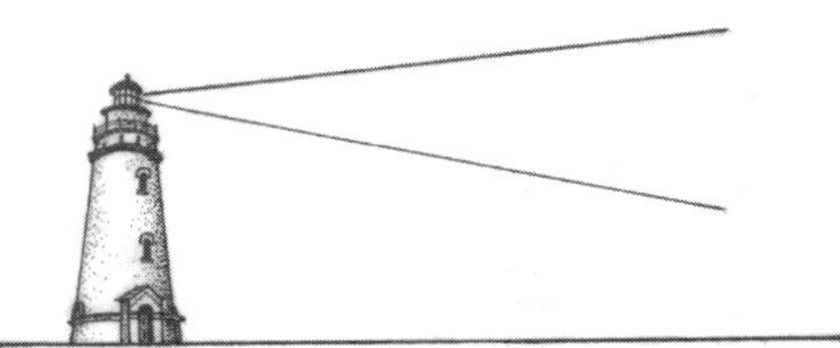

Clam Chowder

Wash one dozen clams, slice an onion; slice two large potatoes; two thin slices of salt pork cut in small squares, and one quart of milk. Fry pork until brown, put in onions and potatoes, four grated crackers, salt and pepper, and one half of a red pepper chopped fine. Boil all in milk. When boiled twenty minutes add clams and boil a few minutes longer. .....Mrs. W. H. Pyburn

Fried Steelhead

Wipe fish dry and if large cut into convenient sized pieces. Dip into sifted cornmeal, rolled crackers, grated stale bread or wheat flour, and fry in butter or olive oil.

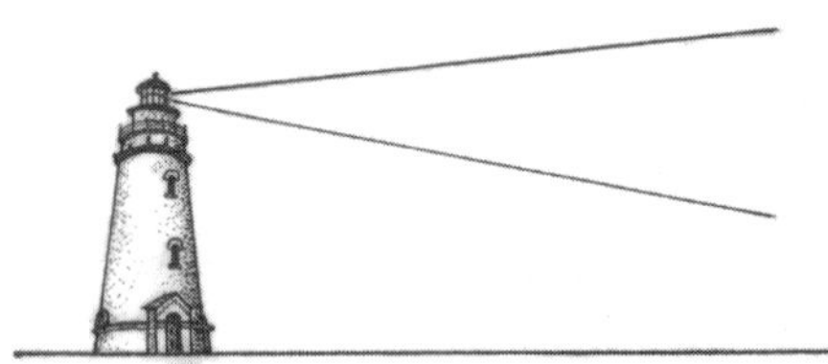

<u>Baked Steelhead(trout)</u>

To bake, soften a little butter and rub over fish, sprinkle with salt and place on a wire stand over a dripping pan. Bake in a quick oven, allowing about twenty minutes per pound.

Note: The fish with the common name steelhead trout is the same species as rainbow trout . The main difference is that the steelhead spends its adult life in salt water only returning to fresh water to spawn. The rainbow remains in fresh water it's entire life. Any recipe for salmon or trout would be suitable. If the fish is over 3 lbs. it would improve the flavor if the fish is skinned. This fish will generally have a high fat content; skinning will help in eliminating the extra fat while the fish is cooking.

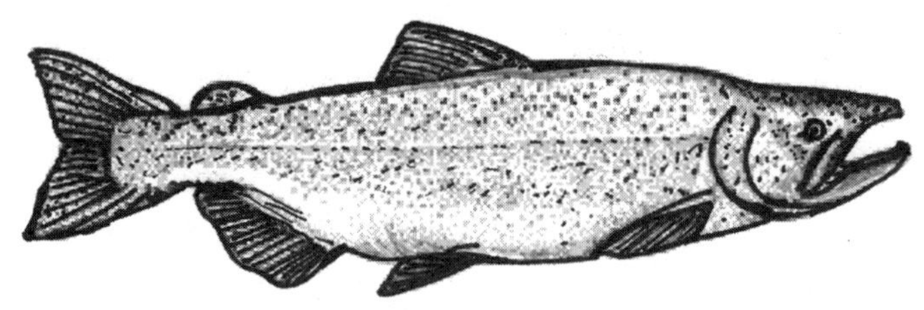

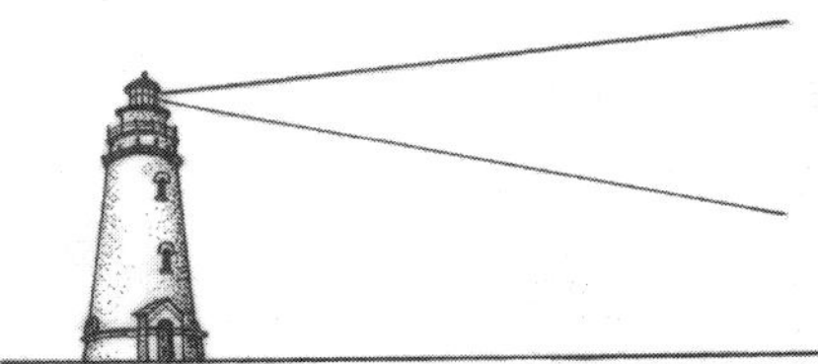

Pan Fried Clams

1 lb. shucked clams
2 cups breading
2 eggs
milk
flour
salt and pepper

Rinse clams under cold water and drain. Mix flour with salt and pepper to taste. Beat eggs with small amount of milk. Place about 1/2 inch oil in a large frying pan on a medium high setting. Dredge the clams through the flour first, then the eggs and last through the breading, making sure the clams are fully covered through each step. Once oil is hot, place the clams in the fry pan. Cook 45 to 60 seconds per side until golden brown. Place fried clams on paper towel to drain excess oil. Makes a yummy pile of clam goodies.

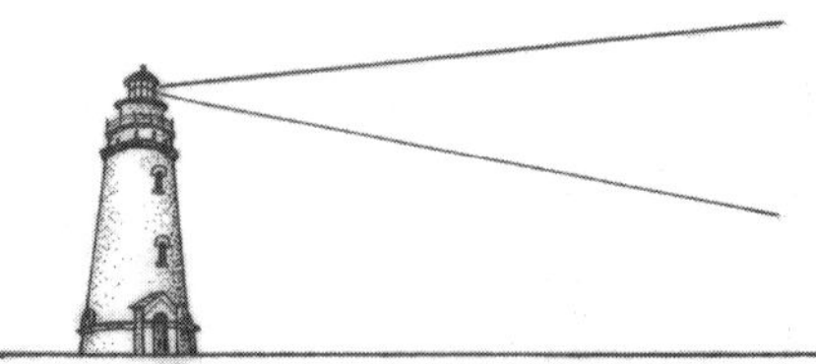

Liver and Onions

2 tablespoons butter
2 large onions, thinly sliced
1 pound beef liver slices
All-purpose flour

Heat the butter in a large skillet over medium-high heat. Add the onions; reduce heat to medium and cook until lightly browned, about 15 to 20 minutes. Remove from pan. Lightly coat the liver with flour. Add butter to the pan if needed and heat over medium-high heat. Add the liver and fry until brown and cooked through, about 5 minutes per side. (Overcooking can ruin liver.) Return the onions to the pan to reheat. Place the liver on a serving dish and top with onions.

Roast Beef Heart

Wash well and clean all the blood from the pipes: parboil it ten or fifteen minutes in boiling water; drip the water from it. Lard the heart and put in a stuffing which has been made of bread

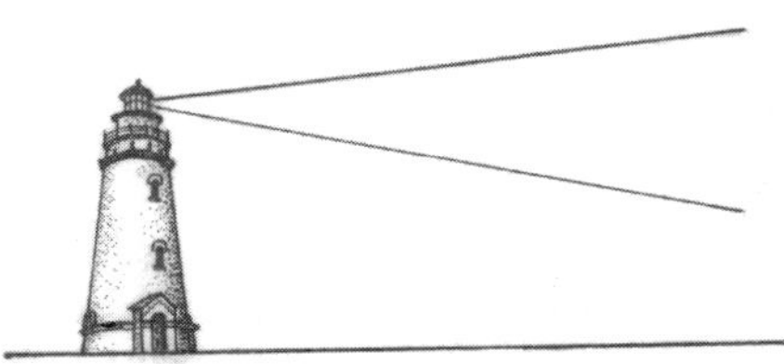

crumbs, minced suet, a little ham, butter, sweet marjoram, thyme, parsley, salt, pepper and a little mustard and onion according to one's taste. Put to roast at once; baste well with suet and butter mixed. Serve with a drawn gravy or currant jelly. To roast allow twenty minutes to the pound.

.....Mrs. J. B. Bennett

Note: This recipe is from "Crumbs from Everybody's Table".

Beef Tongue

2-1/2 lb. beef tongue   1 onion, sliced
2 tbsp. pickling spices

Place tongue in pot. Add onions and spices. Cover with water. Simmer uncovered for 3 hours. Drain and cool. Remove skin and serve.

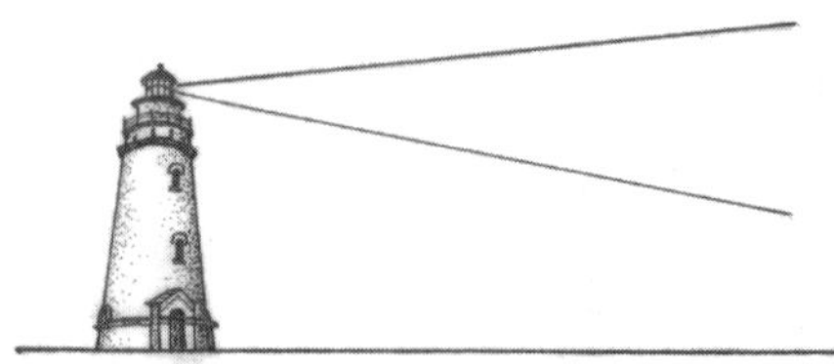

Note: The next two recipes are from "Crumbs from Everybody's Table"

Abalone Fritters

Clean well, remove outside rim. Slice in one-fourth inch slices and pound well with a meat hammer. Dip slices in batter and fry in hot lard until light brown. Batter: one egg, one cupful of sweet milk, one teaspoonful of baking powder and salt to taste. Garnish with limes and serve hot.

.....Mrs. T. Hughes

Abalones Fried

Clean and slice as for fritters; pound well; salt and pepper. Dip each slice in beaten egg, then in cracker crumbs and fry in butter until a nice brown. Serve immediately.

.....Mrs. T. Hughes

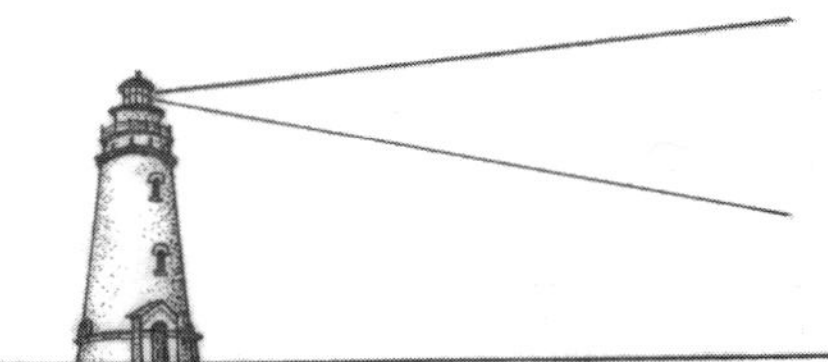

Abalone Chowder

4 slices bacon, diced
6 abalones, pounded and
      cut into small cubes
1 large potato, peeled and diced
1 medium onion, finely chopped
1 garlic clove, crushed
1-1/2 cups hot water
3 cups hot milk
1 tablespoon butter
salt and pepper to taste

Lightly brown the bacon and pour off all but about 2 tablespoons of the drippings. Add the abalone, potato, onion and garlic. Sauté until golden brown. Add the hot water, cover the pan and simmer until the potato is tender. Add the hot milk and butter. Salt and pepper to taste.

Note: The rocks along the coast near the lighthouse teamed with abalone in the 1800s. In 1906 Lorin Jr. bought an abalone-drying operation on San Simeon Point and had 20 divers working for him.

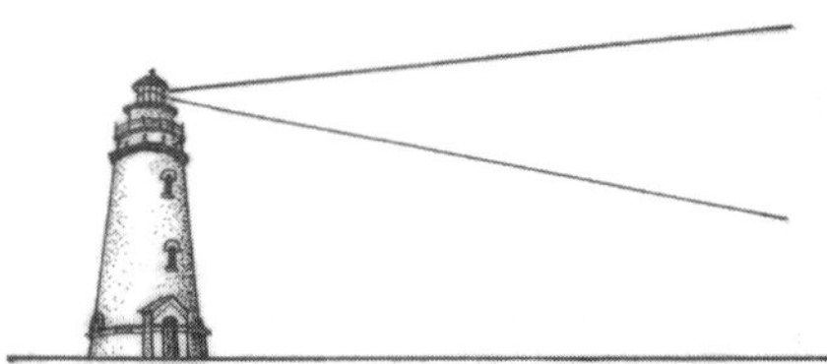

Potato Corn Chowder

3 strips of bacon   1 medium onion, chopped
1 tablespoon flour
1 cup diced potatoes
1-1/2 cups cooked dried corn
1 cup milk   1 cup water

Cut 3 strips of bacon into 1/8" pieces. Fry bacon and remove from pan. Sauté one medium sized chopped onion in the remaining fat. Add one tablespoon flour. Mix flour, onions and fat until thoroughly combined. Add remaining ingredients. Salt and pepper to taste. Simmer all ingredients together for 10 minutes. After cooking, fold in 2 tablespoons of chopped parsley.

Note: Soak corn for 18-24 hrs. in lukewarm water to rehydrate. Some authorities believe that 20 minutes is a sufficient soaking time, I leave the timing to you.

.....Bev Praver

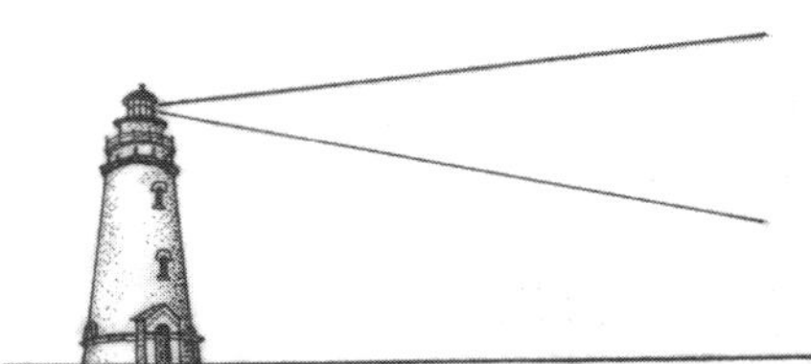

Pioneer Dried Corn and Pork

Use equal portions of corn and salt pork. Cut up salt pork into small pieces, and boil in enough water to cover for 10 minutes. Pour off water and replace with fresh water. Add corn. Originally, the corn used was dried, but you can use either canned or frozen corn. Boil slowly for an hour. Add a small onion, minced finely and cook another half hour. Serve.

Note: This is not one of the uses of dried corn that Donna mentioned but I believe it may have been a recipe typical of the time period.   .....Bev Praver

Dried Apples

There are many schools of thought concerning the proper method of rehydrating dried apples for use in recipes. Soaking time varies from twenty minutes to four hours. The important point seems to be watching them to be sure they are soft but not mushy.

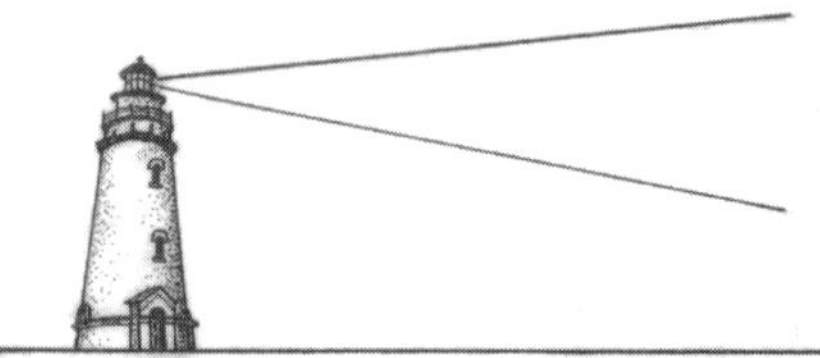

Dried Apple Pie

1-1/2 c boiling water
1-1/2 c dried apple slices
1/3 c sugar
1/2 tsp. cinnamon; ground
1/4 tsp. nutmeg; ground
2 tbsp butter or margarine
1 unbaked two-crust pastry
1 to 3 tbsp heavy cream if desired

Pour boiling water over dried apples and let soak for 3 to 4 hours. Add sugar, cinnamon, and nutmeg. Stir well. Fit half of pastry into a 9-inch pie pan and pour apple mixture into this. Dot with butter or margarine cut into bits. Cover with remaining rolled-out pastry, cut several steam vents in top crust and bake 45 minutes in a 350° F. oven. For an old-fashioned pour-through pie, drizzle the cream into the steam vents 5 minutes before the pie is finished baking. Serve the pie warm with ice cream or sharp Cheddar. Makes one 9-inch pie.

Note: I know one experienced cook who rehydrates dried apples in cider or apple juice.   .....Bev Praver

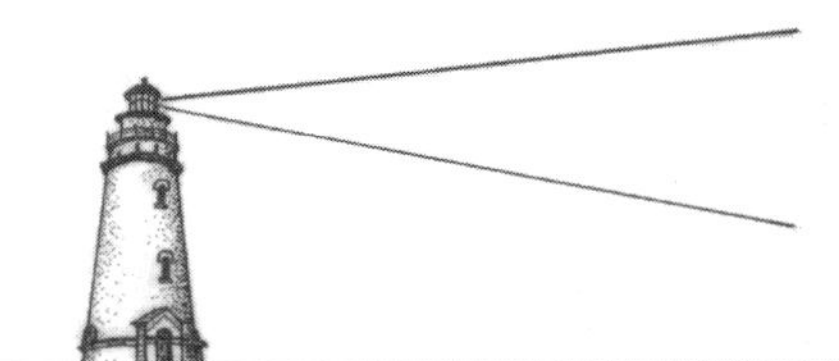

Creamed Potatoes

Put one tablespoon of butter into a frying pan and when it bubbles add one tablespoonful of flour, stirring well. Add gradually one cupful of cream or milk, and season. Onto this pour one pint of cold boiled potatoes cut into small dice and cook until thoroughly hot.

.....Mrs. A.A. Wetherill

Note: This recipe is from "Crumbs from Everybody's Table".

Potato Soup

Boil and mash three or four potatoes. In a medium saucepan melt one tablespoon of butter. Cook 1 teaspoon of chopped onion for a few minutes in the butter; stir in 1/2 tablespoon of flour into the butter and onion mixture. When this is cooked add to it a pint of milk, making a thin white sauce. Add this to the mashed potatoes and pass the whole through a strainer. Return it to the fire for a few minutes to heat and blend it. Season it with salt and pepper. Sprinkle on the soup, chopped parsley and a few croutons.

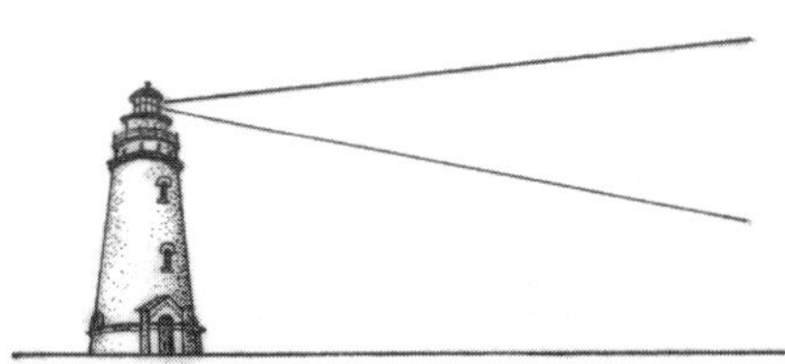

Lyonnaise Potatoes

Cut cold boiled potatoes into dice. Put into a saucepan one tablespoon of butter and one onion sliced. Shake until onion is golden brown. Throw in potatoes so that each piece will come into contact with the butter. Toss and cook until every piece is carefully browned. Serve at once.

.....Miss F.G. Woodcock

Note: This recipe is from "Crumbs from Everybody's Table".

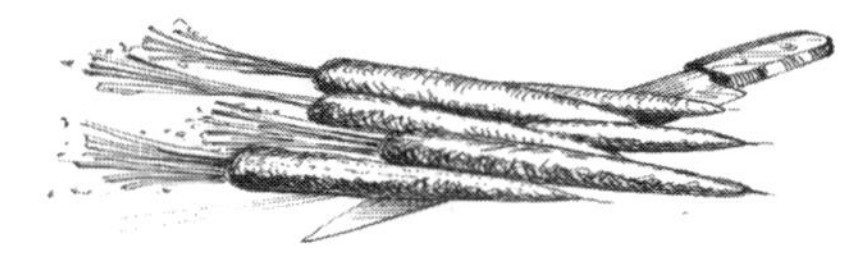

Three Ways of Cooking Carrots

Boil until tender, mash fine, season with salt and pepper, and lastly add a little cream and butter.

After cooking, slice lengthwise, dip in the following batter and fry until brown. Batter: One egg, three tablespoons of milk, a little flour, salt

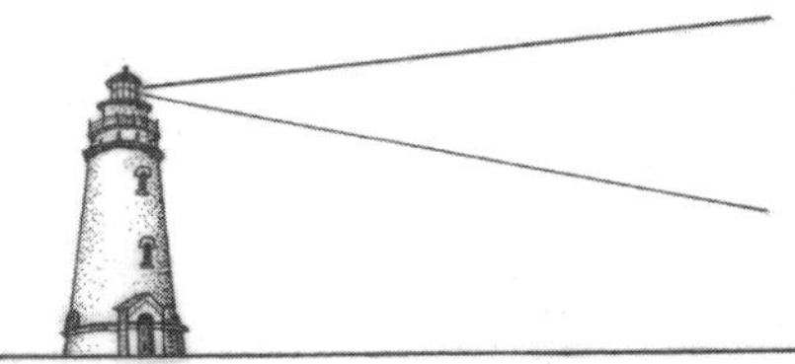

and a pinch of baking powder. Beat well.

When cooked, chop into coarse pieces, add milk, season with salt and pepper, add a small piece of butter and thicken with a little flour or corn starch. Cook a few minutes and serve.

.....Mrs. M.L. Dexter

Note: This recipe is from "Crumbs from Everybody's Table".

Creamed Carrots

1 pound carrots, peeled and sliced
2 Tbs. butter
cream or milk
1 Tbs. flour

Cook carrots in water till tender. Pour off water. Put some cream in a pint jar, add flour and put jar lid on tight. Shake till smooth. Pour into cooked carrots, add more cream or milk. Cook on low heat till thickened. Add butter and mix well. Pour into a bowl and add a pat of butter. Serve.

.....Gerald R. Thorndyke's Kitchen

Note: Gerald R. Thorndyke is a great grandson of Capt. Thorndyke and is Donna Jean Thorndyke Schneider's brother.

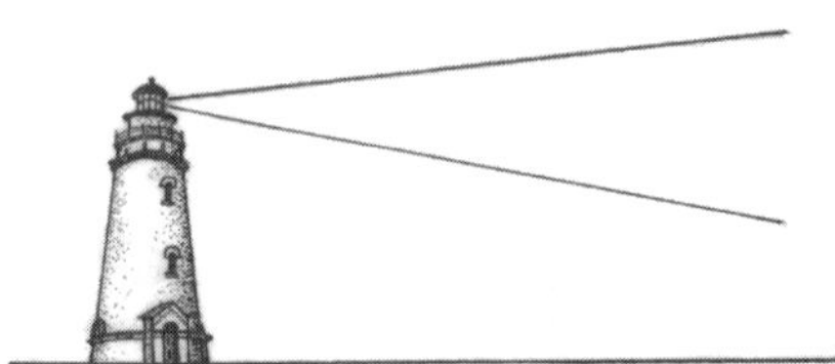

Rice Soup

1 cup rice   1 quart milk

Wash rice till water runs clear. Combine rice and milk. Slow simmer till rice is cooked. Add more milk if needed. Serve with crackers and cheese. Bake lots of cornbread. Have plenty of butter on hand. Make extra to use in rice pudding the next day.

Note: Easy wash day (Monday) supper...family's favorite

.....Thorndyke Family

Rice Pudding

2 cups cooked rice   2 cups milk
3 eggs, beaten   1/2 cup sugar
1 cup raisins   1 tsp. vanilla

Pour into greased baking dish and place in a pan of water 2 or 3 inches deep. Sprinkle with cinnamon. Bake at 350°/ 375° oven for 1 hour. Check using knife blade in the center of the

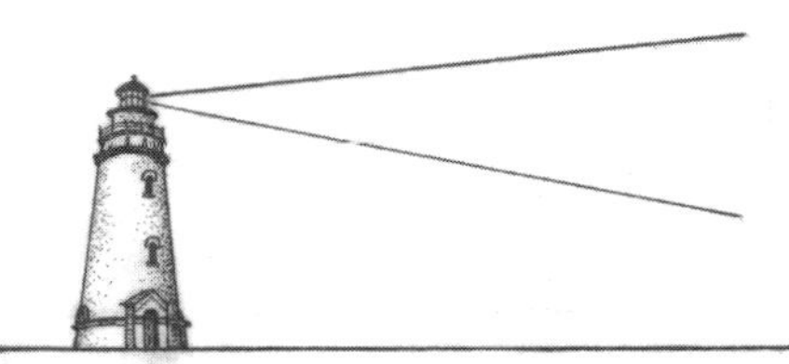

pudding. Keep checking the last few minutes. If custard is too done water seeps from the pudding. Serve with thick cream.

Note: This was made with the plain rice soup leftovers.

.....Thorndyke Family

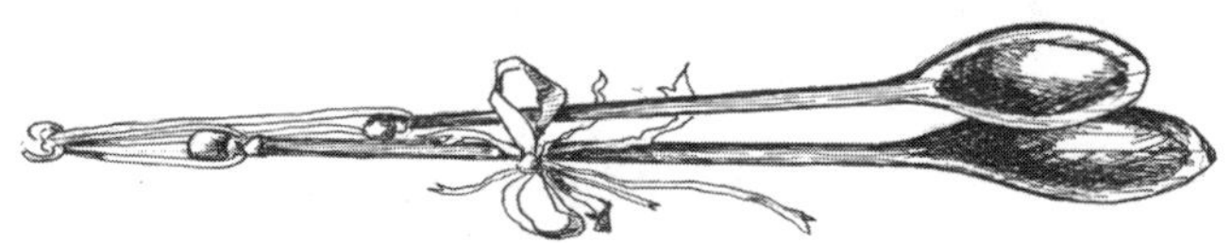

Cornmeal Mush

1 cup cornmeal   1 cup cold water
3 cups water   1 teaspoon salt

1. Stir cornmeal into 1 cup cold water in a bowl. Bring 3 cups water and the salt to a boil in a large saucepan. Add cornmeal mixture to the boiling water gradually, stirring constantly.

2. Cook for 5 to 10 minutes or until thickened, stirring frequently. Serve with sugar and milk or with butter.   Makes 6 servings.

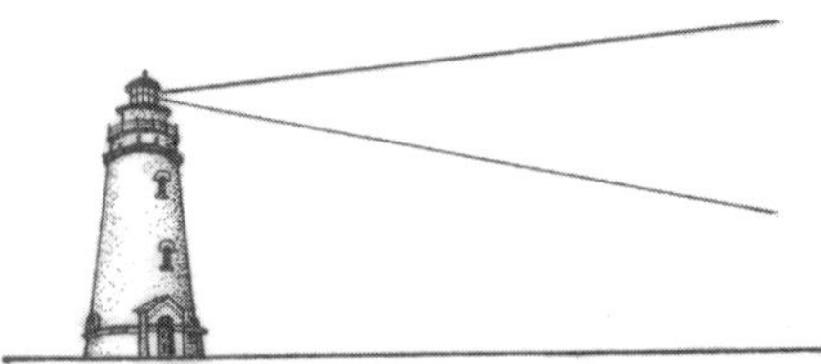

Fried Cornmeal Mush

Pour hot mush mixture into lightly greased loaf pan. Cool at room temperature and then cover and refrigerate overnight. Cut into thin slices. Fry in butter, bacon fat, shortening, oil or lard in skillet over medium-low heat until brown on both sides. Serve with butter and syrup or as desired.

Scrapple

12	cups pork broth, strong (made from pork shoulder meat)
2	cups pork, finely cut
3	cups cornmeal
1	medium onion, chopped
1	teaspoon marjoram
1	teaspoon sage
1	teaspoon thyme
	salt and pepper

In a large saucepan, combine the broth, pork, cornmeal, onion, herbs, salt and pepper. Simmer for 1 hour. Remove pan from heat and pour the

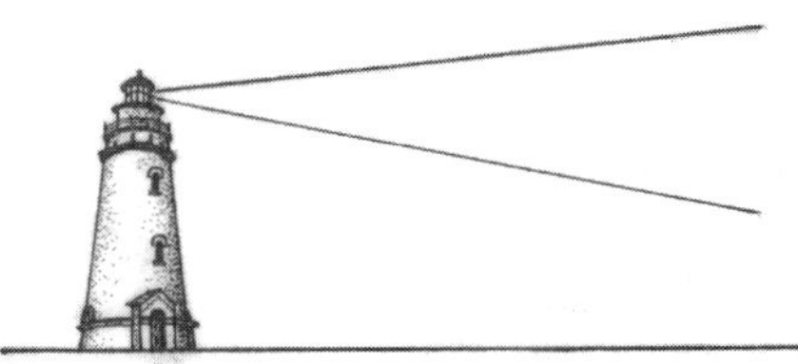

mixture into large loaf pans. Chill until scrapple sets. When ready to serve scrapple, slice loaf into 1/2-inch slabs and sauté in a butter-coated skillet.

8-10 servings   It goes well with syrup, ketchup or applesauce.

Scrapple may be eaten hot or cold. Scrapple is chopped or ground pork and cornmeal mush, cooked and shaped in a loaf pan, cooled, then sliced and browned in butter to serve. It is a true American specialty of the Pennsylvania Dutch (who called it ponhaws or pawnhaus). It was originally made from 'scraps' of pork.

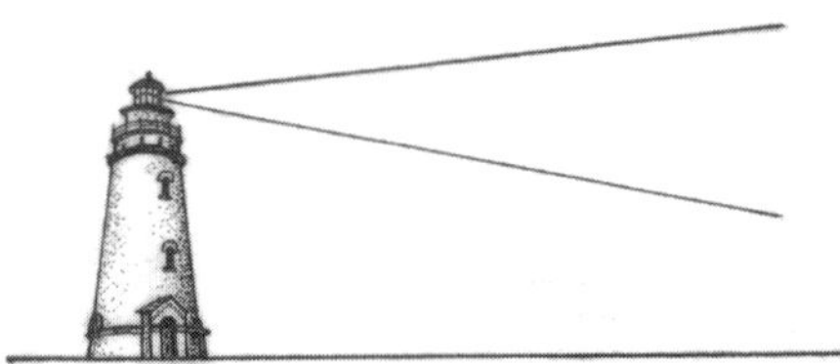

Candied Butternut Squash

*1 butternut squash, halved, seeded, peeled,
	cut into 3/4-inch cubes (2-1/4-pound)
3 Tbs. butter, melted	1/2 tsp. salt
3/4 cup sugar	1/8 tsp. ground cloves
1 tsp. ground cinnamon
1/4 tsp. ground black pepper*

Preheat oven to 375°F. Place squash in 8 x 8 x 2- inch glass baking dish.

Drizzle with butter; toss to coat. Blend sugar, cinnamon, salt, pepper and cloves in small bowl; mix into squash. Bake until squash is tender and syrup bubbles thickly in dish, stirring gently every 15 minutes, about 50 minutes total.

Makes 6 servings.

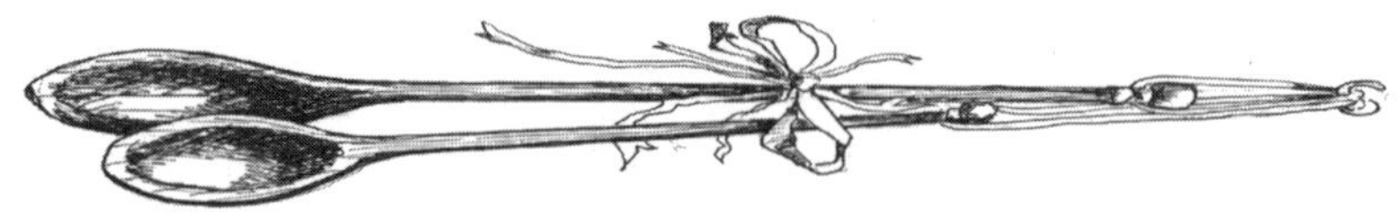

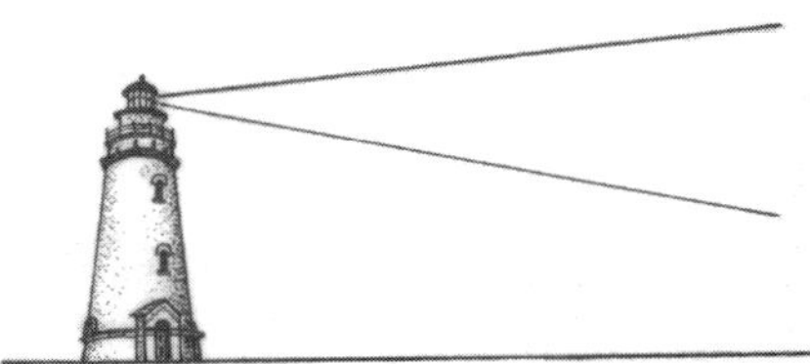

Rhubarb has been a Thorndyke family favorite ever since it was grown at Piedras Blancas Light Station, where it is still growing.

Nine-Inch Rhubarb Pie

4 cups cut rhubarb
1 cup sugar
2 Tbs. flour
1 tsp. cinnamon
1/4 tsp. nutmeg

1 double piecrust
2 Tbs. butter
1 tsp. cream
1 tsp. sugar

Mix rhubarb, sugar, flour, spices in bowl; pour into pie tin with bottom crust in place. Dot butter around rhubarb mixture. Place top crust and crimp. Drop cream over crust and rub gently, lightly sprinkle with sugar. Poke steam holes in top crust. Bake in hot oven, 400° nearly 1 hour.

.....Maud's Kitchen

Note: Maud made 3 pies at a time; one for dinner, one for "3 o'clock coffee time" and one for supper.

.....Donna Thorndyke Schneider

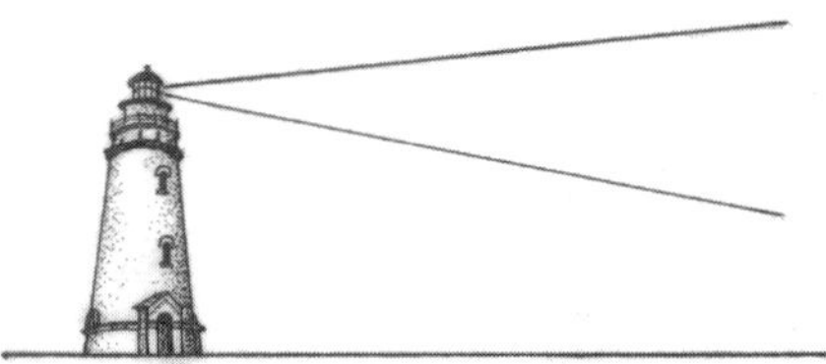

Rhubarb Conserve

2 heaping cups of finely cut rhubarb
2 oranges and rind of one – grind
1/2 cup crushed pineapple
2 or 2-1/2 cups sugar

Cook till thick enough, <u>doesn't take long</u>
Add 1 cup of nuts if you like.

.....Thorndyke Family

Rhubarb Jam

5 cups finely cut rhubarb, add 4 cups sugar. Let stand till it makes some juice (overnight if need be). Cook slowly for 10 minutes. Take off fire and stir in one box of raspberry Jell-O® till dissolved. Put in jars and seal.

3 cups rhubarb and 2 cups strawberries is delicious also.

.....Thorndyke Family

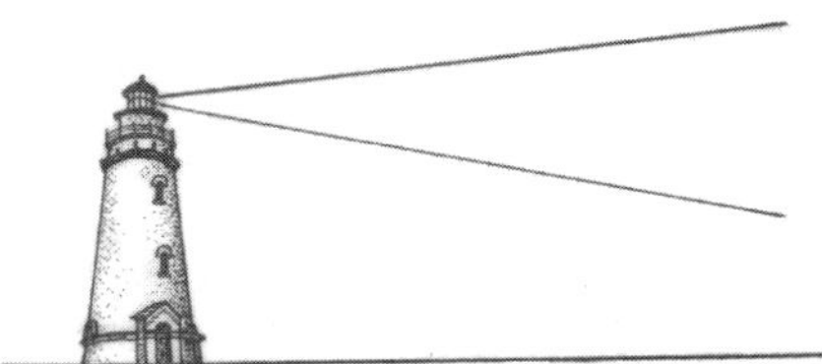

All families have recipes that exist only in their family. Someone made them up long ago and the family liked them, so they were handed down from one generation to the next. This is one of the Thorndyke favorites.

Pullillies (Pa-lee-lees)

Pullillies are made by taking pieces of white bread dough after it has risen twice and deep frying them just before serving. When you get them on your plate you slit them and put butter or jam in them.

....Linda Buttke Thorndyke

Note: According to Linda Buttke Thorndyke, Erma's the one who made pullillies. She doesn't know where the name came from. Linda has made these with her mother-in-law, Marjorie Ingersoll Thorndyke (called Marni). Linda is married to Jim Thorndyke, a great-grandson of Capt. L.V. Thorndyke.

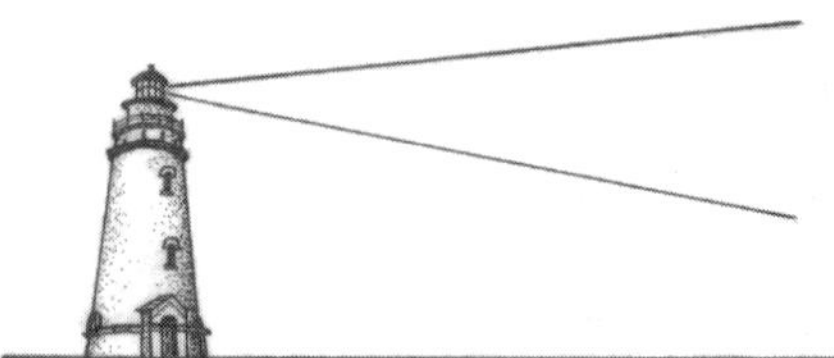

Graveyard Stew

(*So called because you make it when you are too dead to eat anything else.*)

2 pieces of toast	1-1/2 cups milk
1 Tbsp. butter pepper	salt

Scald milk; add butter, salt and pepper. Make 2 pieces of toast, butter them and break into scalded milk.

Here's another recipe for graveyard stew, but this time it's called Milk Toast.

Milk Toast

1 slice white bread	warm milk
sugar	cinnamon
butter	vanilla extract

This really could not be easier! Toast the bread and tear into small pieces. Place in a bowl and dot with butter. Heat milk. Pour over toast and butter. Add sugar, cinnamon and vanilla to taste. Mix well. Allow the toast to absorb the milk and soften before serving.   Serves 1

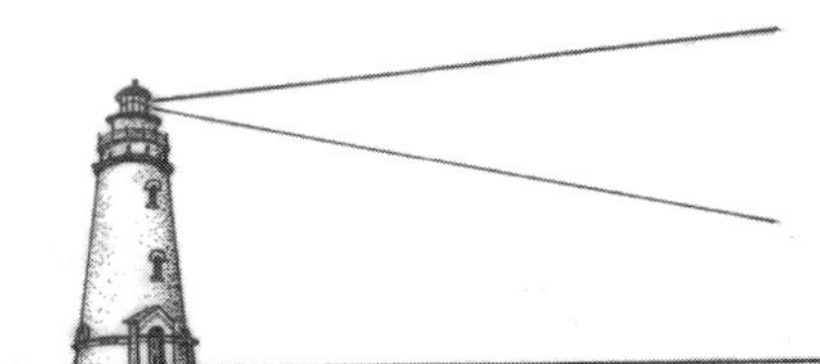

Thorndyke Breakfast

Fried Potatoes

Breakfast potatoes started with melting bacon grease in the pan, slicing 3-5 lbs. of potatoes and frying till brown. Pour off most of the grease, cover pan, turn down heat and finish the rest of the breakfast.

Note: L.V. Jr. liked chopped or sliced onion added while cooking. These were served every morning but Sunday, which was Skinny Hotcake day.

Breakfast was after morning milking: cooked cereal; juice and fruit; pork chops or ham or sausage or bacon; fried potatoes; eggs cooked to each person's likes i.e. fried, scrambled and L.V. JR's favorite, soft boil -three minutes only! - biscuits or toast; jam, honey and butter; coffee, hot tea, milk and cream.

This was all set out on the table each morning. Try not to forget anything. If you had to get up some - times your favorite thing was gone before returning.

.....Donna Thorndyke Schneider

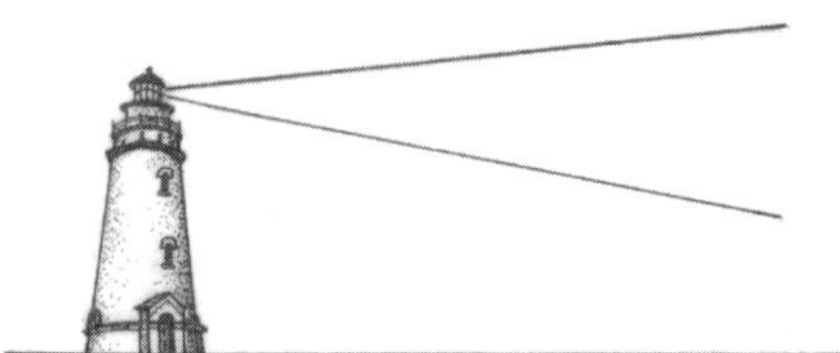

Skinny Hotcakes

6 eggs   2 cups flour
4 cups milk   1/2 cup sugar (optional)

Mix all together to make a thin batter. Heat griddle till smoking. Lightly grease pan. Next, pour 1/2 cup of batter in center of griddle. Then quickly tilt pan around to cover the entire griddle with a thin layer of batter. Brown quickly and flip over till done. Serve on warmed plates. Roll up with butter, Caramel syrup and or fruit.

......Thorndyke Family

Caramel Syrup

1 cup sugar   1 cup milk
1 cup brown sugar   1/2 tsp. vanilla

Combine sugars and milk in a pan, bring to boil, stirring constantly. This is put on simmer, after boiling a couple minutes, while hotcakes are being cooked, stirring occasionally.

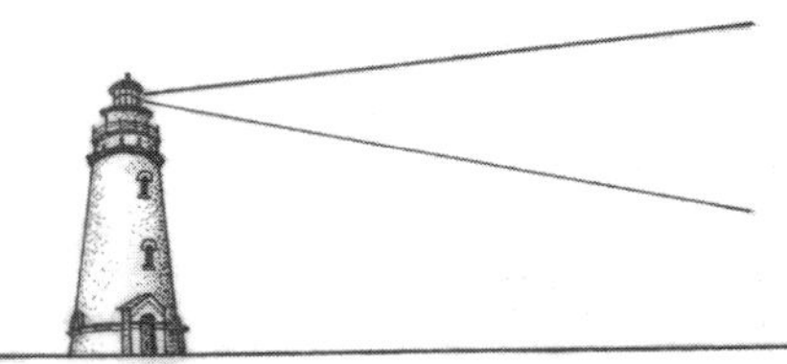

Here are two more of the family recipes.

French Fried Almonds

2 cups whole Almonds, shelled
Boiling water   Salt

Put almonds in small bowl, cover with boiling water, soak till the brown skins, when pinched, slip off of nuts. Dry well.

Fry in hot oil. When browned drain on paper towels. Sprinkle with salt.

—*Daisy Rogers Abbey*

Note: Before her marriage, Daisy worked at the lighthouse cooking for the crews. She and her sister, Maud Rogers Thorndyke, also worked in the hotels in San Simeon as cooks and housekeepers. Daisy later owned an almond orchard in Paso Robles, which still remains in the Abbey family.

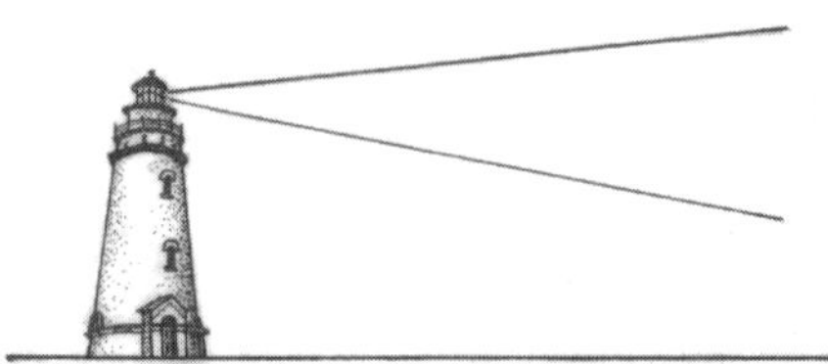

Homemade Ice Cream

6 eggs
6 cups light cream
2 Tbs. vanilla

2-1/2 cups sugar
4 cups heavy cream
Dash salt

Beat eggs; add sugar, vanilla, light cream and salt. Pour into ice cream freezer pail, add dasher, now add last of cream up to full line. Cap and put into wooden bucket. Layer with ice and salt.

Churn until solid. Carefully remove dasher, put cap on and pack in ice again, cover with gunnysacks until needed.

Note: This was made for most outdoor picnics and gatherings. Cream from the Thorndyke dairy was used in everything; breakfast cereal, fruit, soups, gravy, coffee and anything that needed a "little something".

.....Thorndyke Family

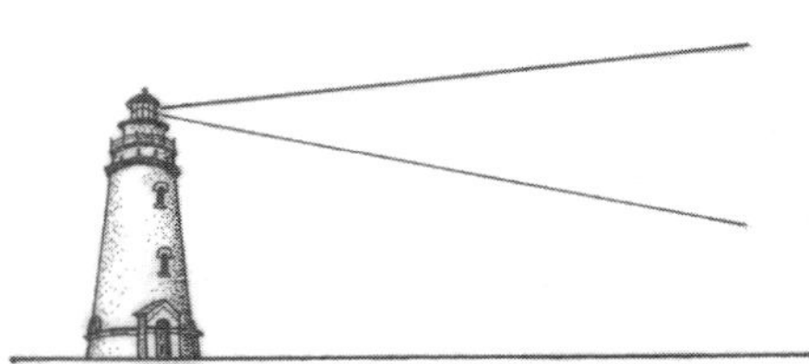

A family gathering in the 1940s L-R : John Rogers, Gene Rogers, Carol Ingles, Sissy Ingles, Nancy Lee Thorndyke.

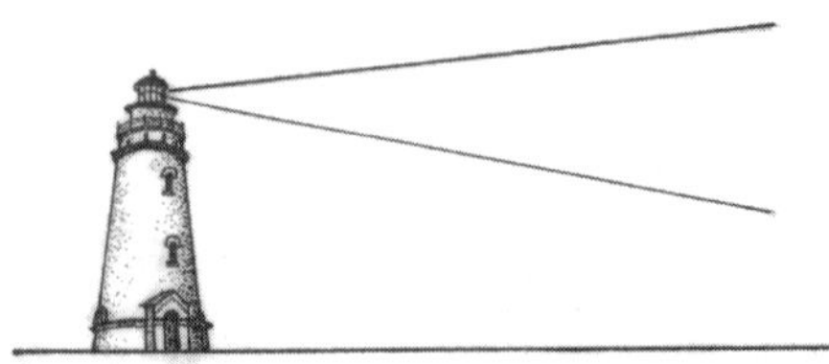

Feather Filling

4 level Tbsp plus 1 1/2 tsp. of flour

Mix slowly with one cup water, then cook until transparent (should be like thick whipped cream). Cool and put in fridge.

When cold, cream 1 cup powdered sugar and 1/2 cup <u>butter only</u> and mix with cooked preparation. Then add 1 cup chopped or ground nuts. Flavor preparation with one tsp. vanilla.

Save out 1/4 cup for topping.

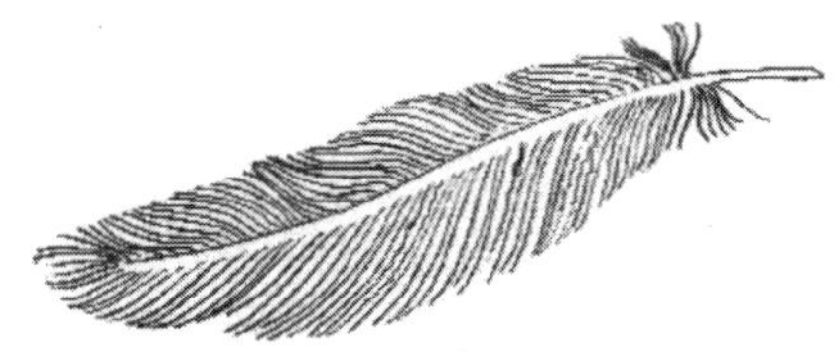

This recipe comes to us from Nancy Lee Thorrndyke Poe, another of Capt. Thorndyke's great-granddaughters. Nancy got it from a dear friend of the family, Linda Luchessa Hampton who was born in this area December 24, 1904. Linda said that the recipe was given to her by Millie Shaug, a half sister of Maud Rogers Thorndyke.

The Descendants

Daisy Rogers Abbey and Maud Rogers Thorndyke in front of the L.V. Thorndyke store in San Simeon circa 1908.

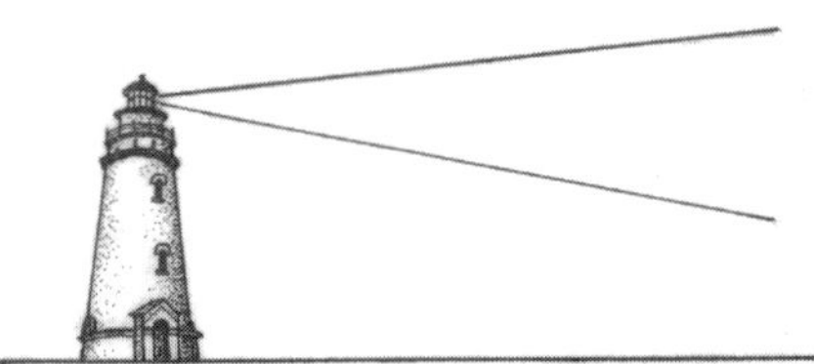

Each generation of the family has added their own recipes and here they share them with you.

Strawberry Fritters

1 quart strawberries	1 tsp. vanilla
1 beaten egg	1-1/2 cups flour
1/4 cup sugar	3 tsp. baking powder
1 Tbs. butter, melt	Dash of salt

Wash and hull berries. Chill. Beat together egg and milk; stir in sugar, butter and vanilla. Combine flour, baking powder and salt; stir into egg mixture, beating till smooth. Dip berries into batter one at a time and deep fry in 375° hot oil till golden brown. Drain well, dust with powdered sugar.

Note: This batter can be used for any fruit cut to bite size.

.....Donna Thorndyke Schneider

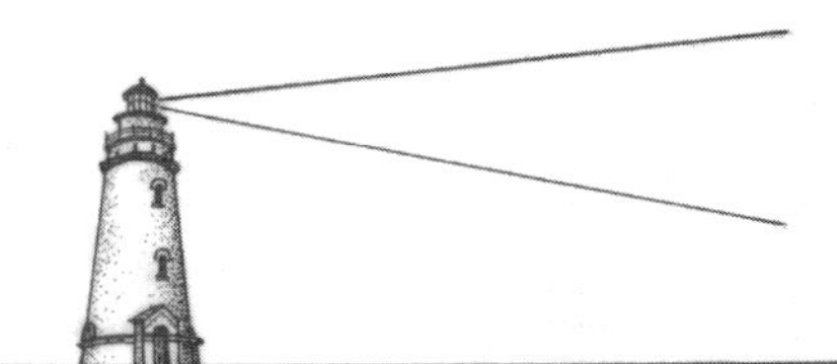

Tamale Pie

1 cup cornmeal (yellow)
2 cups boiling water
1-1/2 tsp. salt
1 onion, chopped
1 cup ripe olives
1 tsp. chili powder

2 Tbs. butter
1 chopped green pepper
1 can corn
2 cups tomatoes
1 pound ground beef

Add 1 tsp. of the salt to the boiling water; slowly stir in the cornmeal. Cook for thirty minutes, and then add the olives. Set aside to cool. Melt butter; add onion, green pepper and meat. Cook till meat is brown. Add tomatoes, chili and corn, remaining salt and cook about 10 minutes. Combine with cornmeal, stirring well. Butter a large casserole, pour mixture into it. Bake at 350° around 1 hour.

Note: Any wild meat may be used. This dish was carried to many family gatherings. A heavy casserole, wrapped in newspaper, put in a heavy cardboard box, then wrapped completely in a blanket. This kept the tamale warm during its journey.

......Thorndyke Family

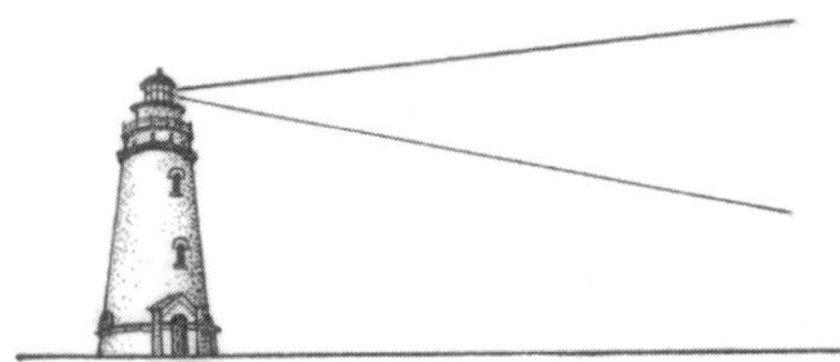

Broccoli & Spinach Casserole

2 pkgs. frozen chopped spinach
2 pkgs. frozen chopped broccoli

Cook according to package instructions and drain thoroughly.

Stir in one pint of sour cream, 1 package of Lipton dry onion soup mix.

Pour mixture in buttered baking dish and top with lots of grated cheddar cheese. Bake 35 minutes at 350°

....Bonnie Thorndyke

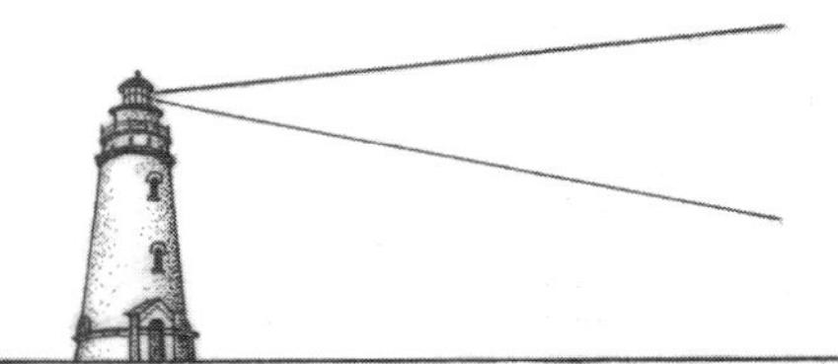

Papa Muir's Meatloaf

1 pound lean ground meat
1 package hot n' spicy sausage
1/4 cup Worcestershire sauce
3 Tbls. garlic salt
1 Tbls. crushed red pepper
4 strips of bacon

Mix together meat, sausage, Worcestershire, garlic salt and red pepper. Form into a loaf and place it in either a glass or metal loaf pan. Top with slices of bacon and bake at 350°F for 40-45 minutes.

....Stephanie & Brian Thorndyke

Note: Brian is a 5th generation Thorndyke and the great-great grandson of Capt. Lorin Thorndyke. Brian's wife, Stephanie Muir Thorndyke, is a fifth cousin to John Muir who founded the Sierra Club.

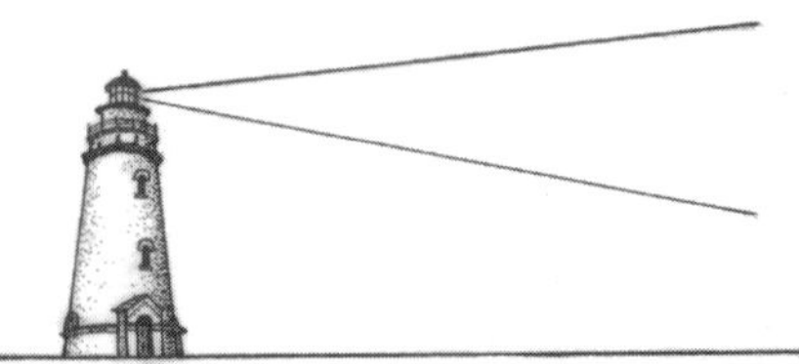

Spicy Pasta Pie

4 oz. broken vermicelli
1 lb. turkey breakfast sausage
1 cup sliced fresh mushrooms
1/2 cup chopped onion
1 – 7 oz. can tomatoes, cut up
1 teaspoon Italian seasoning
1/2 of a 6 oz. can (1/3 c.) tomato paste
1/8 tsp. crushed red pepper
1 clove minced garlic
nonstick spray coating
1 cup shredded mozzarella cheese (4 oz.)
2 tablespoons grated parmesan or
                    romano cheese

Cook vermicelli according to package instructions. Drain well. Set aside. Meanwhile, in a large skillet cook turkey sausage, mushrooms, onion, and garlic until sausage is no longer pink and onion is tender. Drain fat, if necessary.

Stir in undrained tomatoes, tomato paste, Italian seasoning, and crushed red pepper. Spray a 9-inch quiche dish with nonstick spray coating.

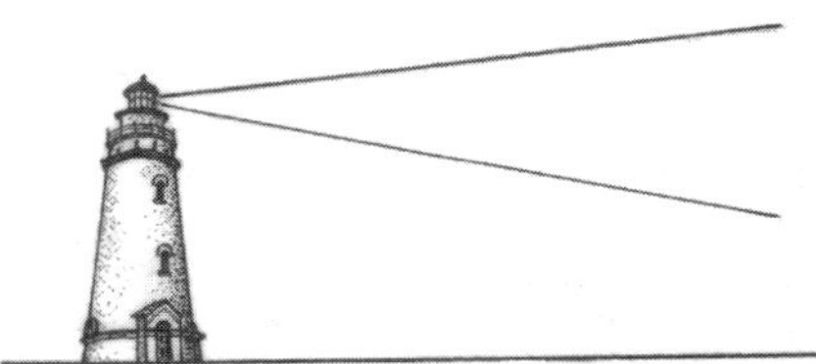

Place half of the cooked vermicelli in the bottom of the dish. Top with half of the mozzarella cheese, and half of the sausage mixture. Repeat layers.

Cover the dish loosely with foil. Bake in a 350°F oven for 25 to thirty minutes or until heated through. Top with Parmesan. Let stand for 10 minutes. Cut into wedges to serve. Serves 6.

....Dana Thorndyke Thiel

Crispy Corn Breakfast Burritos

Fry 2 corn tortillas

Filling: 2 or 3 eggs scrambled with 1/2 tsp. butter, 3 different kinds of cheese, salt and pepper (optional), tomatoes and onions to taste.

Fill tortillas and flip over into a crispy burrito.

....Dana Thorndyke Thiel

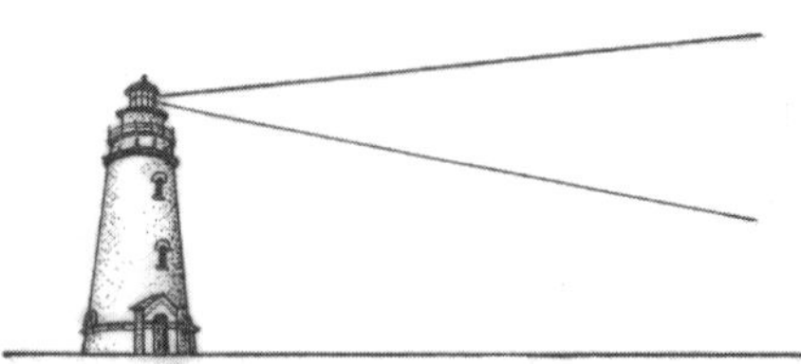

Pot Roast

1 large chuck roast
1 package onion soup – dry
2 onions, quartered
2 stalks of celery cut into 1-inch pieces
whole potatoes
carrots

Brown both sides of roast till very brown. Sprinkle onion soup on top of roast. Add onion and celery. Add water till just to top of roast. Simmer gently 2 hours. Add carrots and potatoes. Put roast on top of veggies. Simmer 1 hour or until everything is tender. Thicken broth with flour to make gravy.

.....Donna Thorndyke Schneider

Note: This is one of George's (Donna's husband) favorites and gives her time to quilt.

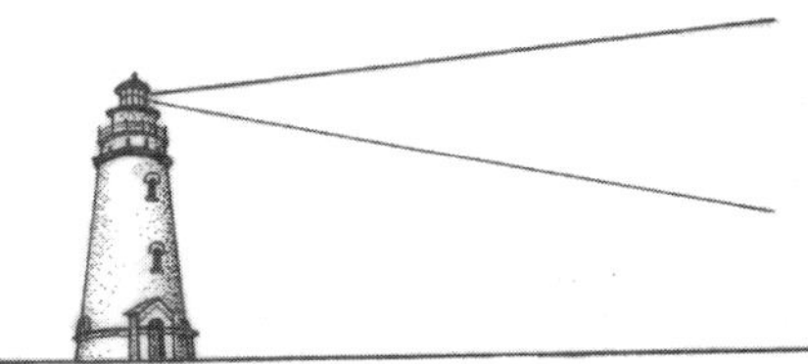

Meal In The Oven

Braised Short Ribs

2-3 lbs. beef short ribs
1 sliced onion
1 tsp. salt
1/2 tsp. garlic powder
3 beef bouillon cubes

Brown ribs on all sides very well. Pour out grease; add onion and the rest of the ingredients. Add water 2 inches over ribs. Bake 2-3 hours at 350°. Lift ribs and onion out of broth onto platter. Remove 1 cup of broth to thicken for gravy. Serve this with potatoes baked the same time as ribs. Also bake one apple per person; serve with cream for dessert.

Save the broth to make onion soup.

.....Donna Thorndyke Schneider

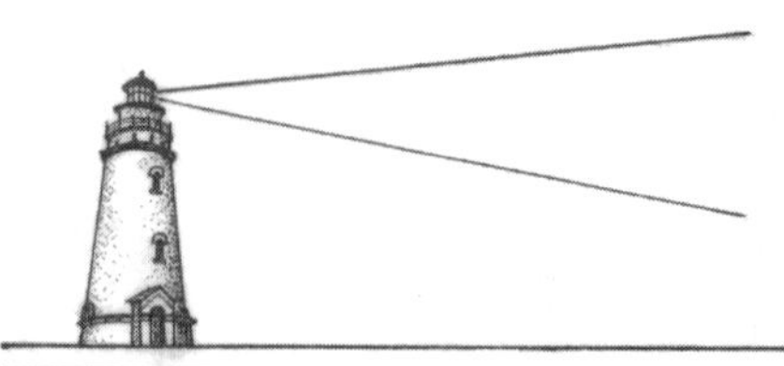

Crockpot French Onion Soup

2 quarts beef broth
6 cups thinly sliced yellow onions
1/2 cup butter   1 Tbs. sugar
2 tsp. salt
2 cups grated parmesan cheese

Pour broth into crockpot. In a large skillet cook onions in butter; cover and cook about 15 minutes. Add salt and sugar, stir well. Add to crockpot, cover and cook on low for 6-8 hours. Before serving add cheese. Serve with croutons.

.....Donna Thorndyke Schneider

Note: This is a favorite of my quilting group. Smelling this simmer all morning while quilting works up the appetite. Someone brings homemade bread, someone dessert. Perfect day. .....D.T.S.

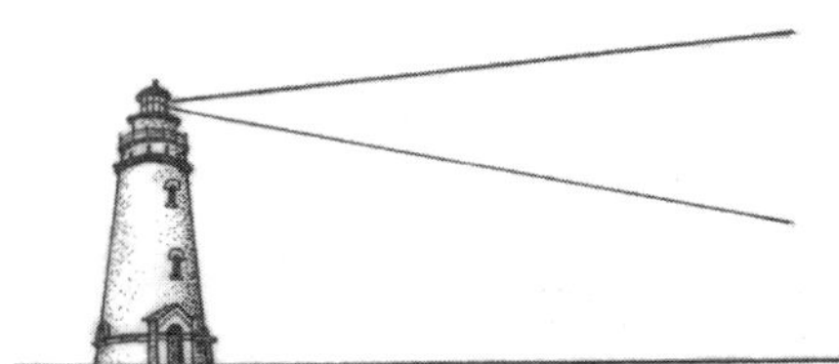

Breaded Tomatoes

1- 16 oz. can of whole tomatoes
2 tsp. sugar   Dash salt and pepper
2 or 3 slices of old bread, pulled into crumbs

Boil tomatoes, sugar, salt and pepper in a pan to mix flavors. Just before serving add crumbs of old bread. Stir gently. Mix well, when completely soaked, the breaded tomatoes are ready to serve. Enjoy!

.....Thorndyke Family

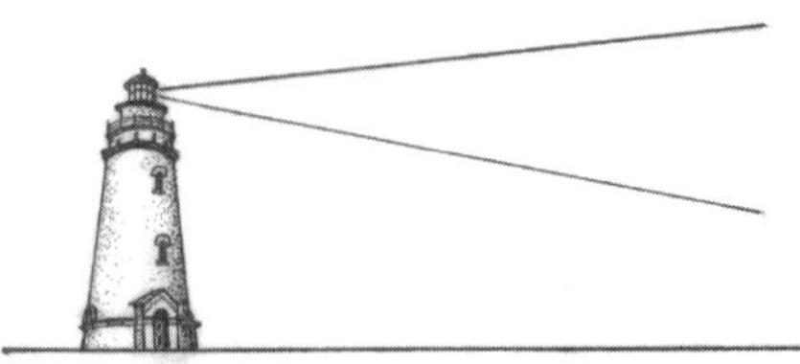

Chard Or Wild Mustard Greens

1 gallon of fresh greens
2 strips of bacon or small bits of ham
1/2 small onion, chopped

Steam greens in small amount of water. Cut bacon into small pieces. Fry slowly, when nearly done add onions. Cook down; add greens to fry pan and simmer covered 10 to 15 minutes.

.....Thorndyke Family

Creamy Lemon Macadamia Cookies

2 cups all purpose flour
1/2 tsp. baking soda   1/4 tsp. salt
1 cup light brown sugar, packed
1/2 cup white sugar   1 large egg
2 tsp. pure lemon extract
1/2 cup salted butter, softened
4 oz. cream cheese, softened
1 1/2 cups whole macadamia nuts, unsalted

Preheat oven to 300 degrees Fahrenheit.

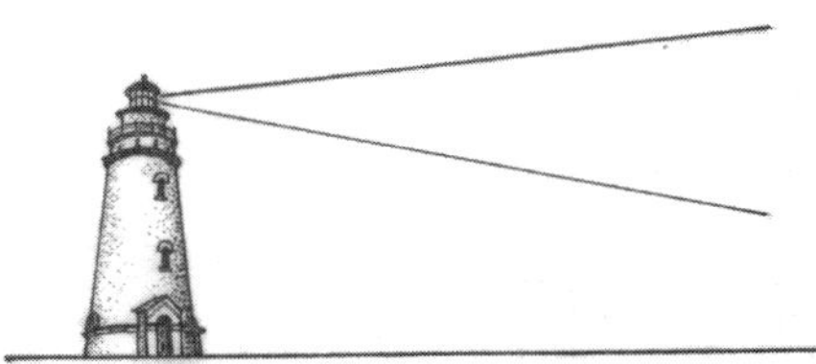

In a medium bowl combine flour, soda and salt. Mix well with wire whisk and set aside.

In a large bowl blend sugars well with an electric mixer set at medium speed. Add the butter and cream cheese, and mix to form a smooth paste. Add the egg and lemon extract, and beat at medium speed until light and soft. Scrape down the sides of the bowl occasionally.

Add the flour mixture and macadamia nuts. Blend at low speed just until combined. Do not overmix.

Drop by rounded tablespoons on to ungreased cookie sheets, 2 inches apart. Bake 23-25 minutes. Immediately transfer cookies with a spatula to a cool flat surface.

....Dana Thorndyke Thiel

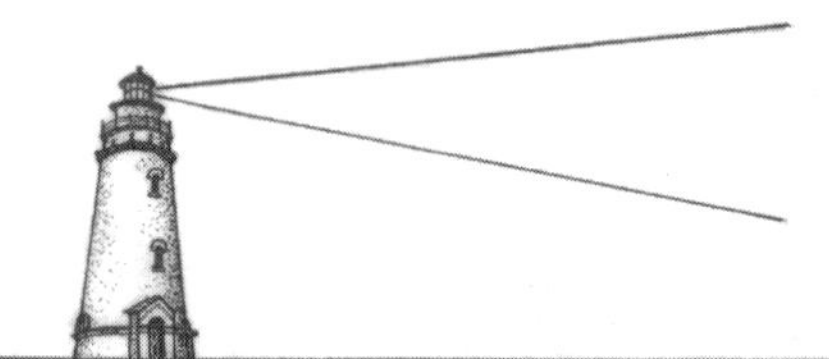

Seafood Stew

4 carrots, peeled and sliced
4 fresh tomatoes, diced   2 Tbs. butter
5 ribs of celery, sliced   1/2 tsp. thyme
4 cups boiling water   1/4 tsp. pepper
4 tsp. salt   2 tsp. lemon juice
1 cup onion, chopped   1/4 cup flour
1 clove of garlic chopped   1/4 cup water
2 to 3 pounds fish, shrimp, crab, oyster or
                    whatever is on hand

Place carrots and celery in large pot; add boiling water, 1 tsp. salt. Cover and cook almost tender. Meantime sauté onion and garlic in butter until limp. Add onion and garlic to carrots and celery, add tomatoes, remaining salt and boiling water, seasonings and lemon juice. Simmer a while.

Mix flour with cold water to a smooth paste. Add to vegetables, blending well. Bring to a boil. Gently add fish combinations and simmer till fish is flaky and shrimp is pink.

Serve as a main course, garnish with parsley. Serves 8

.....Thorndyke Family

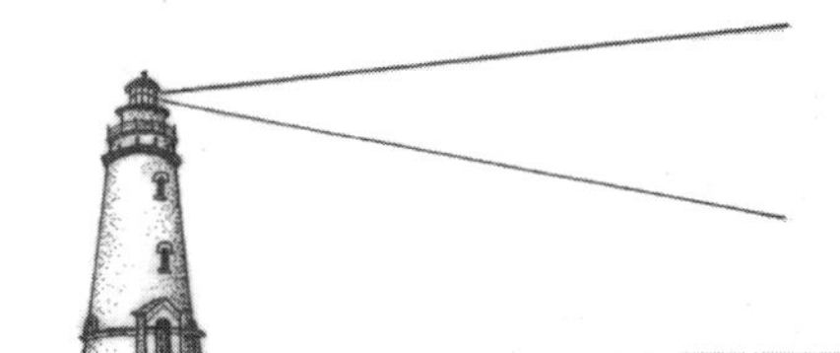

Oven Meal

Pork Roast

1   4-6 lb. pork roast

Rub meat with salt, pepper, onion powder and garlic powder. Sprinkle with rosemary. Bake at 350° for 3 hours or till done (160°-171° F internal temp.).

Last hour add potatoes to bake on lower shelf. Clean half an acorn squash, turn cut side down in baking pan, add 1/2 inch of water to pan. Bake next to potatoes. Test for tenderness, turn over and spoon chunky applesauce into hollow, sprinkle with brown sugar and cinnamon. Bake till all of dinner is ready.

.....Donna Thorndyke Schneider

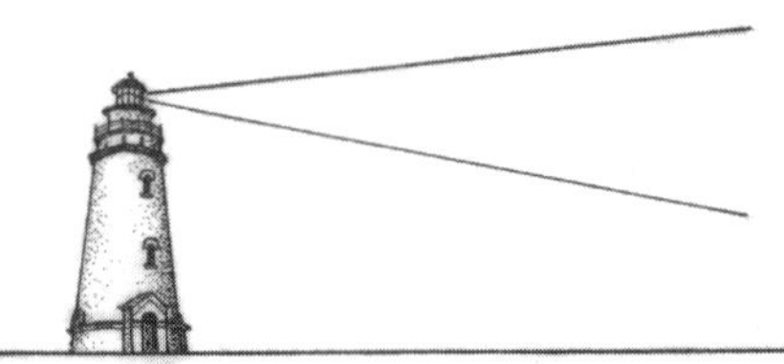

Bread

4 cups warm milk   2 Tbs. dry yeast

Mix in enough flour (4 cups - D.T.S.) to make a sponge. Raise 40 minutes or until doubled.

Add: 1/2 cup sugar, 1 Tbs. salt, 2 eggs, beaten and 1/2 cup melted shortening

Add 3 cups flour for soft dough. Knead.

Raise 40 minutes or until doubled. Shape into bread or rolls. Bake bread at 375°, rolls at 400°.

Yield 2 large loaves of bread or divide one half for bread and half for rolls.

Divide one fourth of dough; roll out to about 16 inches long by 8 inches wide. Spread with soft butter, 3/4 cup of brown sugar, 2 tsp. cinnamon, and 1 cup raisins. Roll up and cut into 9 pieces. Set into 8" x 8" pan, raise.

Use up last fourth of dough making 12 dinner rolls.

.....Donna's Kitchen

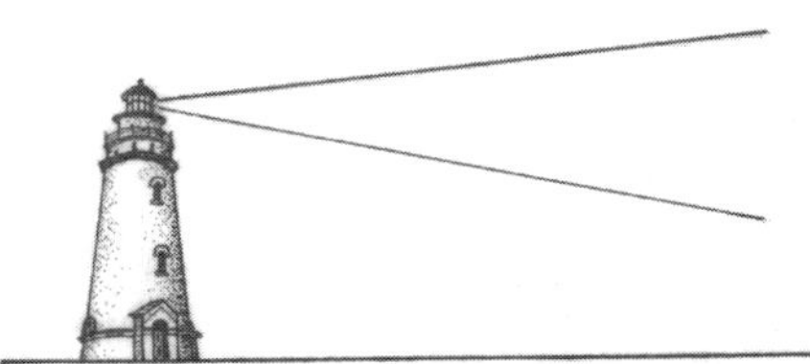

Potato Soup

3 potatoes diced   canned milk
1 onion diced   butter
Dash of salt   cheddar cheese

Combine potatoes, onion and salt in water, barely covering potatoes. Simmer till done. Add milk and butter. This was served with cheese that was crumbled and dropped into soup by each person and eaten as it melted in the hot soup. Bacon was added sometimes or egg dumplings.

.....Thorndyke Family

Potato Chips

Brush thin layers of bacon grease on top of woodstove griddle. Potatoes are thinly sliced (skins on) and laid directly on stove. Brown both sides. Eat right from the stove or wait to put in a bowl, sprinkle with salt.

Note: This is a rainy day treat.

....Donna Thorndyke Schneider

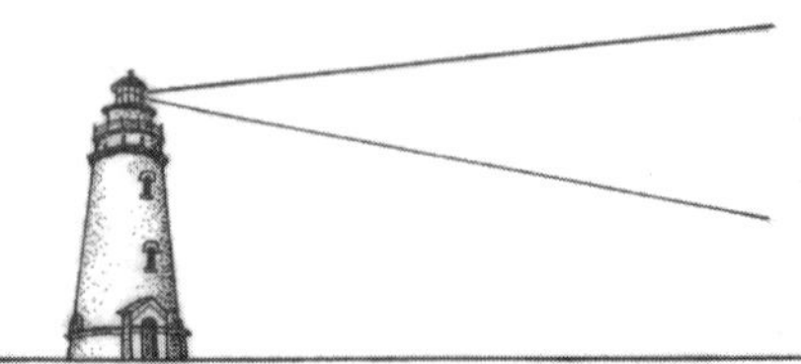

Perfect Potatoes

6 extra large potatoes

1-1/2 cup mayonnaise	1 stick butter
4 eggs	1 cup milk
garlic salt	pepper

Peel and cube potatoes. Add potatoes and eggs to pot of water and boil until potatoes are soft. Drain potatoes when done. Peel and mash eggs at the bottom of a large bowl. Add about half of the potatoes, half of the butter, half of the mayonnaise and half of the milk. Mix together with a hand mixer. Add garlic salt and pepper as desired. Mix together second half of potatoes, butter, mayonnaise and milk along with more garlic salt and pepper. Mix until desired consistency and serve.

.....Stephanie & Brian Thorndyke

The United States Coast Guard Years

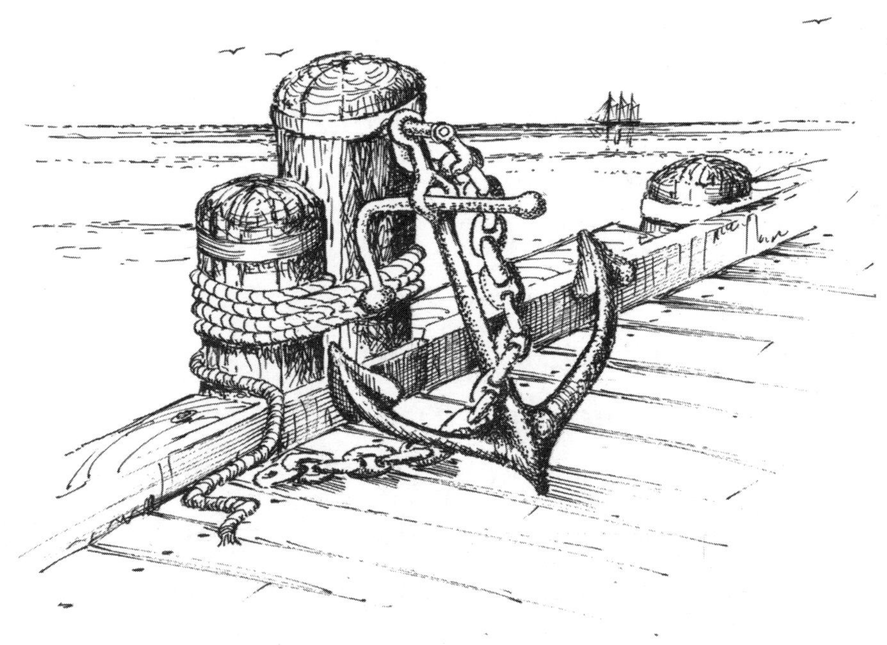

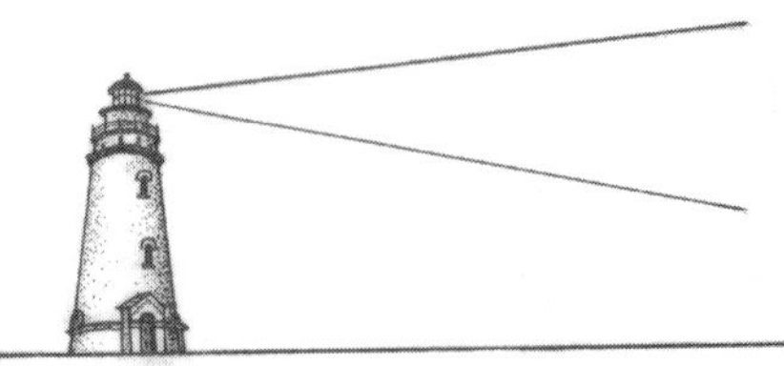

In 1939, the U.S. Coast Guard took over management of all the light stations, at which time officers and enlisted personnel replaced the civilian employees who had been under the supervision of the Bureau of Lighthouses, part of the Department of Commerce.

Norman Francis was the head keeper at Piedras Blancas Light Station from 1934 to 1948. When the lighthouses were transferred to the U. S. Coast Guard, a part of the Department of Treasury, Mr. Francis was already there as the head keeper working for the Lighthouse Service and he was given a rank in the Coast Guard commensurate with his civilian position. He had worked his way up from third assistant to second assistant, then first assistant and Piedras Blancas was his first head keeper position. As head keeper he could elect to remain at his position as long as he wished and, liking Piedras Blancas, he stayed there, with his wife and children, until he retired in 1948.

Norman Francis Jr. recalls eating a lot of "Bullhead" fish and plenty of red abalone. Non-

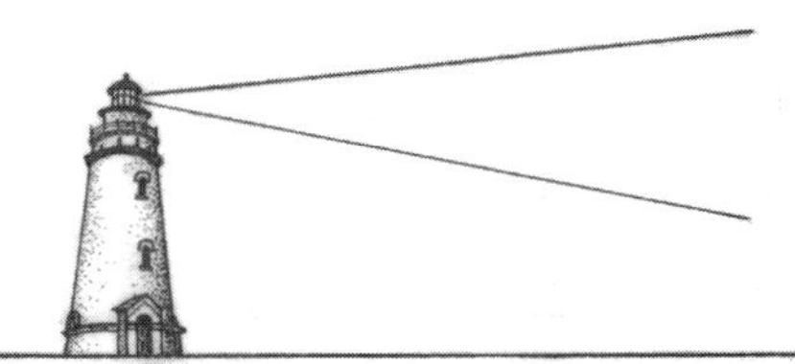

pasteurized milk, beef liver, beef heart, beef tongue and beef tails (which were used to make oxtail soup), came from the Hearst ranch. With the exception of the milk, these things were discarded when the cattle were butchered for the ranch hands.

Jim Lilly served as an assistant keeper for the Coast Guard from 1945 to 1947. He was a young man in his early twenties and didn't know much about cooking. The Coast Guard paid him $1.20 a day for food. This didn't buy much. But, young men are resourceful and he supplemented his food allowance by fishing and growing what he could with the help of the other assistant keeper, Larry Wagner.

Jim didn't care much for Norman Francis. Jim thought Norman was too strict! The only car at the station belonged to the Coast Guard and Norman Francis was the only one permitted to use it. For Jim and Larry this meant a long trip on foot, six miles, to Pete Sebastian's store in San Simeon or 12 miles to Cambria if Sebastian's didn't have what they needed. Sometimes, when Norman

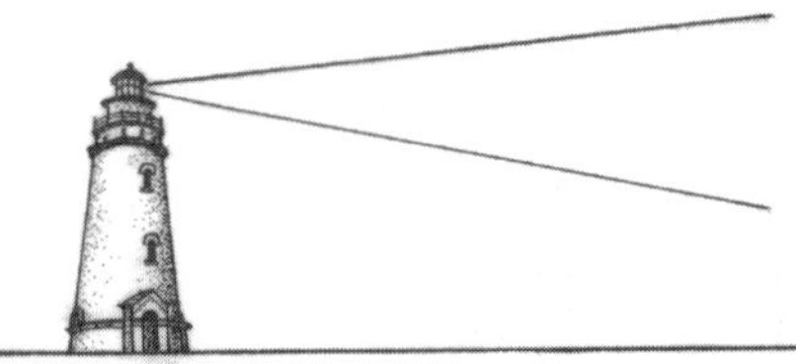

Francis was going into town he would pick up a few things for them, if they gave him the money in advance.

Jim and Larry grew some of their food, mostly root vegetables and crops that grew on vines (they held on tightly to the vine so they weren't blown away by the wind). Their harvest included potatoes, carrots, peas and beans. They did have a problem with blackbirds, who also liked to eat their crops. So these two young men decided to do something about those pesky birds. They got some bare copper wires and attached them to the top of the poles that held the lines for the peas to grow on. Then they attached an old automobile coil and some discarded 24-volt batteries to the grid of copper wires. Jim says when the birds landed on those wires with both feet they flew straight up in the air and they learned not to land on those wires after one or two times.

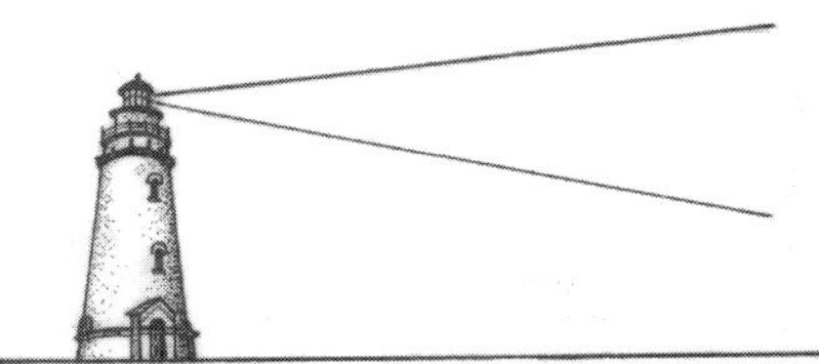

Abalone

red or pink abalone	butter
cornmeal	salt

"Once you've managed to get the abalone out of its shell you peel him a little bit and then get a skillet hot with butter until it's smoking. Coat the abalone with cornmeal and salt, if desired. Put abalone in skillet, cook thirty to forty-five seconds until the milk starts coming out the top. Then flop it over and cook about the same amount of time on the other side. Take it out and it will be tender and good to eat. Be sure to read the note below to find out how to tenderize the abalone before cooking!"

....Jim Lilly

Note: Mr. Davis, another assistant keeper who came over from civilian lighthouse keeping, taught Jim and Larry a way to keep abalone from becoming so tough when you take them out of their shells. He showed the young men a six by six post in the ground. It was about

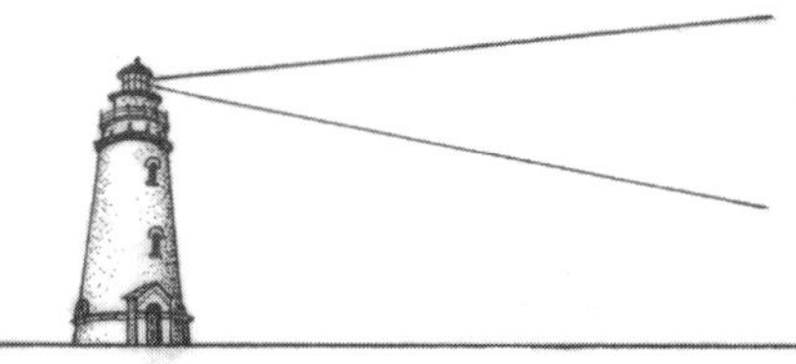

four feet high and had a concave top on it. Mr. Davis told them to keep the abalone in a burlap sack with a little kelp or something to keep them wet and they would live quite a while.

"Then when you get them up near the water tank take them up where that post in the ground is and lay one down there soft side up and over by the water tank, there's a piece of two by six about two feet long. Take that two by six up and smack that abalone as hard as you can. If you break the shell it's alright, but you'll kill it and then when you cut it out it doesn't resist. It just hangs up like a wet sock and it doesn't get all tough from pulling itself up in the shell trying to fight you."

We don't know if this method works or not. Jim swore it did.

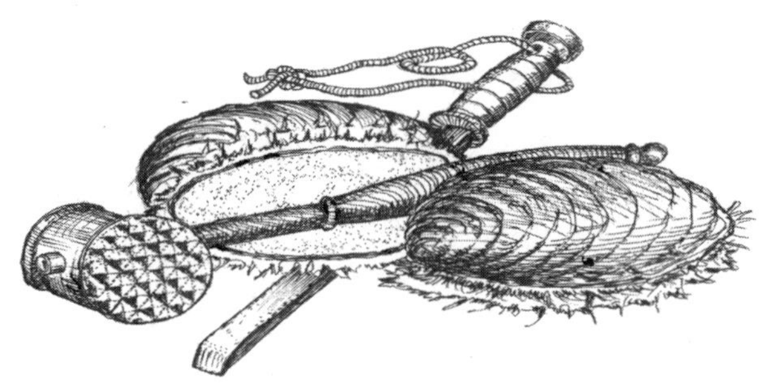

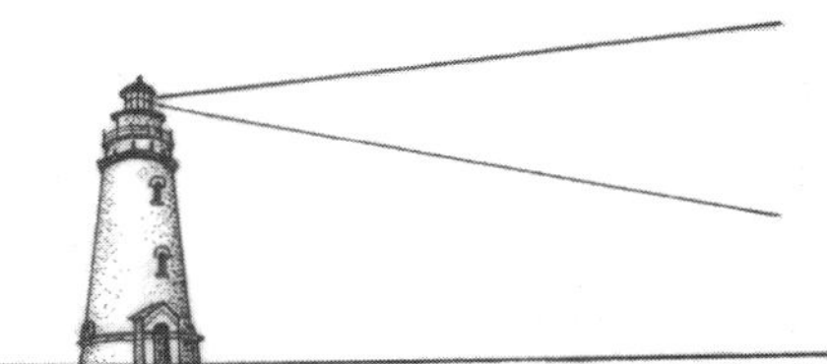

Phony Abalone

boneless chicken breasts
2 cloves of garlic
cornmeal

clam juice
butter
salt

"Flatten those chicken breasts out, real flat, about a quarter or three eighths of an inch thick. Pour clam juice into a bowl and add a piece or two of garlic. Then soak the chicken breasts in the clam juice for about 24 hours. Melt butter in a skillet. Coat the chicken breasts with cornmeal, if desired, and cook for about a minute on each side or until done. When you cook them they are almost exactly like abalone."

....Jim Lilly

Note: This is Jim's recipe, he said , for when you can't get abalone. He said it tastes just like the real thing. With today's prices for abalone, it's a good thing to know.

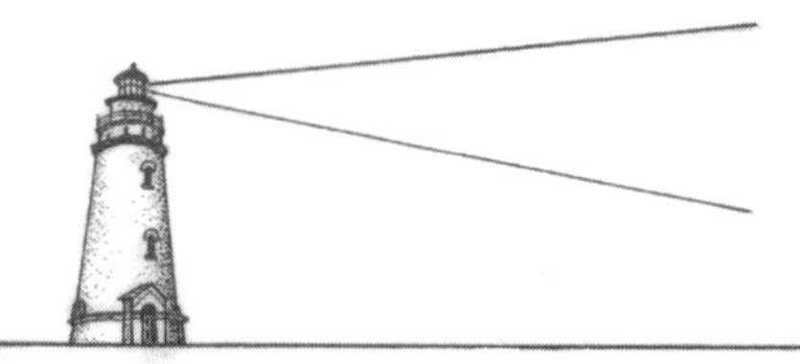

Jim said: "We used to catch cabezone. It's a rock fish and I think here in the bay (San Pablo Bay, where Jim lived at the time) we call them bullheads. They had horns on them about like a Texas steer but right behind their eyeballs they had a little horn that stuck out. If they got you with that thing they'd cut you pretty bad. So we used to go out on the rocks there and catch those cabezone and when you cleaned them they were green and when you cooked them the meat turned white. We'd just take off a fillet down each side of them and throw the rest of them back in because there was plenty of them."

"There were other things out there but we wouldn't eat them. In fact, I was a little leery of the cabezones, again because I was down in the South Pacific (Jim served in the South Pacific during WWII, earning a Bronze star during the invasion of the Phillipines.) and we used to fish a lot down there when we weren't doing more important things. And the natives told us that it was safe to eat any fish that had scales on it. If it had skin on it, it might not be safe to eat. So, if we caught something that didn't have scales we just

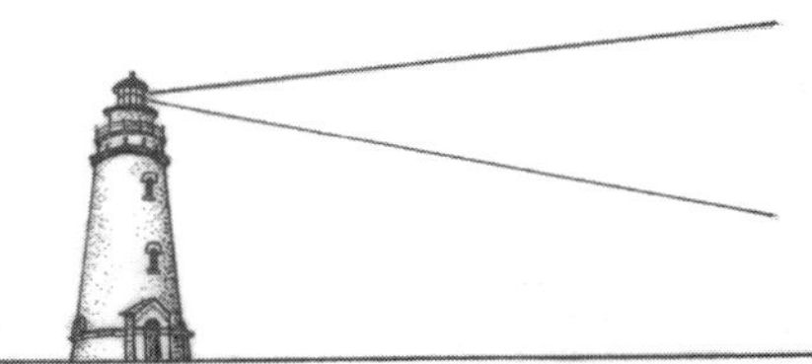

threw it back, but the cabezone didn't. Mr. Davis ate them and he was alright".

The following recipe comes from "Crumbs from Everybody's Table". It's probably not the way Jim and Larry prepared it, but it does look delicious. It should work well with almost any rock fish.

Baked Rock Cod

For a fish weighing about two pounds, chop one onion and a little parsley very fine; mix with one cupful of breadcrumbs, made very fine, and half a cupful of olive oil. Spread this mixture on the bottom of the pan and over the fish after putting it in the pan. Salt and pepper to taste; then pour a cupful of broth over all and bake in a quick oven, basting frequently. When done dish the fish, add a little water, one spoonful of Worchestershire or Bangipore sauce, to the gravy, stir well, boil one moment and pour over fish before serving.

.....Mrs. M. McQuaid

Note: "Bangipore" may be a misspelling of "Singapore". A recipe for Singapore sauce follows.

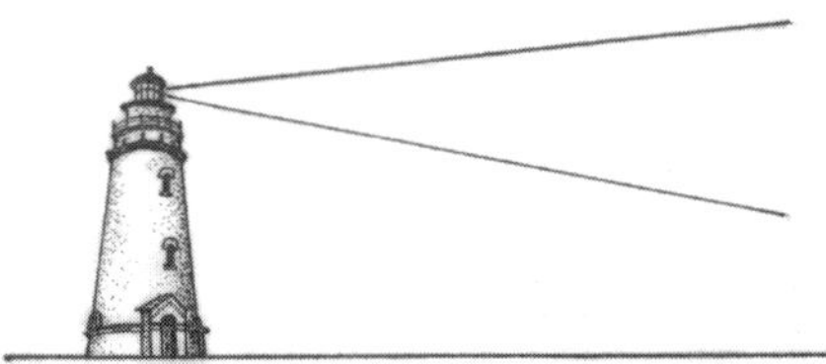

Singapore Sauce

2 T. white vinegar
1/4 cup Madras curry powder
Pinch turmeric (optional)
1/4 cup light soy sauce
1 cup oyster sauce
1/4 cup chile sauce
1/4 cup ketchup

Combine vinegar, curry powder and turmeric (if using). Mix well until powders are well dissolved. Add soy, oyster and chile sauces and ketchup and mix well.
Makes 4 servings.

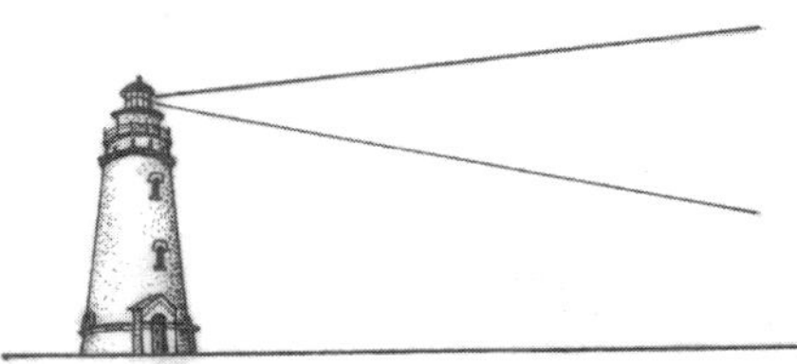

Jim Godsey served with the U.S. Coast Guard and was stationed at Piedras Blancas Light Station in 1949 and 1950. When interviewed recently he said he didn't remember much about the food, his wife fixed everything. He did recall fishing off of Seal Rock and that they had ten hens that laid eggs for all four families that lived there.

Mr. Godsey moonlighted, working the graveyard shift at the Hearst ranch. They ran a trap line to catch the bobcats and coyotes that liked to eat the Hearst's prized peacocks. As part of his job benefits he was given breakfast in the Castle kitchen. He had occasion to meet William Randolph Hearst, Jr. one morning. W.R., Jr. left the gate to the corral open. This was the corral where the prize cattle were kept. Jim, not knowing who W.R., Jr. was, saw him and chewed him out royally for leaving the gate open. It was all taken in good form and Jim did not lose his job.

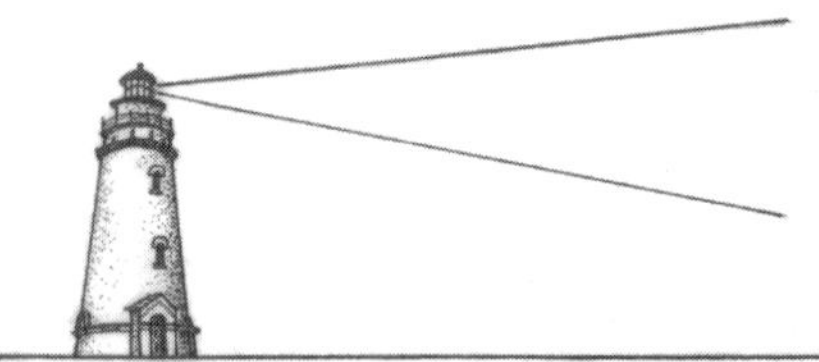

Clifford N. Smith was the Lighthouse Commander at Piedras Blancas from August 1959 to February 1962. One of his daughters, Pat Smith Inabnit, shared some of her mother's recipes and her own reminiscences with us.

Audrey Smith's Angel Food Cookies

3 egg whites
1/2 tsp. vanilla
1 cup chopped dates
1 cup coarsely chopped walnuts
1 cup sifted flour

1 cup sugar
1/2 tsp lemon extract

Beat 3 egg whites stiff, with dash of salt; gradually beat in 1 cup sugar. Add vanilla and lemon extract. Mix in chopped dates and nuts, flour; add to egg whites, mixing well. Drop by teaspoonfuls on greased baking sheets. Bake in moderate oven (350° F.) 10-12 minutes. Remove to rack. Makes about 48 cookies.

....Pat Smith Inabnit

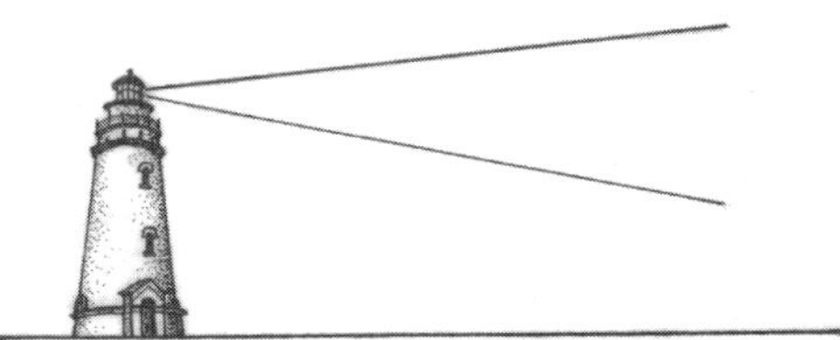

Audrey Smith's Lemon Cream Salad

1 package lemon or lime Jell-O®
1 can #2 crushed pineapple
1 cup grated mild cheddar cheese
1/2 cup walnuts
1/4 cup mayonnaise
1 cup whipping cream (whipped)

Set Jell-O® (1 cup hot water, 1 cup pineapple juice). Add water to this if needed. Let Jell-O® set until jellied. Then fold in rest of ingredients. Save some grated cheese to decorate top.

....Pat Smith Inabnit

"During our stay there we ate mostly spaghetti, tuna casserole, hamburgers, hot dogs, Spanish rice, liver (thank heavens it was only once a month), canned (or frozen) vegetables and fruits, and homemade bread and biscuits. Nothing really out of the ordinary."

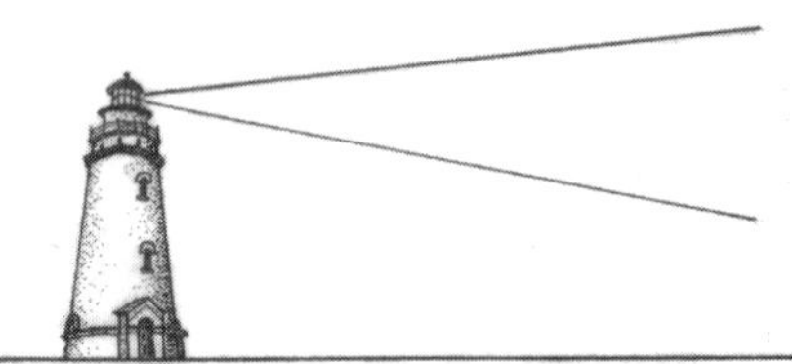

"In their leisure time the adults took my sister and me to the top of the lighthouse and to the beach (we were not allowed to go these two places alone), they played cribbage and pinnacle with the other adults, put together jigsaw puzzles and watched TV and read. Most of the wives at the station sewed their children's and some of their own clothing, knitted, and or crocheted.

My mom was a wonderful piano player, and she played a lot during the day and evening. My favorite was "honkey tonk"- it was so lively and sounded great."

"School was a long trip. My dad would drive us to the gate and wait until the school bus picked us up for the trip to Cambria. On nice days when the bus dropped us off at the gate, we were allowed to walk to the Station."

"At least once a week someone had to search for my sister and me between the station and the outside gate after the school bus left us at the gate. My dad or someone else from the Station would come looking for us if we did not turn up at the

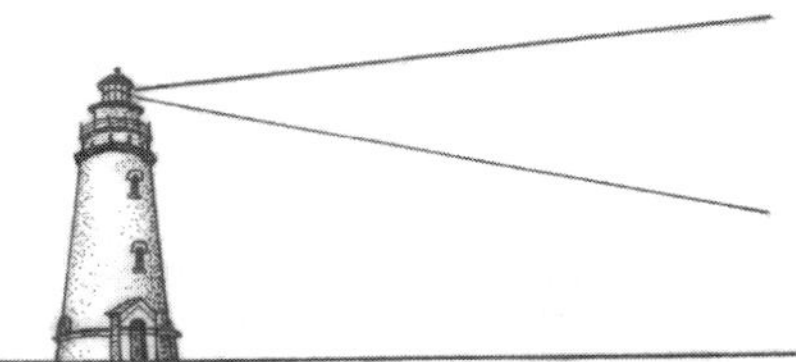

Station within 1/2 hour of the bus dropping us off at the gate. Usually we were playing with the baby cows or the mean old bull had us cornered somewhere - what great fun! If the bull approached us we would hide behind a pole and yell for someone to rescue us."

"There were other children at the station, but they were usually infants or young toddlers. Most often my sister and I were the only children that roamed around outside. We played in the trees at the station, searched for the wild mom cats and their kittens, conversed with the visitors to the station, rode our bikes, and generally played all over the station. I enjoyed walking along the tops of the trees that lined the fence of the station. I could see for miles it seemed like and very often could

spot the place where the wild mom cats had their nest of kittens. I could also "spy" on all that was going on around the station and hide from my younger sister."

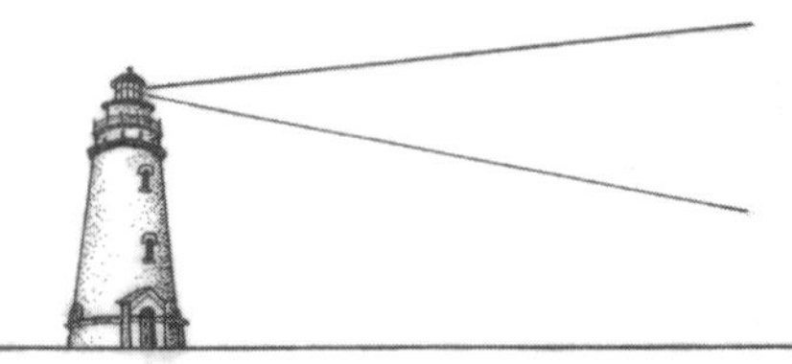

"It seems like we were always so busy playing with dolls, cards, outside, or whatever that we did not have much time to watch television. I do not recall how many channels on TV we had (not very many though, maybe three) or where the signals came from. We did get cartoons on Saturday mornings. I do not recall if we even had a radio to listen to or not in the house. There were, of course, short-wave radios in the office."

"During the winter it rained a lot, and the wind blew very strongly. When the wind was too strong, the men tied a rope from the office around the water tank (both adjacent to the living areas), then to the flag pole ending at a pole that used to be near the living areas in order to be able to traverse the

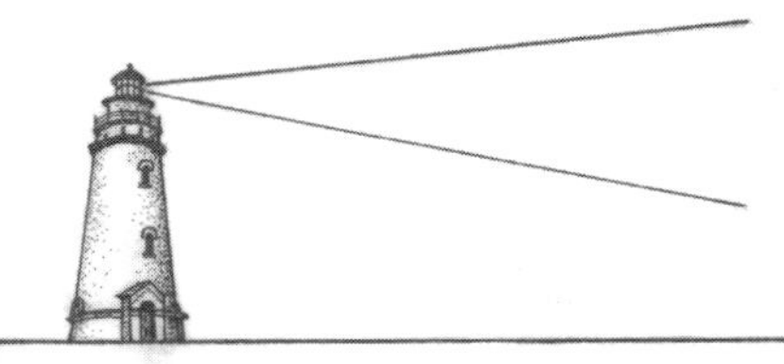

space between the houses and the office. Also during the stormy winter, the waves would wash away the pump house; it used to be on the right side of the field by the ocean as you enter the station, and the men would have to rebuild it once the storm subsided. This happened at least once a year. I have often wondered why they didn't move the pump house."

"Our big weekly excursion was to Sebastian's store in San Simeon where we each got to buy one piece of candy. Once a month my parents went to San Luis Obispo to get groceries for the month. The week following the grocery-getting we had fresh vegetables and fruits."

"The trip to the beach was always a delightful excursion for us. We were not allowed to go down the steps or near the bluff by ourselves. Therefore, during nice weather we were always pestering my dad or mom or anyone else that would listen to take us to the beach. The steps were quite narrow and steep but well worth the effort. It was considerably warmer in the cove

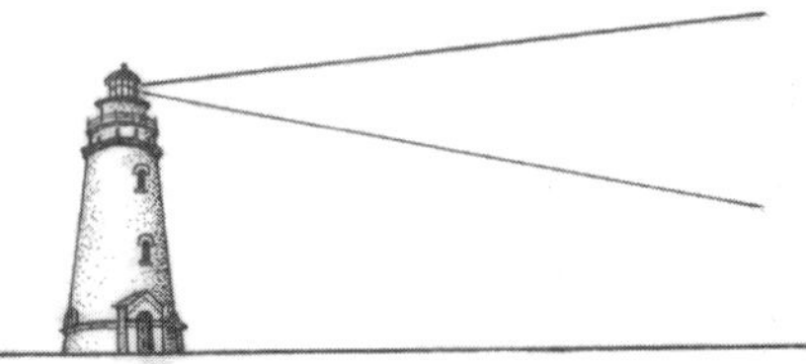

around the beach. During low tide we would go between the rocks to the left of the beach and run up and down the sand dunes. We also played in the ocean a lot and collected sand dollars."

"Once a year, a group of Japanese men would come to the station and harvest kelp and seaweed. They took it away (I do not know where) and made seaweed candy. The following year they would bring us back some of the candy. It looked like a slice of pineapple in shape and was coated a sugary white and tasted rather like coconut."

"The seals or seal lions (I am not sure what they were) made a huge amount of noise all the time. We used to look at them through binoculars, and they were great fun to watch. They lived out on the rocks and only came ashore when they were sick or washed up dead. I remember that when we moved to the Bay Area in 1962 none of us could sleep at night because it was too quiet!"

"Speaking of moving, when my dad was up for transfer from the station we had a family meet-

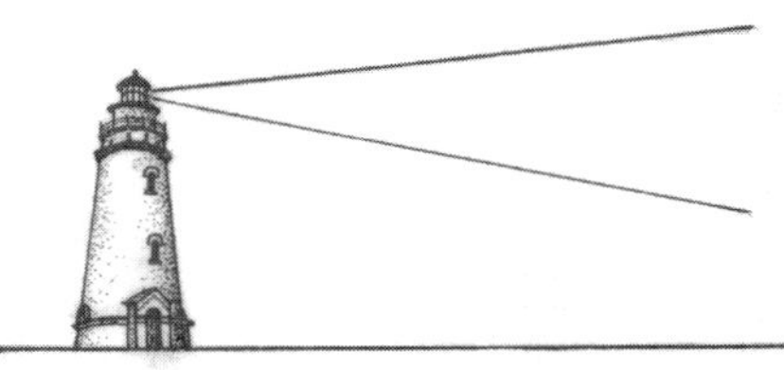

ing to decide where we all wanted to live. Since this was the second light station we had lived on, my sister and I decided we wanted to move to a city. I was 11 at the time and it seemed like a new adventure to me since I had lived in isolated areas, so to speak, since I was 5. Previously we lived at Slip Point Light Station in Washington state for three years."

"At least twice a year a cow would manage to circumvent the cattle guard and come onto the station. It was great fun to watch the men on the station trying to herd it back to the Hearst field. A zebra from Hearst Castle had also taken up residence in the cow field. It kept escaping from the Castle area and they just left it there. They rounded it up once a year probably for a health checkup or possibly shots or something like that, and within a week it was back again."

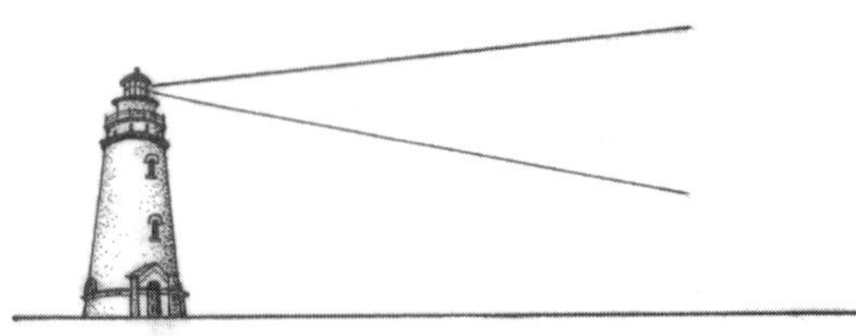

"I remember my dad telling me that it had mated with a horse to make a zebra-horse, but I do not recall ever seeing the zebra-horse."

"Also at least twice a year my mom would get out of the car to open the gate to enter the station and she would jump on top of the gate and yell "rattlesnake." My dad would get out of the car to rescue her, but my sister and I were not allowed to view the rattlesnake."

...Pat Smith Inabnit

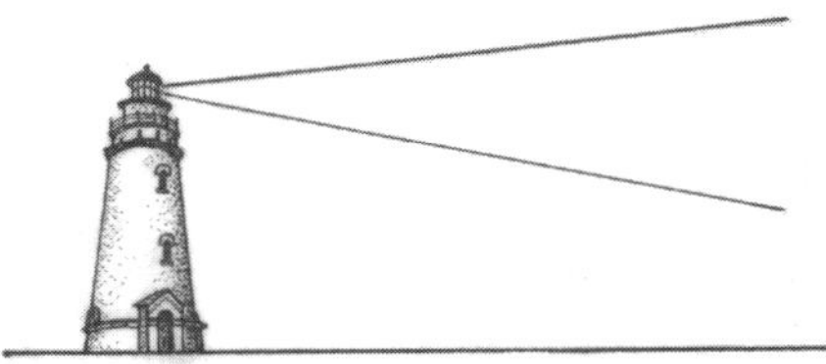

Pam Merrill lived at Piedras Blancas from 1966 to 1969 when her father was the officer in charge.

90-Minute Bread

First mixture:

3 c. very warm water	4 tsp salt
8 tsp. sugar	4 tbsp melted shortening

Next:

4 pkgs. of yeast dissolved in 1 cup, lukewarm water

Put aside:

Approx. 8 c. flour

When the yeast is dissolved, pour into the first mixture. Add flour, a little at a time. Divide into 4 loaves and let stand 15 minutes. Knead each piece 1 minute. Shape for greased pan. Rub top with shortening or oil. Cover and let stand 30 minutes in warm place. Bake at 350° for 30 min.

....Pam Merrill

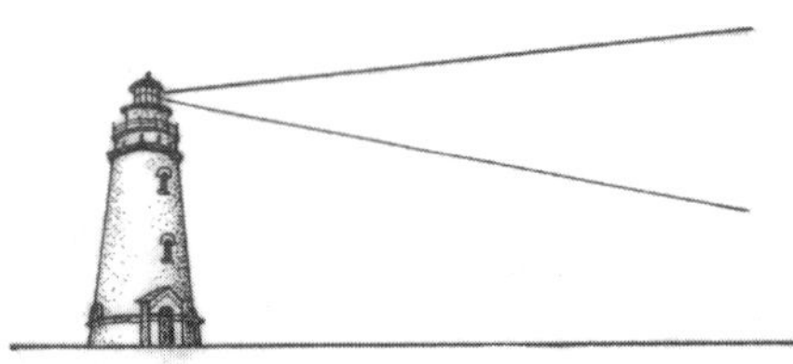

Tanglirini Sauce
(everyone loved this)
(serves 6-8)

1 lb ground beef	1 chopped onion
16 oz tomato sauce	1/4 tsp. pepper
1 clove minced garlic	12 oz. corn
1 can black olives	3 tsp. chili powder
1/2 of the olive liquid	1 c. grated cheese

Brown beef, add onion, garlic - sauté. Add all other ingredients (except cheese). Cover and simmer 40 min. Pour over your choice of cooked-and-drained noodles. Sprinkle with cheese. Bake at 350° for 1 hour.

....Pam Merrill

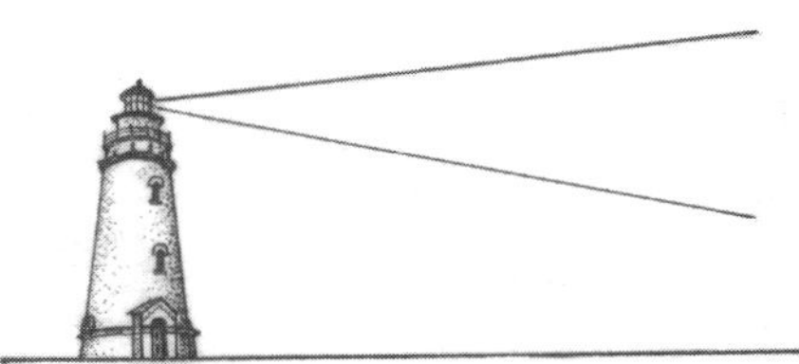

Enchiladas

(I got this from Mary Valenzuela when she visited her son Jesus, aka "Val", who lived at Piedras Blancas Light Station with his wife)

1 lb ground beef	1 chopped onion
1 can black olives	1 can tomato sauce
1 tsp. chili powder	grated cheese
1 pkg. tortillas	

Brown ground beef, drain and add onion and chili powder. In another frying pan (one big enough to fit tortilla) heat the tomato sauce. Put in tortilla and turn so both sides have tomato sauce on it. Remove tortilla and put into it a couple of tbsp. ground beef, a couple of olives and some cheese. Roll and put in an ovenproof pan. Repeat until all tortillas are in pan. Spread remaining tomato sauce on tortillas. Sprinkle with cheese and bake covered for 45 minutes at 350°.

....Pam Merrill

The Bureau of Land
Management,

BLM Volunteers,

Wildlife Researchers

and

U.S. Representative
Lois Capps

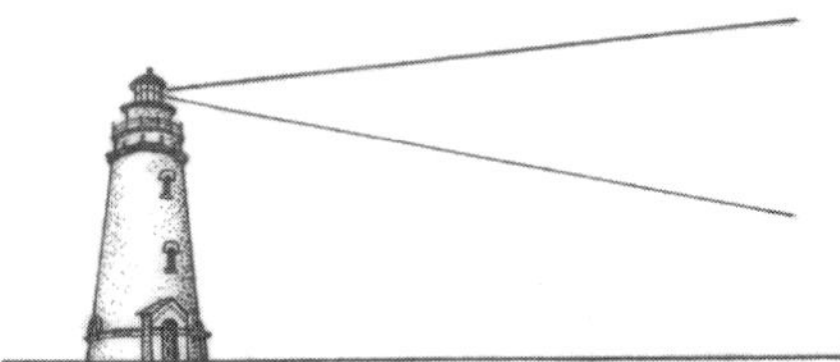

Congresswoman Lois Capps was instrumental in encouraging the Bureau of Land Management to request transfer of Piedras Blancas Light Station from the U.S. Coast Guard to the BLM.

U.S. Representative Lois Capps

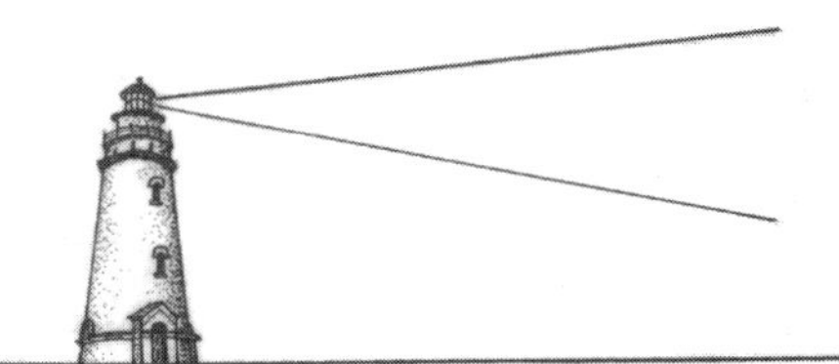

Swedish Oven Pancakes

A Capps' Family Favorite Recipe

Put 1/4 cup of butter in a 9"x 13" pan and place in hot oven (450°F) to melt the butter.

In a medium bowl, beat 3 eggs. Add the following ingredients in the order listed and mix well:

    2 cups of milk
    1/8 cup of sugar
    1 teaspoon of salt
    1 cup of flour

Pour the batter over the melted butter in the baking pan and return to the hot oven for about 20 minutes until puffy and golden brown. Serve immediately with any fruit or syrup topping. We like to sprinkle it with powdered sugar and squeeze a lemon over all. Serves 6-8

....Lois Capps, U.S. Representative,
California 22nd Congressional District

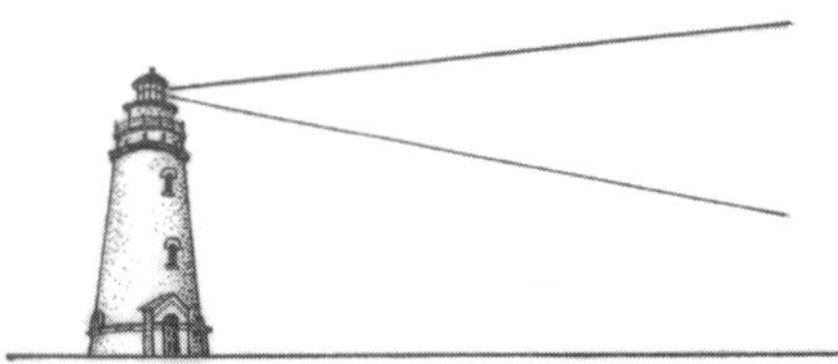

Broccoli Salad-Pennsylvania Dutch Style

2 heads raw broccoli   1/2 cup raisins
8-plus slices bacon, fried and crumbled
1 small onion
Dressing:
2 cup mayonnaise   1 cup or less sugar
4 Tablespoons vinegar

Mix bacon with dressing before mixing with rest of ingredients. The dressing keeps well in the refrigerator and is tasty on lettuce or spinach salads.

Chop broccoli into small bite-sized pieces. Pour on dressing and mix. Mmmmm. Try garnishing with hard-boiled egg slices. The salad tastes better as it marinates. Try different ingredients like cauliflower, cheddar cheese or chestnuts.

"This recipe comes from the New Guilford Brethren in Christ Church in Chambersburg, Pennsylvania. My family and ancestors are from this part of southeastern Pennsylvania where the table spread is based on the eating philosophy of hav-

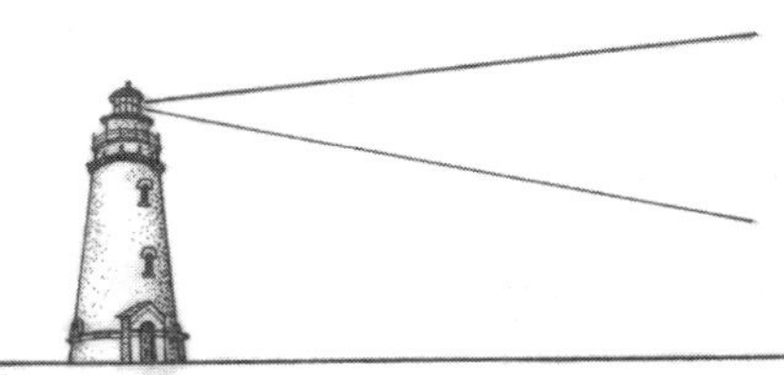

ing 'seven sweets and seven sours.' This salad could be one or the other depending on your measurements. The men in the field, mostly dairy farmers, needed a hardy "supper" (lunch) and broccoli salad provided a filling dish. As we say in our family, 'there's more back.' "

....Greg Haas
Aide to U.S. Representative Lois Capps

John H. Bogacki's Piedras Blancas Light Station White "Chikin" Chili

"The Piedras Blancas Light Station was established in 1875 just north of San Simeon on the central coast of California. The centerpiece of this wonderful place is one of the most beautiful lighthouses ever constructed on the west coast. The Bureau of Land Management took over the site in 2001, and I have the honor to be the station's Lightkeeper. I fine-tuned my regular White 'Chikin' Chili recipe for our first volunteer meeting. Folks seemed to like it! Make in "multiples" for big gatherings! I hope you enjoy it!" ....John

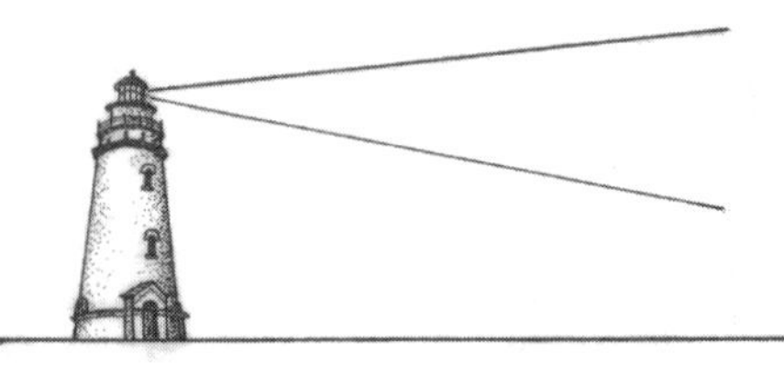

Quantity	Unit	Ingredient
1	tablespoon	olive oil
1-1/2	pound	boned, skinless chicken breast, (cut to 1/2" cubes)
1	cup	chopped onion
1	16oz. can	chicken broth
1	4oz. can	chopped green chilis
1	tablespoon	garlic powder
1	tablespoon	ground cumin
1	tablespoon	oregano leaves
1	tablespoon	cilantro
1	tablespoon	ground red chili powder
1	19oz. can	great northern white beans (un-drained)
2-3	tablespoons	lime juice
2	stalks	celery, finely-chopped
1	16oz. can	fat-free refried beans
1	16oz. can	diced, stewed tomatoes
1/2	each	bell pepper, finely diced

Optional:

1 bottle of your favorite beer per recipe (add to chili after adding chicken, beans, and lime juice). Spikes the flavor up a bit!

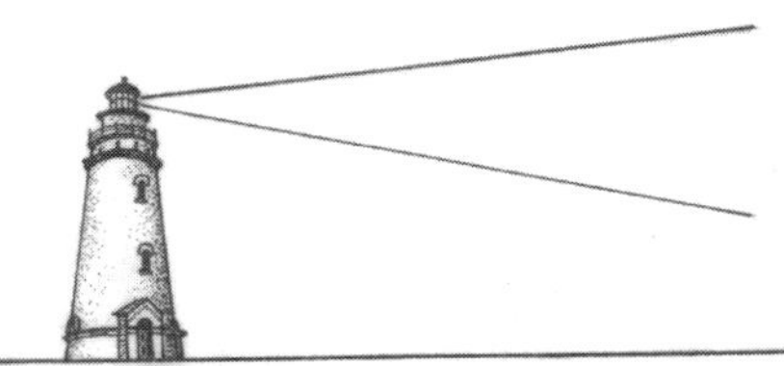

Optional:

8 cloves of crushed, fresh garlic is better than the garlic powder.

Optional:

Substitute skinned, boneless and de-fatted chicken thigh meat in place of chicken breast for a richer flavor and a different texture!

To Taste for garnish:

> *Monterey Jack cheese (shredded)*
> *chopped green onions*
> *chopped, fresh cilantro*

Lastly: Heat up all the flour tortillas you can eat and serve with chili. (who ever heard of eating chili without them?)

Directions:

1). *Heat olive oil in a 3-quart saucepan over medium-high heat.*

2). *Add chicken; cook 5 to 7 minutes, stirring often.*

3). *Remove chicken with slotted spoon, cover, and keep warm.*

4). *Add chopped onion, bell pepper, and cel-ery to saucepan; sauté about 2 minutes.*

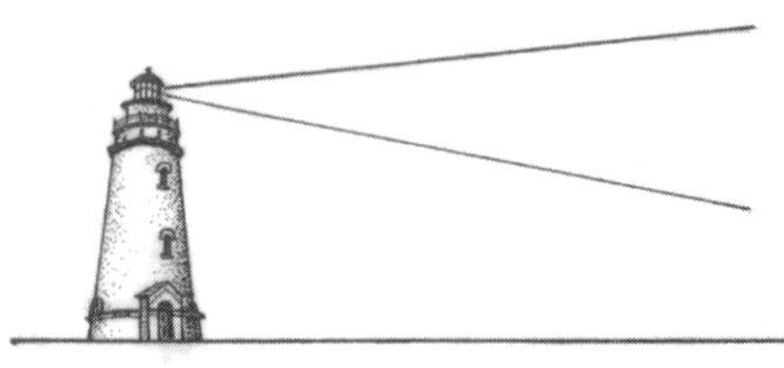

5). Stir in chicken broth, green chilis, garlic powder, ground cumin, oregano leaves, cilantro, and ground red pepper; simmer for 30 minutes.

6). Stir in chicken, great northern white beans, refried beans, and lime juice; simmer for 10 minutes. Garnish with cheese, cilantro, and/or green onion.

Basic recipe serves 5!

Tip: Heat up leftover chili the next morning and fold into a 3-egg omelet. Use the leftover cheese, onions and tortillas too (why waste them?). (Leftovers also make a pretty decent burrito)!

Another Tip: For large groups, (20 or more people), try mixing pinto, great northern, pinquitos, and cannellini beans together for a little different taste treat!

A good, (2002) cervesa Negra Modelo® or Dos Equis® will round out this epicurean adventure!

....John H. Bogacki, Light Keeper

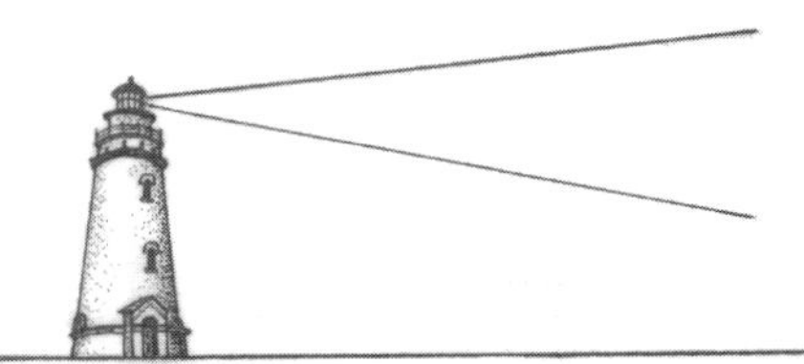

John Bogacki's wife, Toppy, is an architect and has been invaluable in designing our future visitor facilities. She's also a fine cook and shared one of her favorite recipes with us.

Toppy's Chinese Chicken Salad
Bakersfield, California
09-02-00

This is everyone's favorite! If you are on a diet, it won't do you a bit of good, but you sure feel like you're behaving when you eat it!

Dressing:

In a quart jar or wide-mouth bottle mix together: 1/3 cup rice vinegar, 1/2 cup sesame oil, 1/3 cup vegetable oil (or olive oil if you are health-conscious), 2 cloves crushed garlic (John would add two more), 1 teaspoon fresh-ground ginger, 15 drops Tobasco sauce, 1 teaspoon sugar, 1/2 teaspoon salt, 1/2 teaspoon ground black pepper.

Replace lid and shake all ingredients well for about 30 seconds.

(continued on page 222)

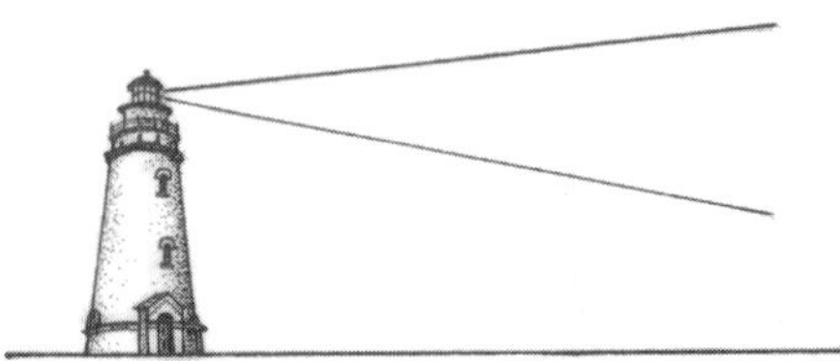

Salad:

4-5	boneless/skinless and boiled chicken breasts (cooled), chopped into cubes
1/4	cup toasted slivered almonds
1	package Top Raman® noodles (toss the flavor package), or crispy canned chow mien noodles

2 teaspoons sesame seeds

1-1/2	bags angel-hair cole slaw (or one very thinly-sliced head of cabbage)
1-3	chopped green onions

In vegetable or olive oil or Pam®, sauté 1/4 cup slivered almonds till lightly toasted. Set aside.

In a large mixing bowl, hand-toss the cole slaw/cabbage with the chicken, green onions and sesame seeds. Add the slivered almonds and blend together.

Add the pre-mixed dressing and toss the whole thing until your arms get tired. (just kidding).

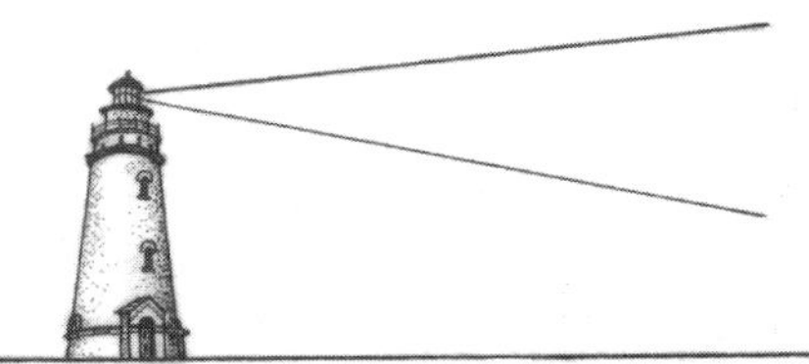

Lastly, break up the noodles and add into mix just before serving, (if using chow mien noodles open can and add to salad.)

....Toppy Bogacki

Makes a meal all by itself! Enjoy!

Turkey Tacos

John and Toppy Bogacki
Bakersfield, California

We've been perfecting this recipe for thirty years now and we think it's just about "right"! We used to use very lean ground beef as the "base" (guess you still could), but we discovered ground turkey and it elevated the flavor tremendously! Hope you think so, too! The basis for this recipe is the meat filling. Here goes:

Quantity.	Unit	Ingredient
2-3	pounds	premium ground turkey
2	tablespoons	peanut oil
1	each	large yellow onion, finely chopped
1	(4 oz.) can	diced green chilis
4	cloves	garlic, peeled and crushed

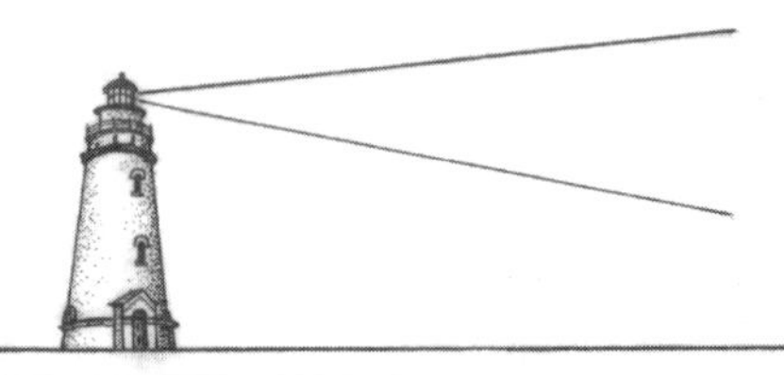

1	(16 oz.) can	refried beans, (fat-free if possible)
1	(16 oz.) can	flat, stale beer (open can, leave on kitchen counter overnight)
*	to taste	ground cumin
*	to taste	cilantro, (fresh) finely chopped
*	to taste	ground red chili powder

In a cast-iron skillet (preferably), heat the peanut oil till it starts to smoke over a medium heat. Add the onion and sauté till it becomes clear. Add the garlic. Break up the ground turkey and continue to break up in the skillet with a wooden spoon until the meat starts cooking evenly. When the meat appears to be cooked, add the cumin, cilantro, chili powder and stale beer (1/4 can at a time to keep meat moist). Mix well. Add in the refried beans and fold in until the mixture is fully mixed and even-textured (we use a potato masher to grind everything into a nice consistency, but it's not entirely necessary). Simmer over a low heat for about 20 minutes, uncovered. Set aside, covered until ready to serve.

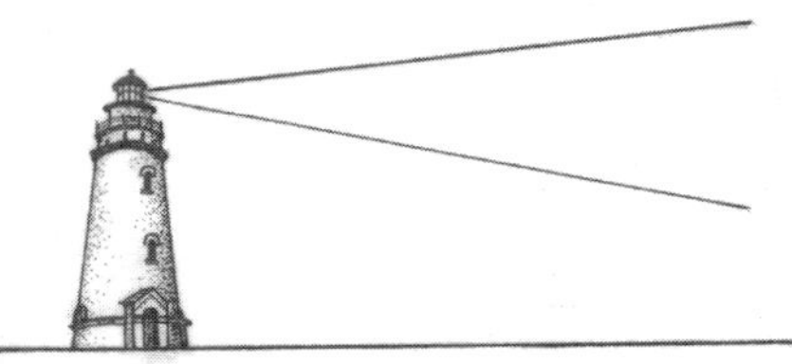

Condiments:

Quantity.	Unit	Ingredient
2	each	ripe, red tomatoes, chopped
1	each	large yellow onion, finely chopped
2	(8 oz.) cans	black olives, chopped
1	head	lettuce, finely chopped
1	pound	jack cheese, grated
1	bottle	McClintock's® Hot Sauce or your favorite taco sauce or salsa

Tortillas

We like them soft, but you can fix them as you like! We start by heating about 1/4 cup of peanut oil in a small cast iron skillet. Remember that this is the hairy part of the operation because of the hot oil. Be cognizant of what you are doing!

Once the oil is heated up, we slip the corn tortillas in, one at a time, and turn them immediately (this keeps the oil absorption to a minimum), then

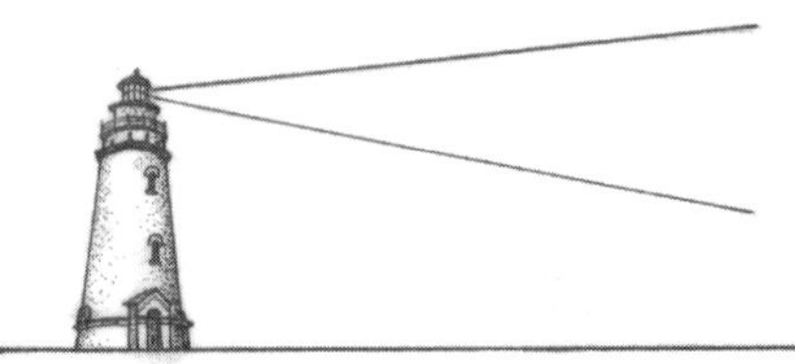

we "pat" the tortilla dry with paper towels and store them in a tortilla "safe". (You can also use a paper-lined bowl.)

We cook a dozen at a time and find this adequate for four hungry people. As soon as you are done with the hot oil, set it to the back of the stove to cool, then discard.

<u>Serving</u>
Place the tortillas on a plate, spoon on a generous dollop of meat filling and then mix and match ingredients to suit. Cold beer or your favorite non-alcoholic beverage goes great with this dish as long as the drink is ice cold! Enjoy!

....John and Toppy Bogacki
Piedras Blancas Light Keeper and wife

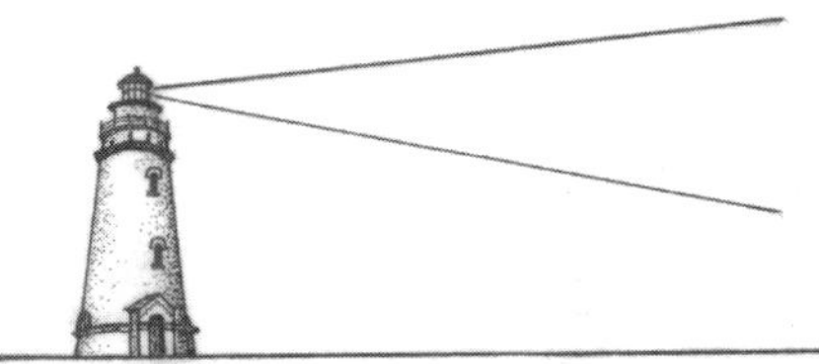

Bev's Chicken Tortilla Bake

1 15 oz. can of black beans
1 15 oz. can of refried beans
1 or 2 7 oz. cans of Oretga® diced green
          chiles (according to taste; I use 1)
2 cups grated Monterey jack cheese
1 medium white onion, diced
approx. 2 cups cooked, shredded meat
                    (pork, chicken or beef)
Santitas® white corn tortilla chips

Preheat oven to 350° F. Spray 9"x 13" pan with vegetable oil. Place a layer of corn chips in the bottom of the pan. Mix refried beans and black beans together in a separate bowl. Pour 1/2 of the bean mixture on top of the chips. Spread meat over the beans. Spread 1/2 of chiles over the meat. Place another layer of chips over the chiles. Pour remaining 1/2 of beans over the second layer of chips and put the remaining chiles over that. Top with cheese and chopped onions. Bake uncovered at 350° for 30 minutes or until warmed through.

...Bev Praver, BLM Volunteer

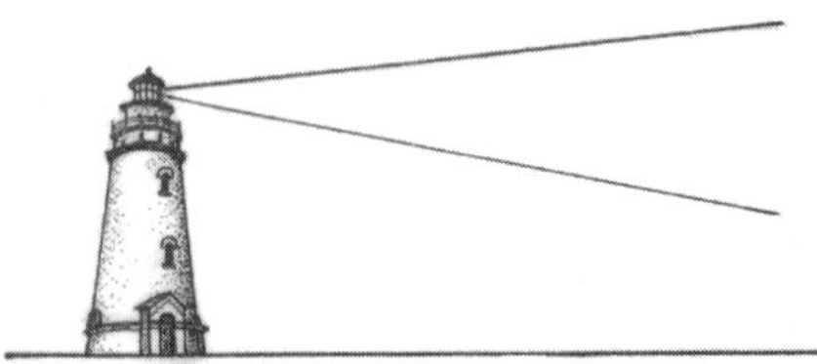

Zucchini Casserole

1-1/2 lbs. zucchini (sliced)
boiling salted water
1 onion (chopped)
1 teaspoon garlic salt
2 cups cottage cheese
1 cup grated cheddar cheese
1 can mushroom soup
1 teaspoon oregano

1 lb. ground beef
1 cup instant rice

Preheat oven to 350 degrees.

Cook zucchini till tender, drain. Sauté beef with onion till brown. Add rice and seasonings. Place half zucchini in bottom of 2-1/2 quart casserole. Cover with beef and cottage cheese. Add remaining zucchini. Spread soup over all. Sprinkle with grated cheese. Bake uncovered 35 to 40 minutes till bubbly.

....Diana Clark
BLM Volunteer

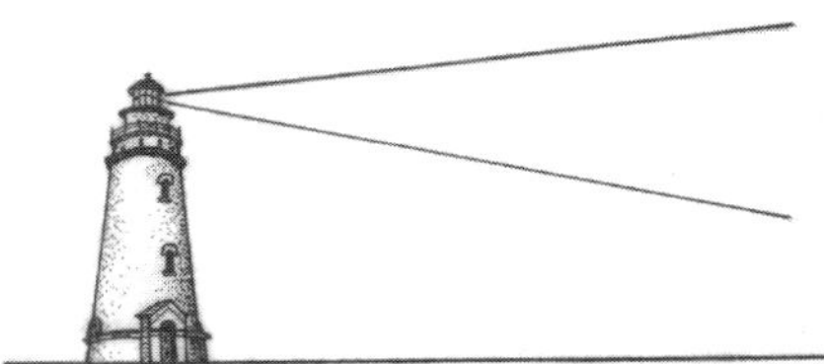

"Here is one of my favorite recipes - White Chili. My husband says it should be called 'Whili' because it is white. Whatever it's called, it's good. Even people who think chili has to be red to be good have been converted by this one."

....Carole Adams
BLM Volunteer

White Chili

3-4 chicken breasts	2 cups chicken broth
1 tablespoon salad oil	2 large onions sliced
1 clove garlic, minced	1/2 tsp. ground cumin

2 15 oz. cans cannellini (white) beans, rinsed
and drained

1/4 cup lime or lemon juice
1 can diced green chilis
1 small fresh jalapeno chili, stemmed,
seeded, and minced
1 cup shredded jack cheese
condiments (listed below)

Cook chicken in broth, drain and cut or tear into chunks. Save broth.

(Continued on page 230)

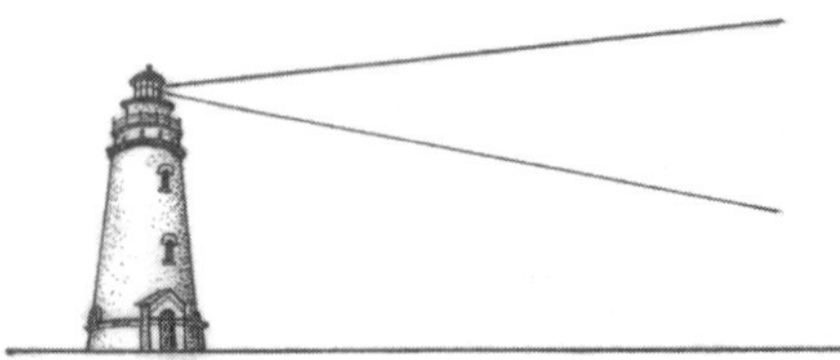

Heat oil, add onions and garlic and stir until soft.

Add reserved broth plus extra broth to make 3 cups. Add beans, lime juice, green chilies, jalapeno, seasonings. Simmer for 15 minutes. Stir in chicken and cheese and heat until hot.

Ladle into bowls and serve with condiments if desired: Diced roma tomatoes, shredded jack cheese, sliced ripe olives, fresh cilantro sprigs, sliced green onions.
Serves 4-6.

(Optional seasonings to use during the last stage of heating: 1/4 cup minced cilantro, 1 teaspoon oregano, 1/4 tsp cinnamon. I'd probably throw in some chili powder. Another option is to substitute one cup of dry white wine for one cup of the broth.)

....Carole Adams
BLM Volunteer

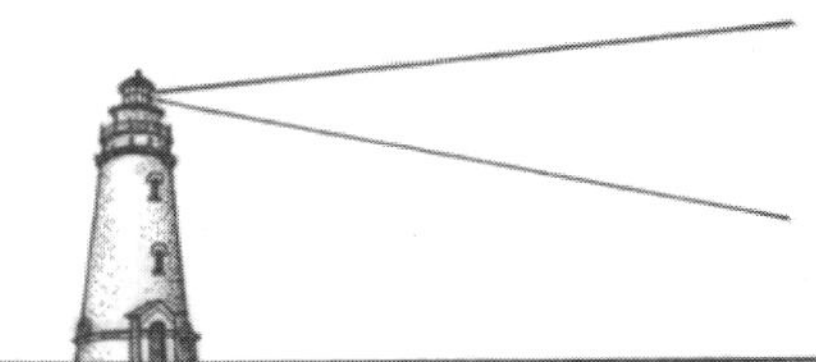

Here is an appetizer recipe that has been passed around a lot during the last 20 years or so. There are probably many variations of this. It could be called ....

"The Tower"

Mexican Layered Dip

1 can bean dip
2 avocados mashed, with a squeeze of lime
1/2 cup sour cream and 1/4 cup mayo
1 large tomato, diced
3-4 green onions chopped
1 can sliced black olives

Layer above as listed and top with grated cheeses - Jack or Cheddar (or Longhorn) or a combination.

Serve with tortilla chips.

....Carole Adams
BLM Volunteer

231

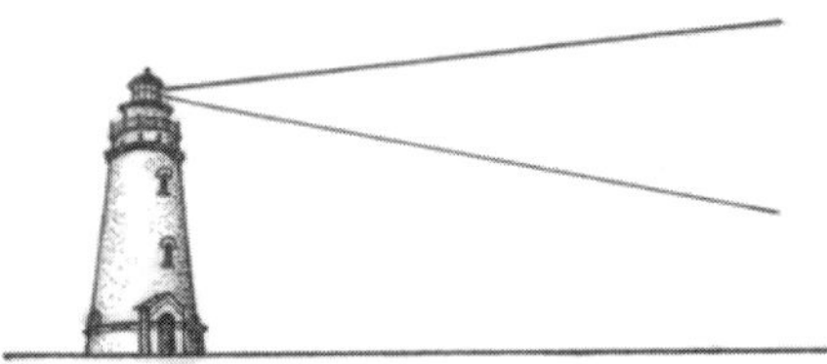

Lighthouse-Keepers' Slaw

1 head of cabbage, shredded
1 onion, sliced
3/4 cup sugar

Mix together: 1 tsp. dry mustard, 1-1/2 tsp salt, 1 tsp. celery seed, 1 cup of vinegar. Boil. Add 1 cup vegetable oil and blend. Pour the hot mixture over the cabbage, onion, sugar mixture. Chill 24 hours.

"I brought this slaw to several lighthouse volunteer potlucks, and it has always been well received."

....Carole Adams
BLM Volunteer

Carole's Corn Bread Casserole

2 large onions, chopped
6 tablespoons butter or margarine
2 eggs   2 tablespoons milk
2-17-oz. cans cream-style corn

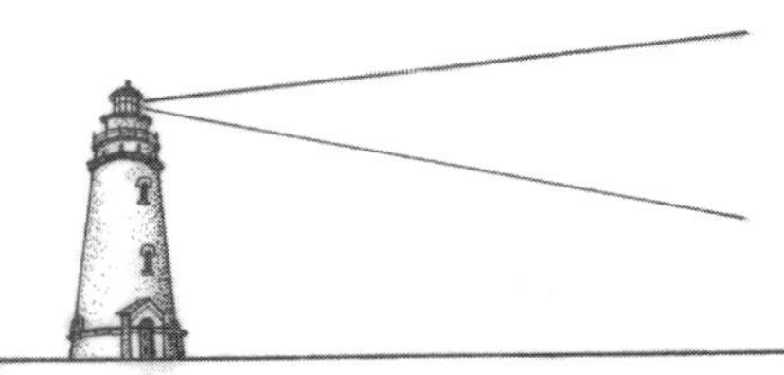

1 (1-lb) pkg cornmeal muffin mix (Jiffy® is
great!)
1/2 pint dairy sour cream (1 cup)
2 cups (8 oz) shredded , sharp Cheddar
cheese

Preheat oven to 425 degrees. Butter a 13"x 9"
baking dish. In a medium skillet sauté onion in
butter or margarine until golden; set aside. In a
medium bowl mix eggs and milk until blended.
Add corn and muffin mix. Mix well. Spread corn
bread batter into prepared baking dish. Spoon
sautéed onion over top. Spread sour cream over
onion. Sprinkle with cheese. Bake 35 minutes or
until puffed and golden. Let stand 10 minutes
before cutting into squares. May be refrigerated
or frozen and reheated. Makes 16 servings (not
in my household it won't, but that's what the recipe
says.)

....Carole Adams
BLM Volunteer

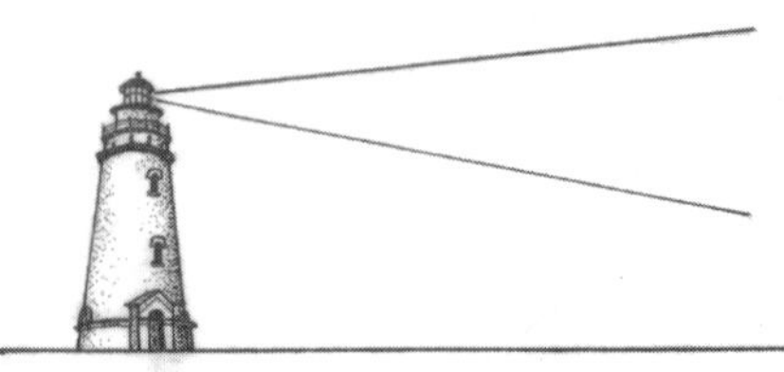

"This is one of our favorite recipes from our lighthouse days – 1980-1986. During this time I (Jim) was studying sea otters and doing graduate work on kelp-forest fish communities, some of which included catching and measuring mid-water rockfish such as Blues, Blacks, Olives & kelp. Having two small children, born 1980 and 1982, and working only part time, a few of those fish made it to our dinner table. Following is what evolved into one of our favorite dishes (only now we use Alaskan Halibut):

Place one pound of rock fish filets (skinned and boned) in the bottom of a baking dish. Brush with olive oil. Season with dill and oregano.

On top of this place 1 sliced medium zucchini.

On top of this put a layer of mozzarella cheese.

On top of the mozzarella cheese is a layer of thickly sliced tomatoes which have been brushed with crushed garlic and seasoned with more oregano, dill, black pepper and splashed with lemon juice.

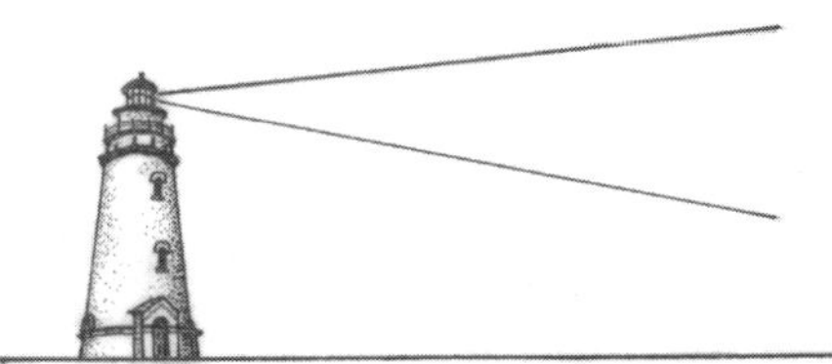

The tomatoes are then covered with another layer of grated mozzarella cheese.

Bake at 350° uncovered for about 20 minutes. We serve it with or without rice.

We also occasionally enjoyed meals of red abalone, sliced thinly and tenderized thoroughly, dipped in egg batter and coated in bread crumbs. We would then lay avocado and Monterey Jack cheese on the abalone and roll it up. These would be baked at 350° for about 20 minutes. A real treat, but abalone took a little effort to get."

....Jim and Donna Botkin,
Marine Biologist, currently living in Alaska

Note: Rock fish have a varied look depending on type ranging from blues to yellows and reds and weigh around 10 pounds. Rockfish is excellent baked, poached and sautéd. Fillets are very delicate and need to be handled with care or they tend to fall apart.

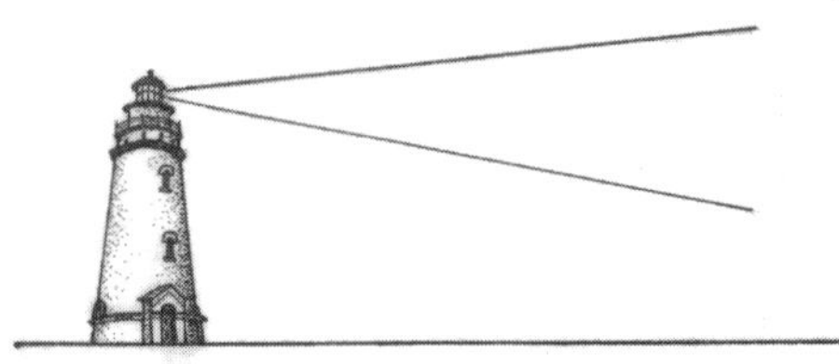

Susan Wright worked as an administrative assistant in the office of the wildlife research station at Piedras Blancas from 1983 until she retired in 2002. Here she shares with us some of her memories and recipes:

"I felt very fortunate to have a job at such a beautiful and unique site. Being the only female in the office, I soon found myself baking a cake whenever there was a birthday to celebrate. (I must give biologist Tom Murphey credit for baking some of those cakes, however, especially when it was my birthday being celebrated!). I often used the following recipe—a family favorite for over 30 years."

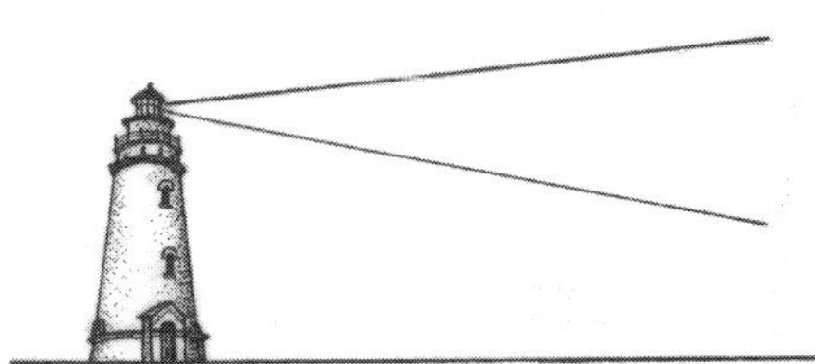

Red Devil's Food Cake

1/2 cup shortening	2 cups flour
1-1/2 cups sugar	1/2 cup milk
1/2 cup cocoa	2 teaspoons baking soda
2 eggs	1 cup boiling water
1 teaspoon vanilla extract	

Cream shortening and add sugar and cocoa. Cream thoroughly and then add eggs and beat well. Stir flour into mixture alternately with milk in which soda has been dissolved. Stir in boiling water and vanilla. Line bottoms of two 8-inch cake pans with waxed paper. Turn batter into cake pans. Bake in moderate oven (350 degrees F.) 30 minutes. Frost as desired.

....Susan Wright

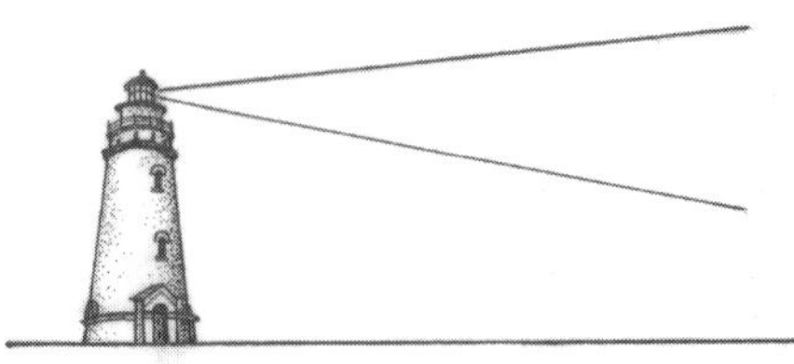

"I commuted from Cambria to work until 1990 when one of the four government housing units became vacant. Soon after moving into 'Quarters B' I brought home a new puppy, Molly, to keep me company and drive my three cats nutty! Molly and I enjoyed many walks down the road to the main gate and back again, and along the beach, tossing and fetching sticks from the ocean, that is, until the elephant seal population grew so large as to take over the entire beach for themselves. The elephant seals brought other Piedras Blancas activities to a stop, too, such as our many barbeques at "the cove" and the after-Christmas tradition of tossing our Christmas trees down to the beach for fueling a very hot bonfire. Our barbeques moved from the beach to our backyards. My standard dish for those great times was my mom's potato salad that she served hundreds of times back in Kansas where she lives to this day. The recipe was never written down —so I do it here for the first time. The measurements are only approximate—but close enough."

....Susan Wright

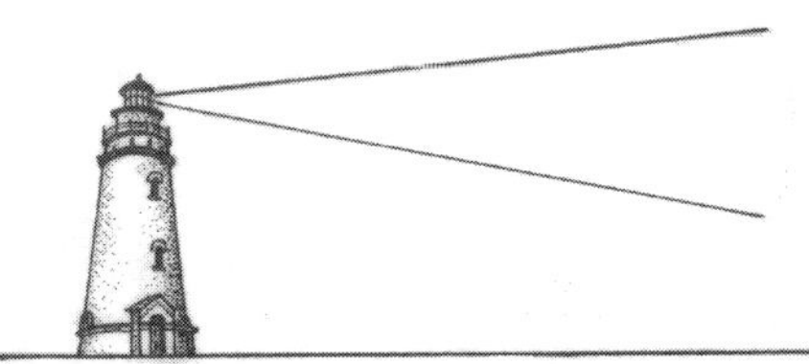

Mom's Potato Salad

3 lbs. potatoes, cooked, cooled, peeled and
        cubed (1/4-1/2 inch cubes)
8 to 12 hardboiled eggs, shelled and cubed
        (1/4-1/2 inch cubes)
1 to 2 cups chopped celery
1 to 2 cups chopped onion (scallions are best)
1/2 cup diced dill pickles (I prefer kosher
        style)
1/4 cup pickle "juice" from pickle jar
2-3 tbsp. prepared mustard
1 cup, more or less, of mayonnaise (I prefer
        Miracle Whip®)
Salt and pepper to taste

Mix all in large bowl, refrigerate till ready
to serve (best if made the day before).

....Susan Wright

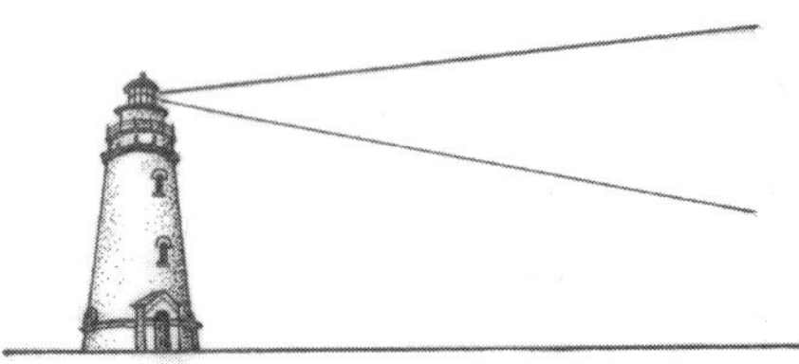

"Being so isolated was an inconvenience, but the major drawback about living at the lighthouse was the weather and climate. Those cold northwesterly winds blowing most days of the year often made staying indoors preferable to enjoying the beautiful out-of-doors. Not that it rained that often, but when it did, I would be drenched from the windblown rainstorm on my 2-minute walks between home and office. The salty, damp air rusted everything made of metal, indoors and out, and some of the closets in my house smelled of mold and mildew (yuck). If we left our jack-o-lanterns outside only for a day or two after Halloween they became soft and mushy (double-yuck), which inspired another Piedras Blancas tradition of dropping them from the top of the Lighthouse. What a mess! (That's how I learned that Molly loved the taste of pumpkin!) I'd try to remember to bring my jack-o-lantern indoors before that happened so that I could use it in the following recipe. I'd cook the pumpkin right away, freeze it, and thaw it in late November for making pies for Thanksgiving."

.....Susan Wright

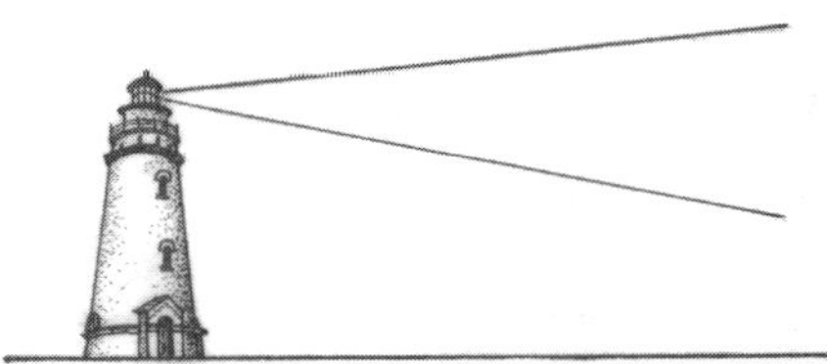

Jack-o-Lantern Pie

3/4 cup brown sugar
1 tbsp. flour
1/2 tsp. salt
2 1/4 tsp. pumpkin pie spice
1-1/2 cup cooked mashed or food-processed
   pumpkin (o.k., so open a can if you must!)
1-1/2 cup evaporated milk
1 slightly beaten egg
2 tbsp. dark molasses

Mix well all ingredients and pour into unbaked pastry-lined pan. Bake at 375 degrees F., 40-45 minutes or until knife inserted into center of pie comes out clean. Serve with or without whipped cream.

....Susan Wright

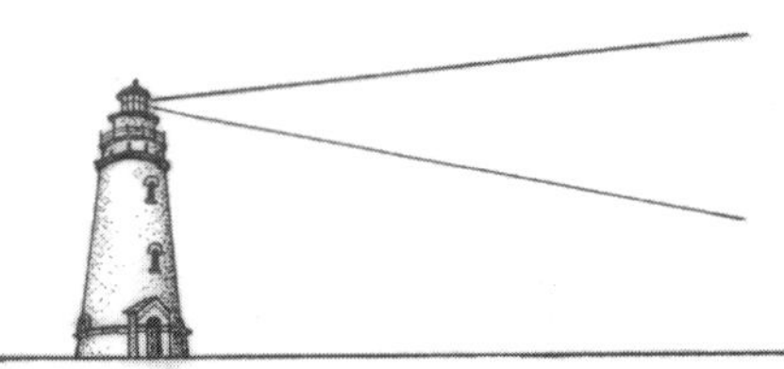

Banana Nut Tea Bread

1-3/4 cups sifted flour	1/2 tsp. salt
2-3/4 tsp. baking powder	2/3 cup sugar
1/3 cup shortening	
2 eggs, well beaten	
1/2 cup coarsely chopped nuts	
1 cup mashed, ripe bananas (2 to 3 bananas)	

Sift together flour, baking powder, and salt.

Beat shortening until creamy in mixing bowl.

Add sugar gradually to shortening and continue beating until light and fluffy.

Add eggs and nuts and beat well.

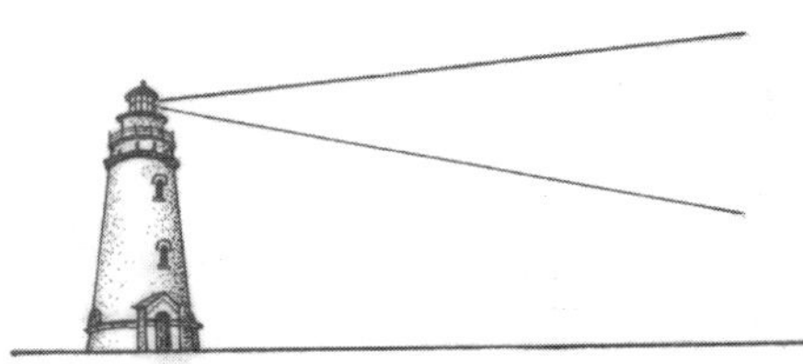

Add flour mixture alternately with bananas, a small amount at a time, mixing after each addition only enough to moisten dry ingredients. Turn into a greased bread loaf pan and bake in a moderate oven (350 degrees F.) about 1 hour and 10 minutes or until bread is done.

....Susan Wright

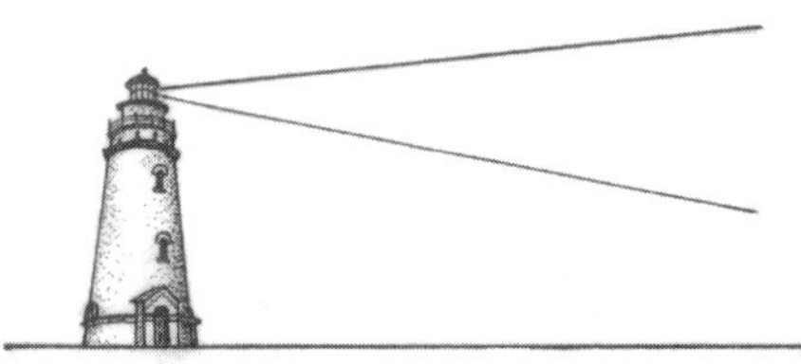

"*One biologist whose name shall remain anonymous brought a fresh frozen lobster tail to my house one evening to share with all the Piedras Blancas residents. I tried to think of the best way to share one lobster with several people and decided to get out my favorite pizza recipe. I cut up the thawed, raw lobster tail into chunks and put the chunks on the pizza before sticking it into the oven and it turned out to be a great hit!*"

....Susan Wright

Susan's Pizza

Dough:
1 cup warm (not hot) water
1 package active dry or 1 cake compressed
  yeast
1 tsp. sugar
1 tsp. salt
2 tbsp. olive or salad oil
2 cups sifted flour
Additional 1-1/2 cups sifted flour (about)

244

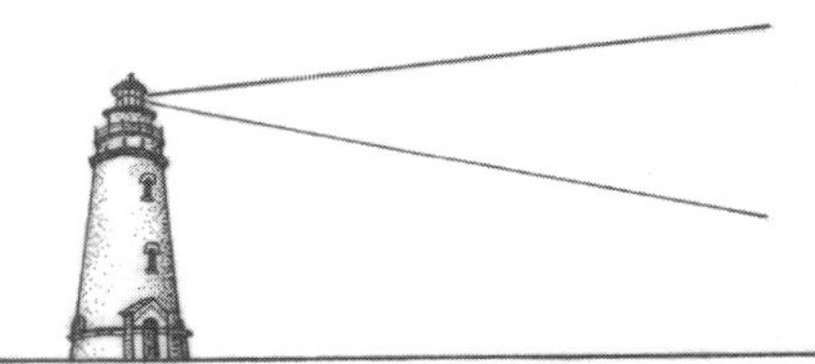

Topping:
1 6-ounce can (2/3 cup) tomato paste
1/2 cup water
1 tsp. salt
1 tsp. crushed oregano (I'm more generous with
the oregano)
Dash of pepper
1/2 pound mozzarella cheese, sliced about
1/8 inch thick
4 tbsp. olive or salad oil
4 tbsp. grated Parmesan cheese

Sprinkle or crumble yeast into the water and stir until dissolved. Stir in sugar, salt and oil. Add the 2 cups sifted flour and beat until smooth, then gradually stir in the additional flour. Dough should be as soft as biscuit dough. Turn out on lightly floured board and knead until smooth and elastic. Place in greased bowl; brush top with soft shortening. Cover and let rise in warm place (85 degrees F.) free from draft, until doubled in bulk, about 45 minutes. Mix together the tomato paste, water, salt, oregano, and pepper. When dough is doubled in bulk, punch down and divide

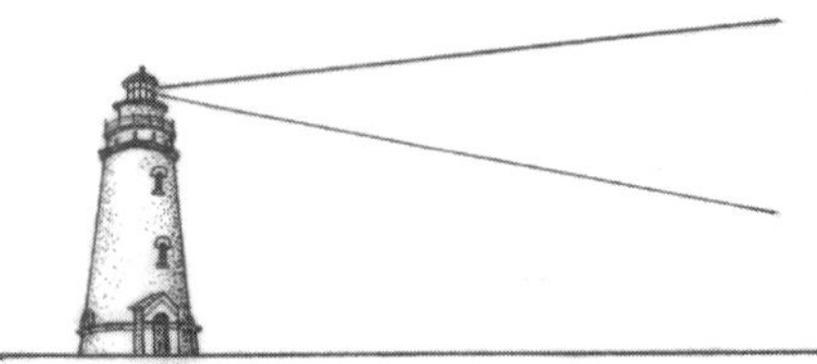

in half. Form each half into a ball and place on greased baking sheet. Press out with palms of hands into circles about 12 inches in diameter, making edges slightly thick. On each circle of dough arrange half of the Mozzarella cheese. Spread evenly half of the tomato mixture; sprinkle evenly 2 tablespoons oil and 2 table-spoons grated Parmesan cheese. (Note: You may add your favorite toppings after spreading the tomato mixture.) Bake in hot oven (400 degrees F.) about 25 minutes. Serve hot. Makes two 12-inch pizzas.

...Susan Wright

"Sara, my middle daughter, lived with me one summer between semesters at San Francisco State. One Saturday she suggested we try fishing off the rocks behind the house. It wasn't long before we had lost all our tackle to the many snag-ups on the rocks below the ocean's surface. Sara did manage to catch one rock cod though (no pun intended). If you ever need to feed a bunch of people on one little fish you might want to try the following recipe. It's delicious and perfect for a Christmas eve or New

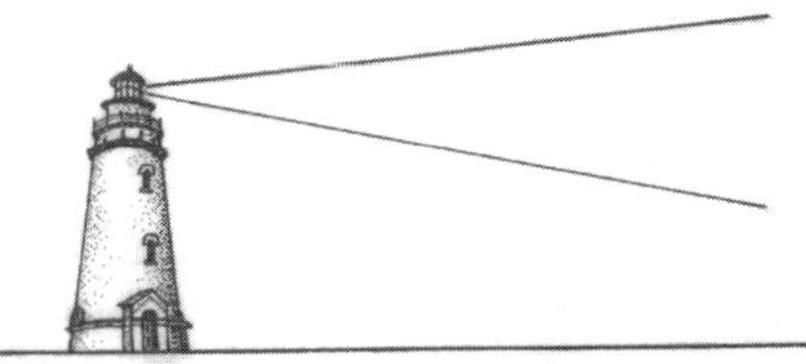

Year's eve supper. I recommend doubling the recipe
if you're serving more than 4."

....Susan Wright

Cioppino

1 lb. firm fleshed fish (cod, turbot, haddock,
etc.) and/or seafood (raw shrimp, scallops,
steamed clams)

2 tbsp. butter or margarine

1 large onion, 1" diced

1 cup water

1 large green pepper, 1" diced

2 cloves garlic, finely chopped

1 - 1 lb. can tomatoes, chopped, with juice

1 tbsp. Old Bay® seasoning (it's often hidden
   in the meat, fish or deli section of your super
   market)

1/4 tsp. basil

3/4 cup red wine

1/4 tsp. marjoram

6 or more mushrooms, halved

Cut deboned fish in large bite-size pieces. Sauté
vegetables in butter until crisp-tender. Add water,
(continued on page 248)

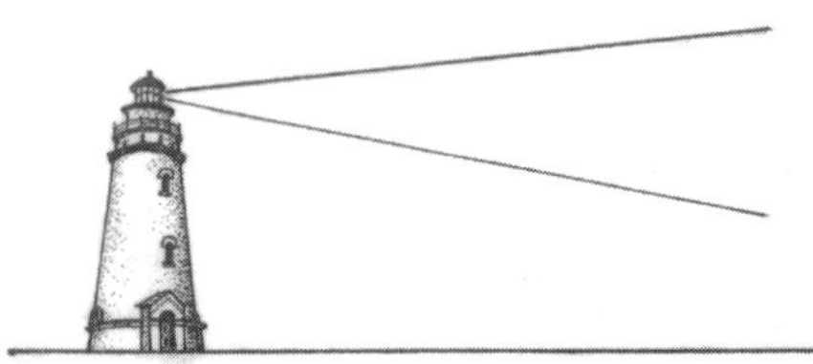

tomatoes with juice, and seasonings; heat to boiling. Reduce heat, cover and simmer 10 minutes.

Add wine and mushrooms; bring to boiling. Reduce heat, cover and simmer 10 minutes. Add fish, shrimp and/or scallops, cover and simmer until done, about 8 minutes. Clams (if used) should be added during last 3 minutes. Serve in soup bowls and with yummy sour dough bread or rolls.

....Susan Wright

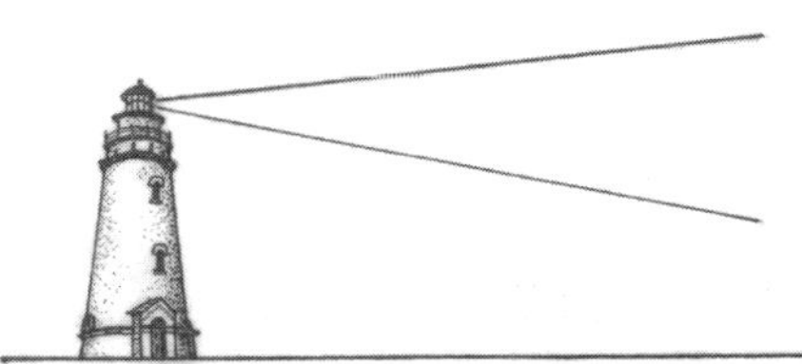

"This is a recipe passed down to me by my mother. It makes a tasty side dish and is easily portable for potlucks or picnics. It is good to eat at room temperature."

.....Barbara Akle, BLM Volunteer

Rice Salad

Ingredients:
1 cup raw rice
1/4 cup butter or margarine (1/2 stick)
1 1/2 tablespoons lime juice
1 cup thin sliced celery
1 green onion, sliced
1 can mandarin oranges
1/2 cup mayonnaise (or to taste)

Directions:
Cook rice. Stir in butter and lime juice. Cool to room temperature. Add remaining ingredients. No need to heat or chill to serve. Serves 6 or more.

.....Barbara Akle, BLM Volunteer

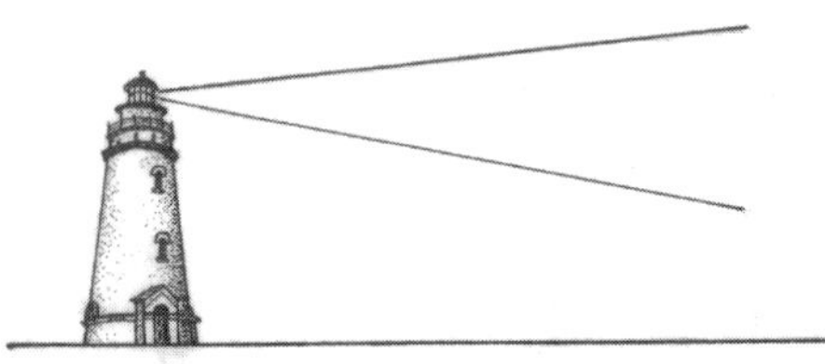

Piedras Blancas Special Banquet

In 1992, Lynn and Galen Rathbun hosted a banquet for 8 guests in the tower at Piedras Blancas Light Station. The event took place in order to reward several Cambrians who had distinguished themselves in a local conservation effort. The formal candle-lit meal started at the lowest level of the tower with hors d'oeuvres and with each course progressed a level up in the tower, culminating with a dessert at the top. Lynn was the cook for the evening, while Galen and Cynthia Hawley climbed the spiral stairs too many times to count in order to serve the meal. Below are recipes for the hors d'oeuvres and dessert, as prepared by Lynn.

Artichoke Cocktail Spread

1 cup mayonnaise
1 cup parmesan cheese
1 15 oz can artichoke hearts (or you can
use a package of frozen artichoke hearts
that have been thawed and drained)

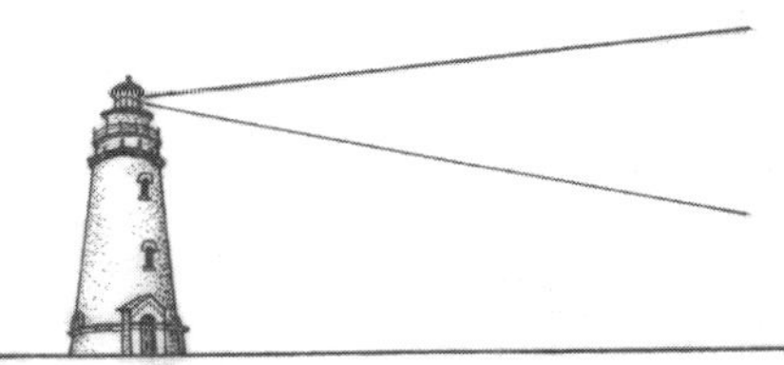

Mix together the ingredients thoroughly and heat (microwave works best).
Serve on heart-shaped crackers.

....Lynn Rathbun
Artist and wife of Galen Rathbun,
Marine Biology Researcher

Apple/Raisin Pie

Stir and Roll Pie Crust:

1-1/3 cups Flour	1/3 cup canola oil
1 tsp. salt	3 Tb. cold milk

Yield one 9" pie crust

Prepare 2 pie crusts. (You can double the recipe or make each one separately.)

Mix flour and salt. Pour oil and milk into one measuring cup. Do not stir; add all at once to flour. Stir until mixed. Roll between 2 pieces of waxed paper. Arrange in 9" pie plate and place in 400 degree oven for about 7 minutes until it starts to bake. Remove and fill with apples.

Note: This crust is light and flaky and is wonderful for both sweet and savory pies. It does

(continued on page 252)

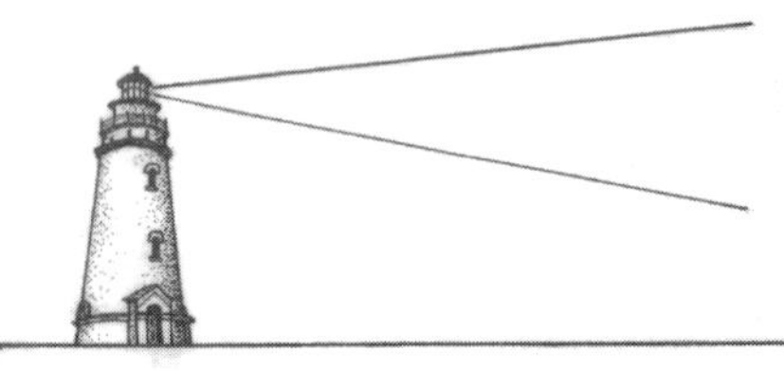

not do well if made ahead of time and placed in the refrigerator. Also, it is very healthy as it contains no saturated fats.

Filling:
6-8 medium sized apples, such as Pink
 Lady, which are sweet and crunchy
Juice of 1 lemon   1/3 cup flour
1/2 cup sugar   1/2 tsp. cloves
1 tsp. each cinnamon, nutmeg
2 T. butter, cut into small pieces.
Optional: 2 small boxes SunMaid® raisins (soaked for 10 minutes in boiling water and then drained.)

Preparation: Peel, core and cut apples into slices about 3/8" thick and place in bowl. Sprinkle lightly with juice of lemon. Mix flour, sugar and spices and pour over apples, so that each is coated.

Arrange apples in pie shell until mounded up in center. If you are using raisins, sprinkle them on top of each layer of apples. Dot with small pieces of butter.

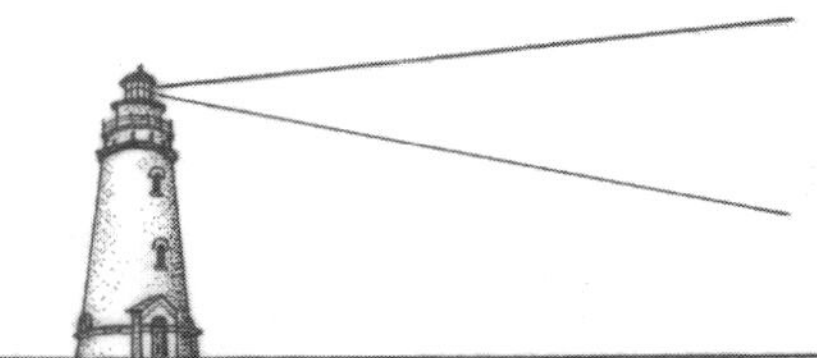

Cover with second crust, pinch edges and trim excess, and make cuts in top to release steam. Bake at 375 degrees for 45 minutes or until crust turns light brown. Remove and let cool for 20 minutes. Serve with ice cream or frozen yogurt.

....Lynn Rathbun, Artist and wife of Galen Rathbun, Marine Biology Researcher

Three Bells
(Red Bell Peppers with Cherry Tomatoes)

3 red bell peppers, parboiled and cut in half lengthwise

For Dressing:
2 tsp. extra virgin olive oil
2 Tblsp. balsamic vinegar
2 cloves garlic, minced
2 oz. can anchovies, rinsed & chopped (opt.)
1 Tblsp. fresh thyme leaves
1 Tblsp. small capers
1/4 Cup fresh basil, cut in strips

Mix together ingredients for dressing. Toss with 1 lb. cherry tomatoes, stemmed and halved.

(continued on page 254)

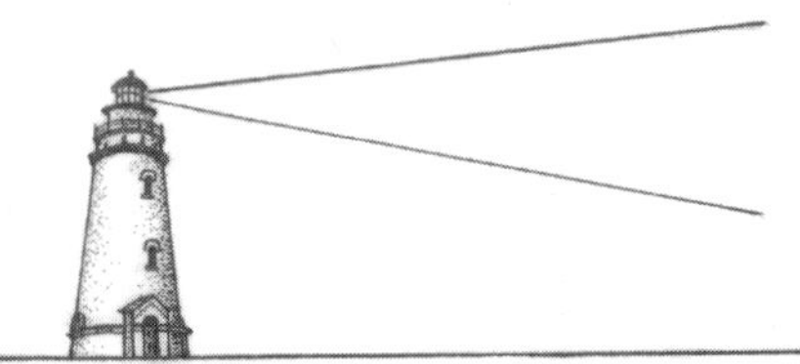

Stuff peppers. Bake in 450° oven for about 30 minutes or until the peppers are tender when pierced with a fork.

Grated mozzarella may be sprinkled on top.

....Jean Hernandez, BLM Volunteer

Polenta with Gorgonzola, Green Onions and Pine Nuts

3 cups chicken broth	1 cup polenta
4 cloves garlic, minced	1/2 cup milk
4 T. (1/2 stick) butter	1/2 t. pepper

Boil broth with garlic and gradually stir in polenta. After polenta begins to thicken, stir in milk. Continue stirring and cooking 10 minutes. Add butter and pepper and cook until creamy and smooth, about 5 minutes. Pour mixture into shallow ovenproof pan.

Sprinkle with: 1/4 cup crumbled gorgonzola cheese, 1/4 cup green onions, sliced; and 1/4 cup toasted pine nuts

Bake in 325° oven or microwave to heat.

Serves 6

....Jean Hernandez, BLM Volunteer

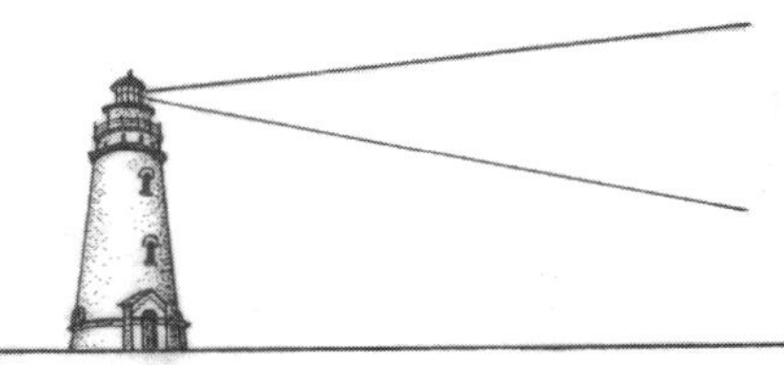

Smokey Split Pea and Root Veggie Soup

6 T. (3/4) stick butter   3 bay leaves
3 medium carrots, chopped
2 large parsnips, chopped
2 medium leeks, white light green parts,
                                          chopped
1 large onion chopped
2-1/2 teaspoons dried thyme, crumbled
2 teaspoons dried marjoram, crumbled
11 cups chicken stock
3 c. golden split peas
1-1/4 lbs. smoked ham hocks
1/2 c. chopped fresh Italian parsley

Melt butter in a large pan. Add carrots, parsnips, leeks, onion, thyme, marjoram and bay leaves. Cook about 20 minutes, covered. Add stock, peas and ham hocks; simmer covered 45 minutes until peas cook. Remove ham hocks and cut meat into small pieces. Add meat to soup.

Serves 6

....Jean Hernandez, BLM Volunteer

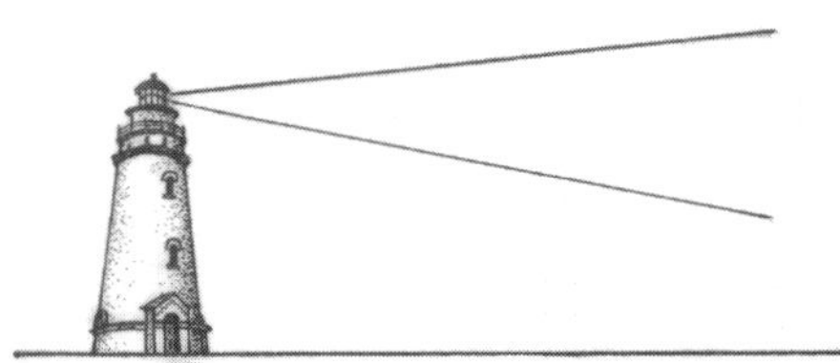

Caper Chicken

3 T. butter   6 chicken half breasts
1 cup heavy cream   3 T. capers
3 T. caper juice   Freshly ground pepper
3/4 tsp. dried oregano   1 bay leaf

Preheat oven to 350°. Melt butter in a large skillet. Add the chicken pieces and brown well on all sides. Remove chicken to a baking pan. Pour fat off skillet. Add remaining ingredients and bring to a boil. Reduce heat and simmer 2 minutes. Remove bay leaf.

Pour sauce over chicken. Bake 30 - 40 minutes until chicken is cooked. Baste occasionally while baking.   Serves 4 - 6

....Jean Hernandez, BLM Volunteer

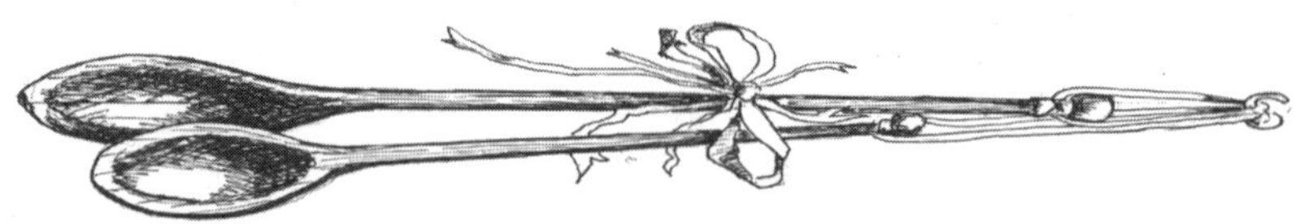

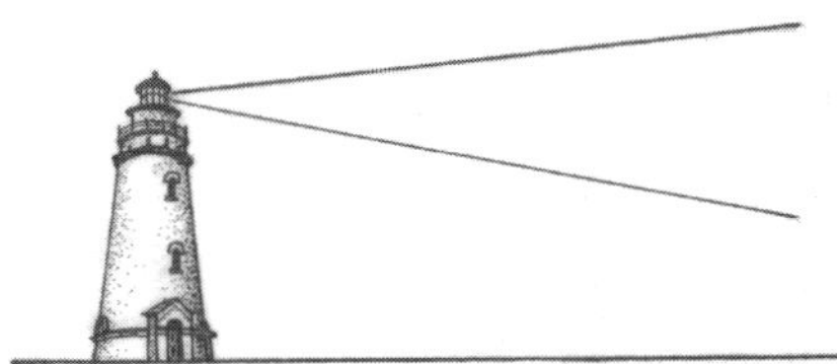

Cashew Shrimp & Pea Salad

1-1/2 cups roasted cashews - divided
16 oz. pkg. frozen petite peas, thawed and
drained
1 cup thinly sliced green onions
2 large stalks celery, cut in thin pieces
3/4 cup small cooked shrimp
salt and pepper to taste
Set aside 2 Tblsp. cashews for garnish. Combine remaining ingredients. Add dill dressing and mix lightly.

Dill Dressing: Mix 1/4 cup each, mayonnaise and sour cream, 1 T. lemon juice and 1 T. fresh dill or 1 tsp. dill weed.

Line a serving bowl with 6 - 8 large butter lettuce leaves. Spoon salad into center; garnish with reserved cashews and, if desired, dill.

Serves 4
....Jean Hernandez, BLM Volunteer

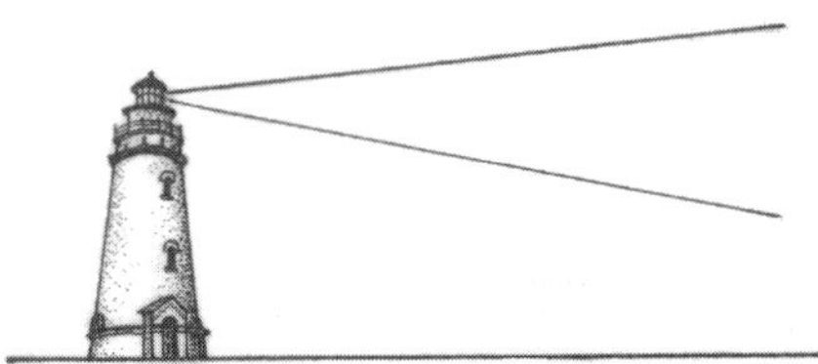

Shrimp with Feta Cheese

1 tsp. olive oil   1 T. butter
1/4 tsp. dried oregano 1/2 tsp. salt
1/4 tsp. crushed red pepper
1 lb. medium shrimp, peeled and deveined
3 garlic cloves, minced

Sauté 2 - 3 minutes until shrimp is cooked. Remove shrimp from pan. Reduce in same pan: 1/2 cup dry white wine to 1/4 cup.

Stir in 3 cups diced plum tomatoes. Cook 3 minutes. Combine with shrimp. Serve over 4 cups cooked pasta. Sprinkle with 1/4 cup minced fresh parsley and finely crumbled feta cheese.
Serves 4

....Jean Hernandez, BLM Volunteer

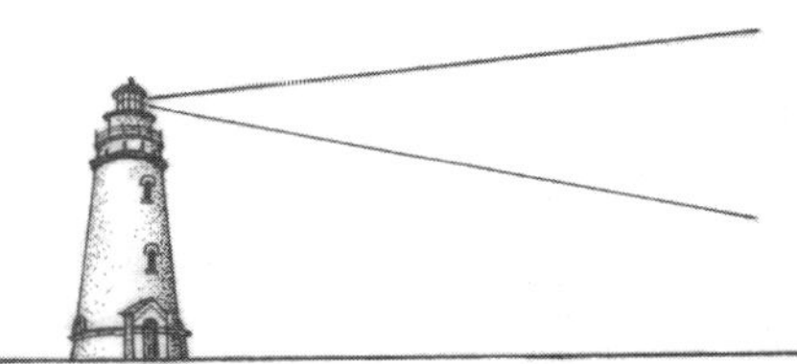

Irish Soda Bread

3 cups all-purpose flour   1 tsp. salt
1/4 cup granulated sugar
3 tsps. baking powder
1 tsp. baking soda
1-2/3 cups buttermilk   1 cup raisins
1/4 cup margarine, softened
1 large egg, beaten
2 Tbsps. caraway seeds

Preheat oven to 350° F. In a large bowl mix together flour, sugar, baking powder, baking soda and salt. Stir in buttermilk, margarine and egg; mix well. Add raisins and caraway seeds. Equally divide dough into 2 pieces; place each piece in a greased 9 inch pie pan. ("Cut a cross in the top of each loaf to let the devil out" that is the way I was taught!) Bake until golden brown, 30-40 minutes. Cool before slicing.   Makes 2 loaves.

"This is a recipe for Irish Soda Bread that I made for the potluck at Piedras Blancas Lighthouse."

.....Maryann B. Mullen, BLM Volunteer

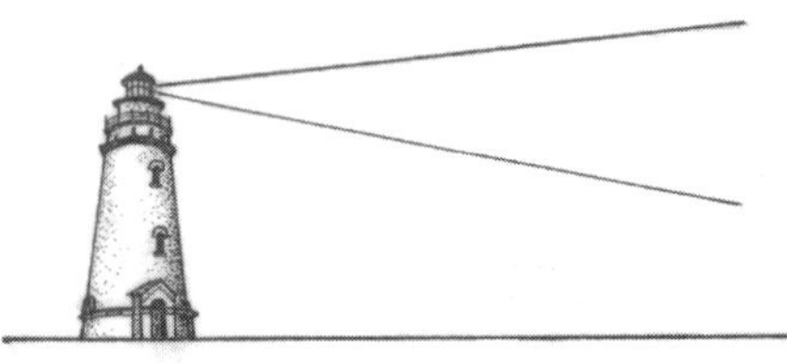

Parmesan Polenta Pizzas with Slow-roasted Pesto Tomatoes

2 tubes prepared polenta, cut into (24) 3/8"
          thick slices, discarding ends
12 roma tomatoes   fresh-ground pepper
1/4 cup purchased or homemade pesto
1 cup grated fresh parmesan/reggiano cheese

Cut rinsed tomatoes in half lengthwise and place cut side up in an oiled 10" x 15" pan. Sprinkle lightly with pepper. Spread about 1/2 tsp. pesto onto cut side of each tomato half. Bake in a 350° oven until browned on top and slightly shriveled – 1-1/2 to 2 hours. If pan juices begin to scorch, add a little water. Let tomatoes cool about 10 minutes.

Place polenta rounds slightly apart on an oiled 12" x 17" baking sheet. Sprinkle 1/2 cup parmesan cheese evenly over rounds. Set a tomato half, pesto side up, on each and sprinkle remaining cheese on top. Bake in a 450° oven until cheese is melted and beginning to brown – 10-13 minutes.

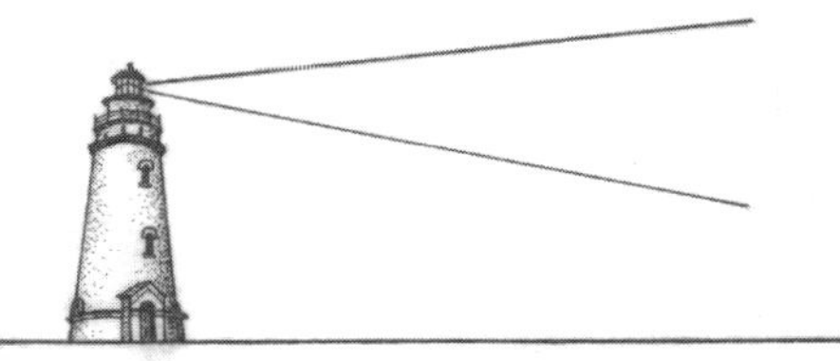

Let cool 2-3 minutes then transfer with a spatula to a platter.

....Jackie Kane, BLM Volunteer

Chicken-Chile Casserole

4 cups diced, cooked chicken or turkey (3-4 whole chicken breasts)
a 7 oz. can diced green chiles
1 medium onion, finely chopped
1 can cream of chicken soup
9 tortillas, buttered and cut in half
1 pound sharp cheddar cheese, grated
1 cup regular strength chicken broth

Combine chicken, chiles, onion and soup. Arrange 6 halves of tortillas over bottom of casserole, buttered side down. Spread 1/3 chicken mixture over tortillas and top with 1/3 of the cheese. Repeat twice more. Pour broth over all. Bake at 400 for 25-30 minutes. Serves 6

....Jackie Kane, BLM Volunteer

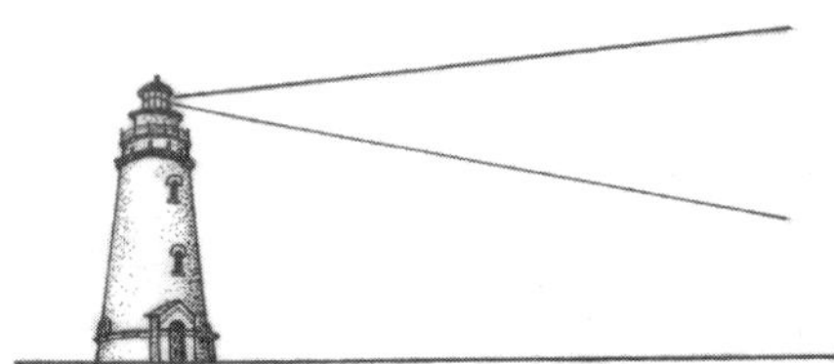

Artichoke Salad

Combine:
4 small or 2 large jars
            marinated artichokes, drained
2 cans plain artichokes
2 baskets cherry (halved) or olive
                            tomatoes
1 (tall, skinny) jar pimento stuffed
                            olives
1 lb. sliced fresh mushrooms

Toss with marinade:
1 cup olive oil   1/2 tsp. dry mustard
2 tsp. oregano   1/2 tsp. pepper
1 tsp. salt   1/3 cup wine vinegar
2 cloves garlic, pressed

Serves 16 to 20 and is easily halved for
            fewer servings.

....Jackie Kane, BLM Volunteer

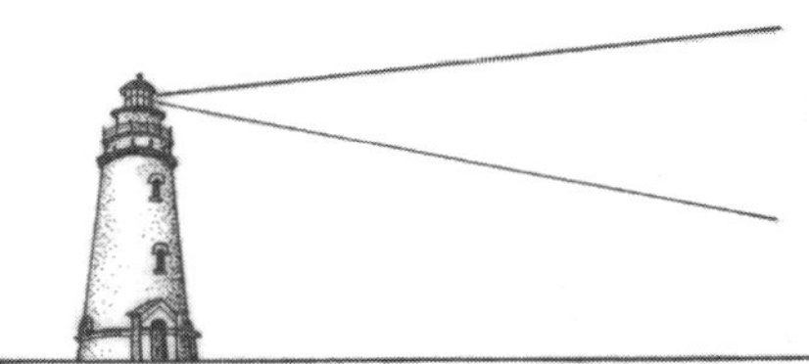

Tomato Lasagne Rolls

8 pieces curly edge lasagne, uncooked
12oz. jar of Classico® Tomato-Basil sauce
15 oz. container Ricotta Cheese
10 oz. pkg. frozen chopped spinach, thawed
and well drained
1 cup shredded mozzarella cheese, divided
1 egg, slightly beaten
2 Tablespoons grated parmesan cheese
1/2 teaspoon salt   1/4 teaspoon black pepper

Cook pasta according to package directions; drain. Lay flat on foil to cool. Heat oven to 350° F. In bowl, stir together ricotta cheese, spinach, 1/2 cup mozzarella cheese, egg, parmesan cheese, salt and pepper. Spray 12x8-inch baking dish with cooking oil. In bottom of baking dish spread 1/4 cup tomato sauce. Spread about 1/3 cup cheese filling on each noodle to within 1-inch of ends; roll up. Place rolls in prepared dish; top with remaining tomato sauce. Cover. Bake 35 minutes or until hot and bubbly. Sprinkle with remaining 1/2 cup of mozzarella; bake until cheese melts.

....Bev Praver, BLM Volunteer

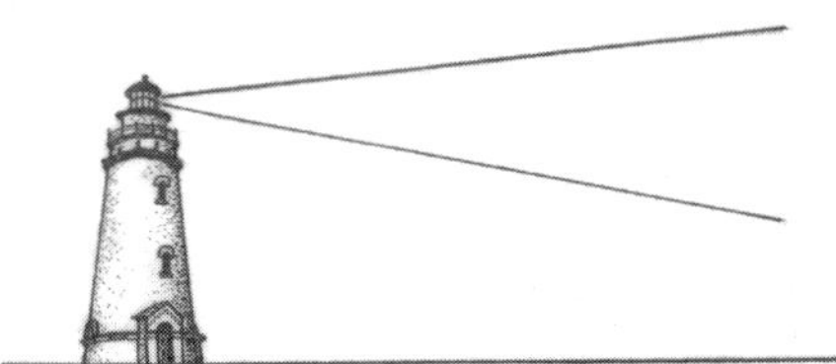

Turkey Hawaiian

15-1/4 oz. can pineapple chunks
3 T. butter or margarine   1/3 cup flour
1/2 tsp. salt   1/2 tsp. ground ginger
14-1/2 oz. chicken broth
1-1/2 cups diced cooked turkey
8 oz. can sliced water chestnuts
1/4 cup sliced green onion
1/2 cup green pepper, cut in large chunks
1 medium tomato, sliced in thin wedges
1/3 cup slivered almonds   chow mein noodles

Drain pineapple, save syrup. Melt butter in skillet. Stir in flour, salt and ginger. Add chicken broth and pineapple syrup. Cook and stir until smooth and thick. Stir in turkey, water chestnuts, green pepper, green onions and pineapple; heat through.

Stir in tomato wedges and heat through. Serve immediately over noodles or rice. Sprinkle with almonds.

....Bev Praver, BLM Volunteer

Family

Trees

The family trees presented here are not complete and are given only as a guide to help in understanding the relationship between the recipe contributors from the extended Thorndyke family.

The names of Thorndyke family members who have contibuted recipes to this book are printed in italics on these charts.

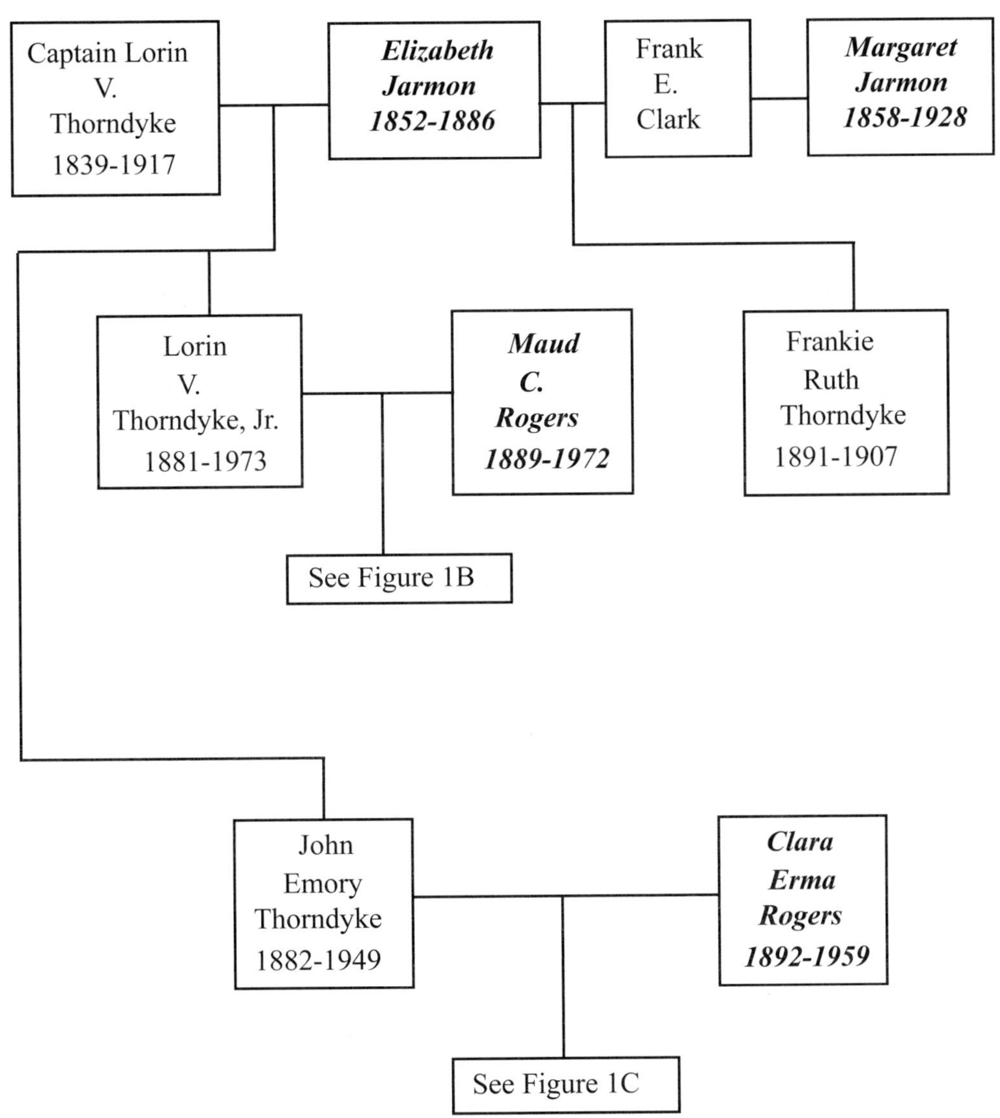

Figure 1A . Thorndyke Family Genealogy

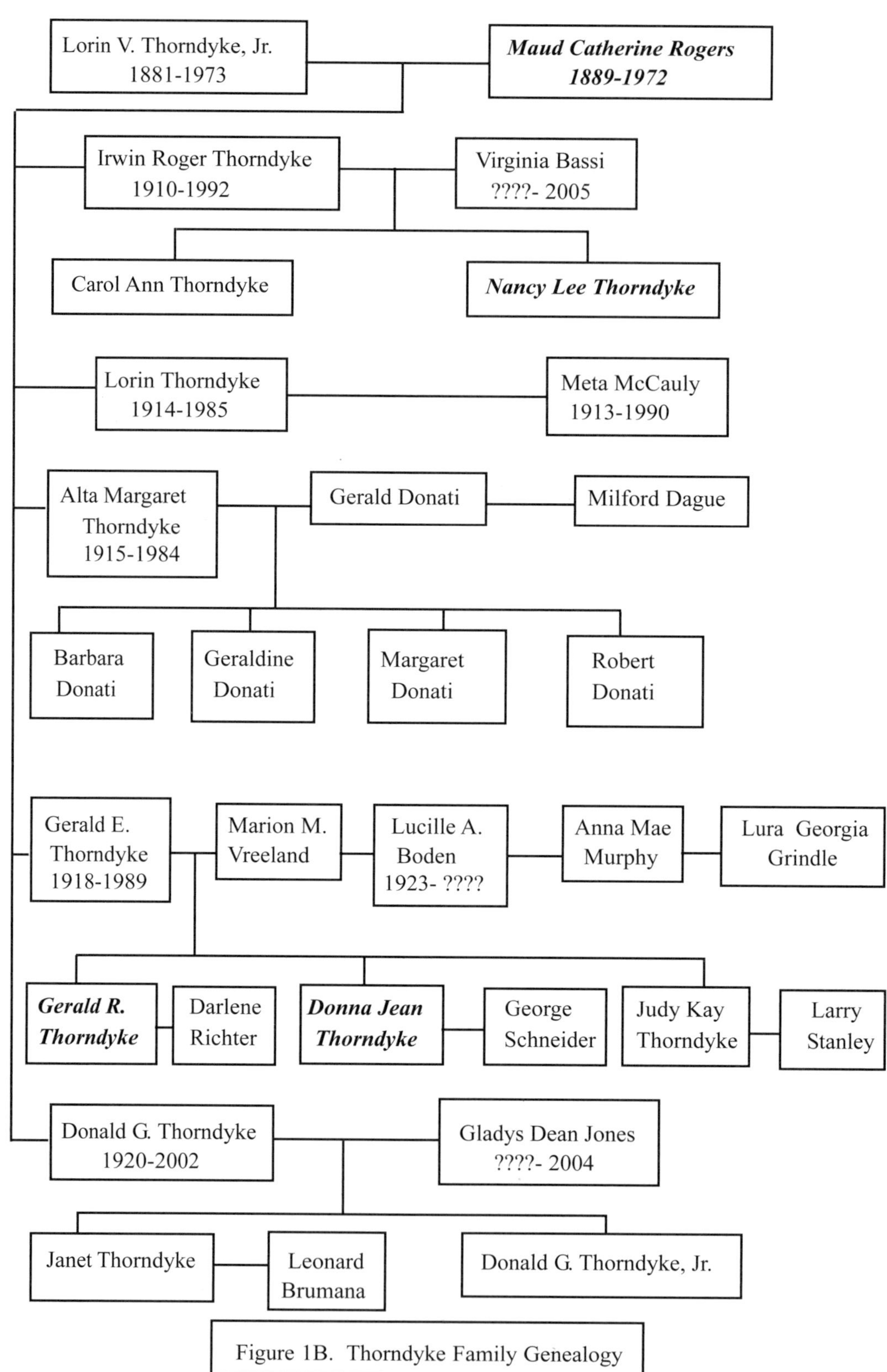

Figure 1B. Thorndyke Family Genealogy

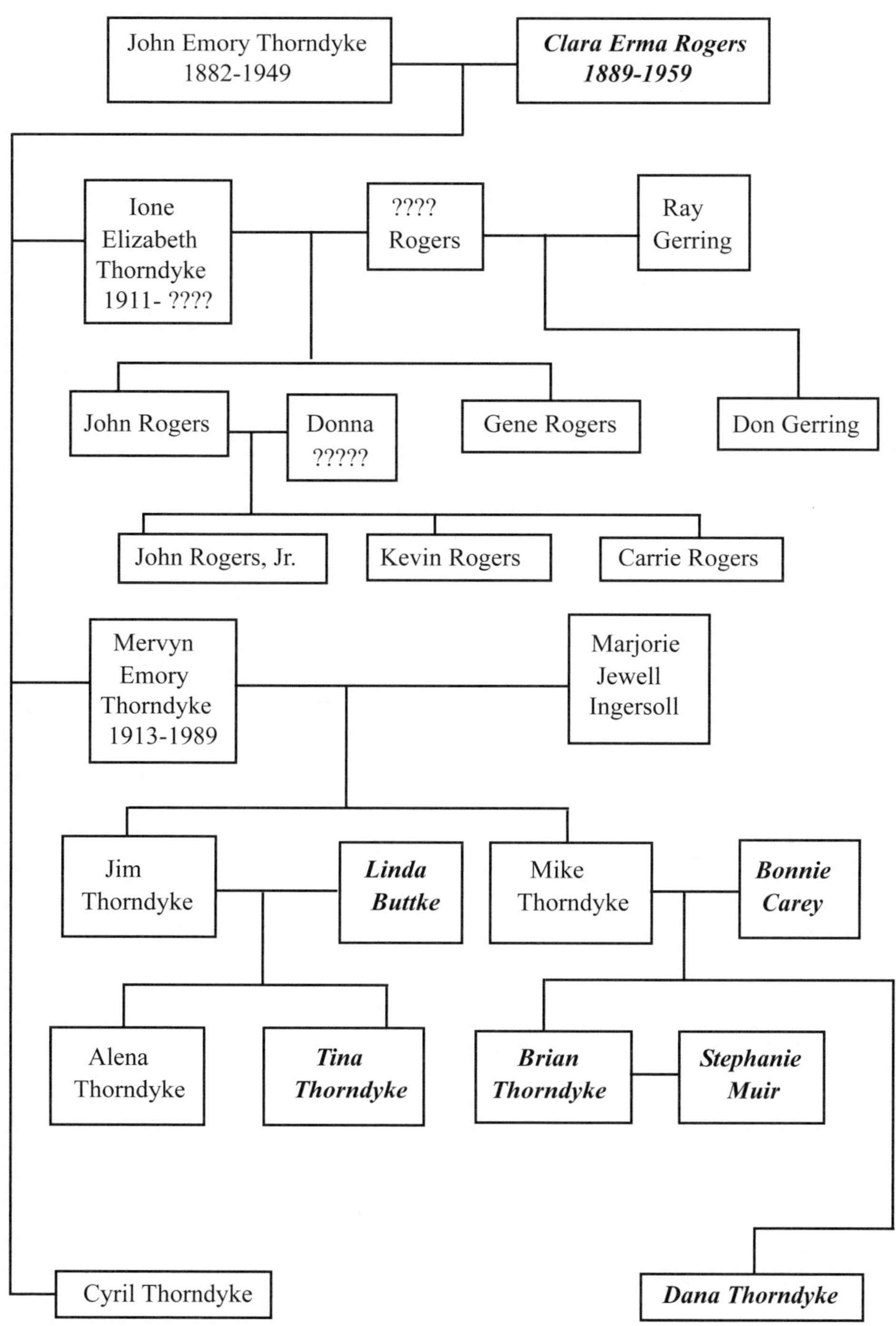

Figure 1C. Thorndyke Family Genealogy

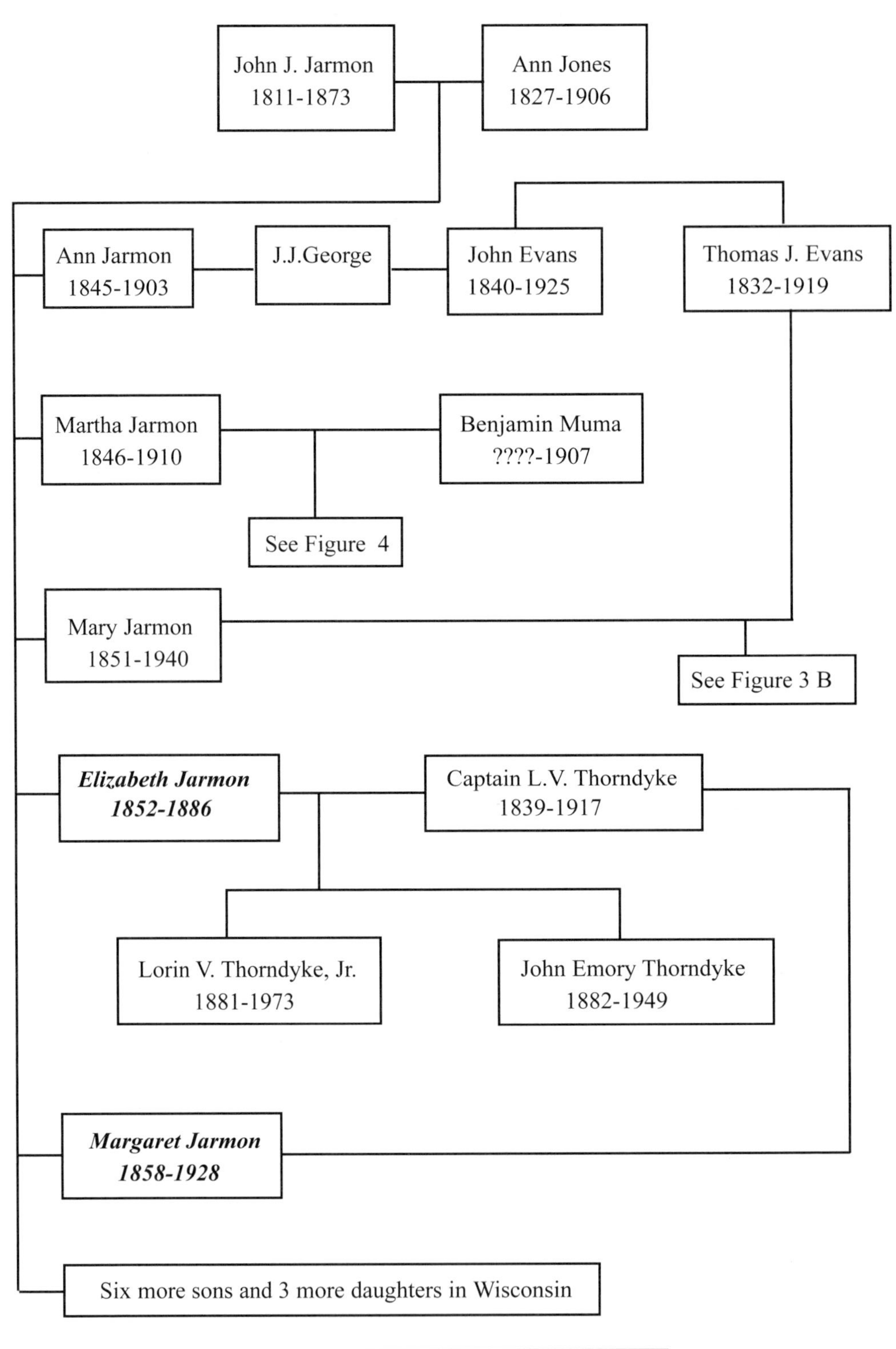

Figure 2. Jarmon Family Genealogy

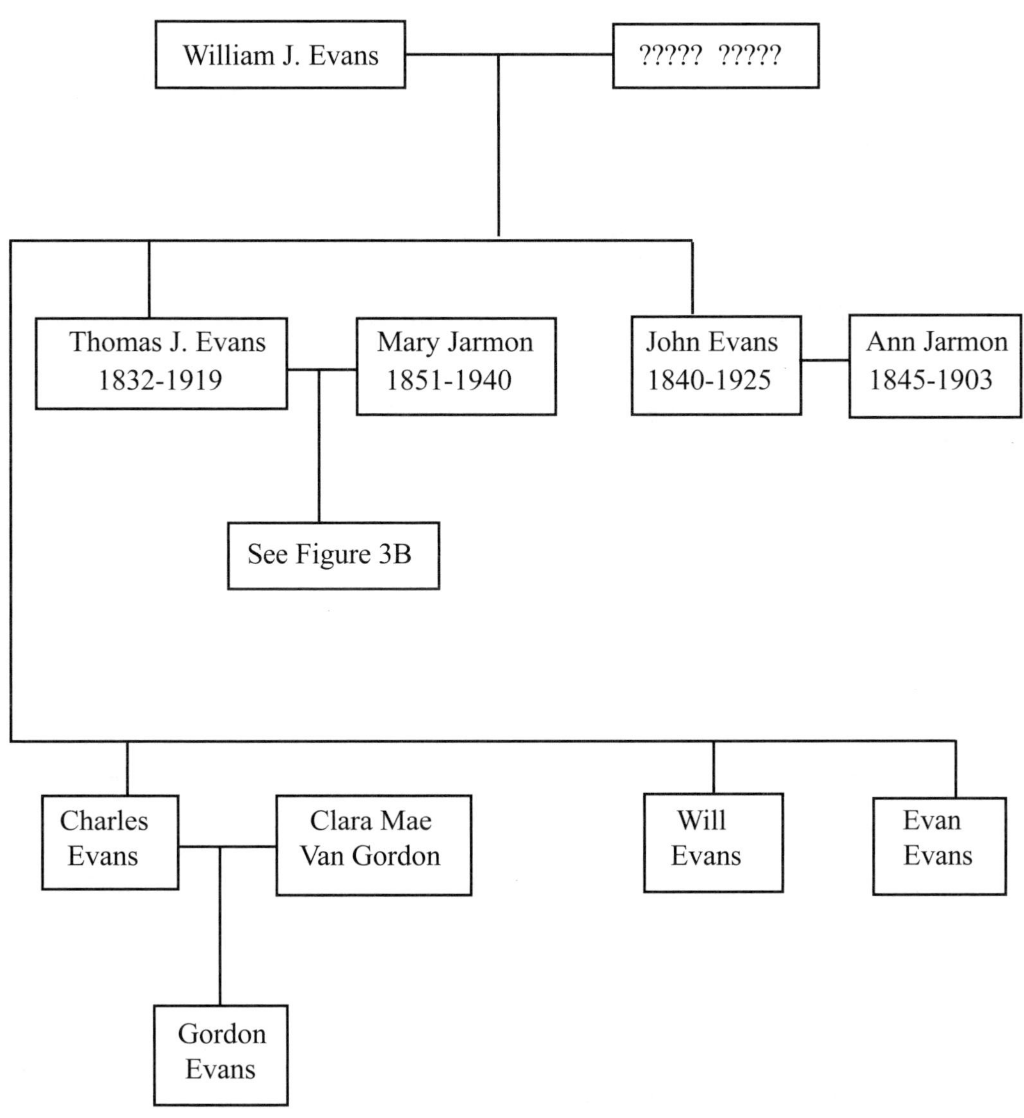

Figure 3A. Evans Family Genealogy

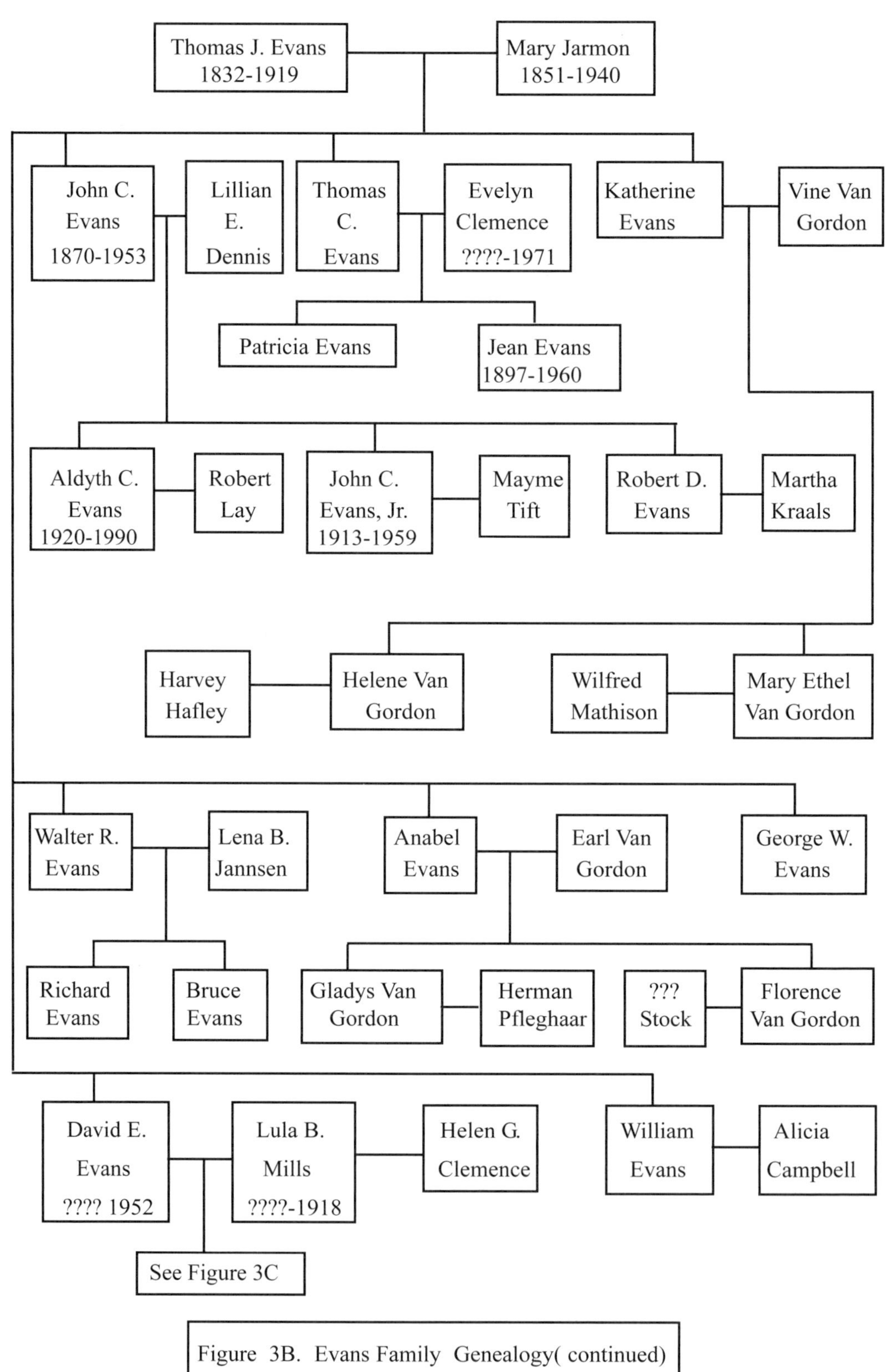

Figure 3B. Evans Family Genealogy(continued)

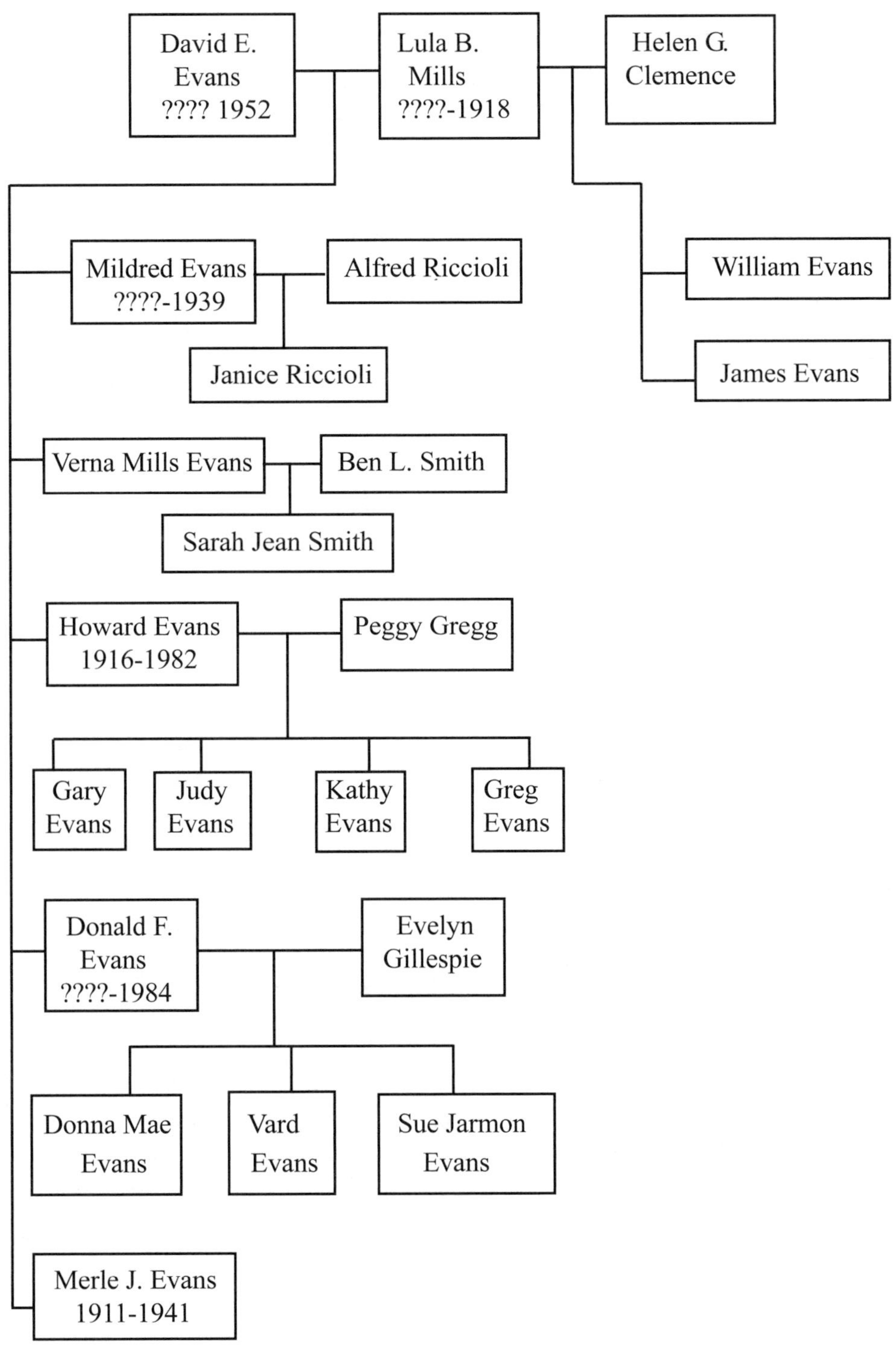

Figure 3C.   Evans Family Genealogy(continued)

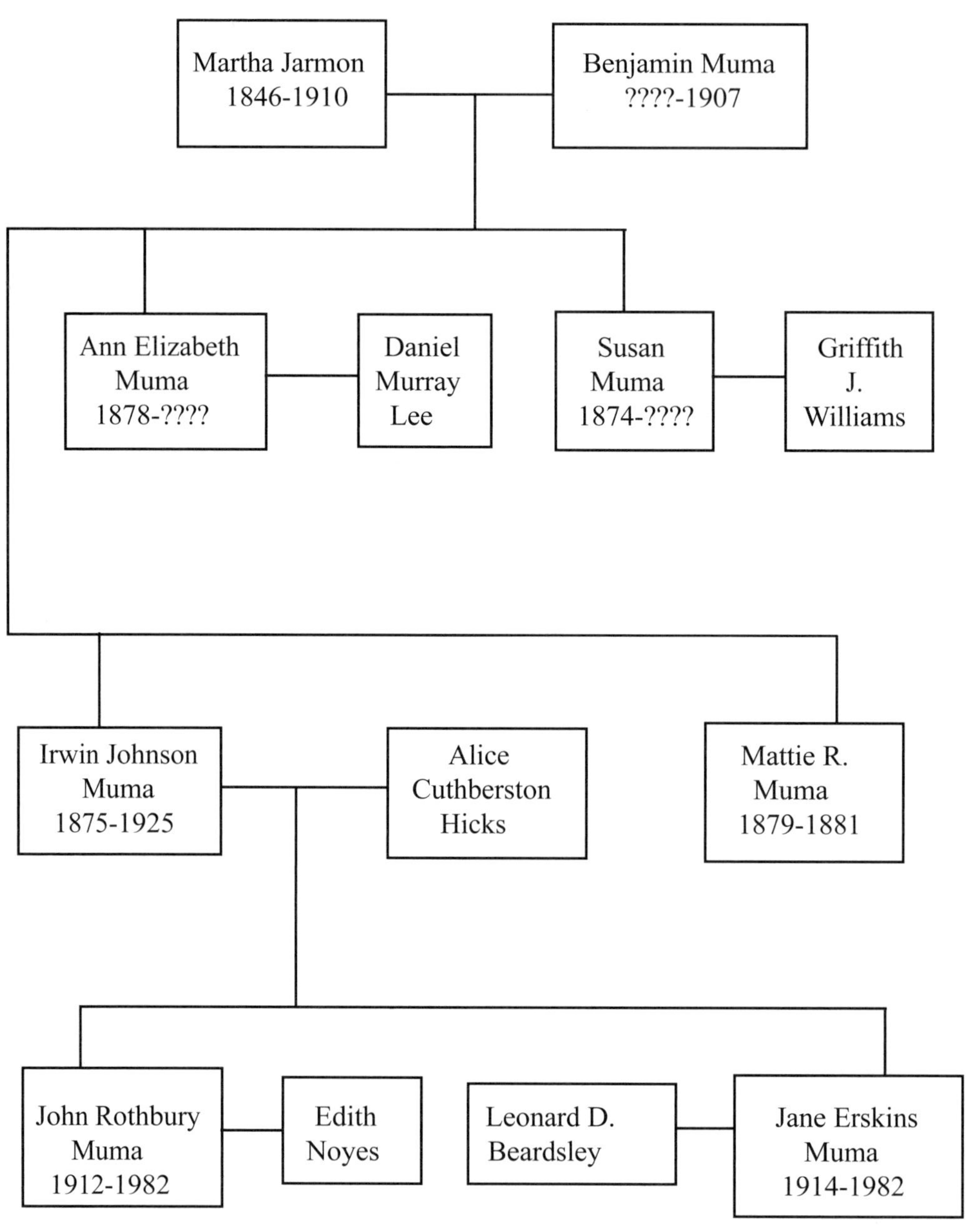

Figure 4. Muma Family Genealogy

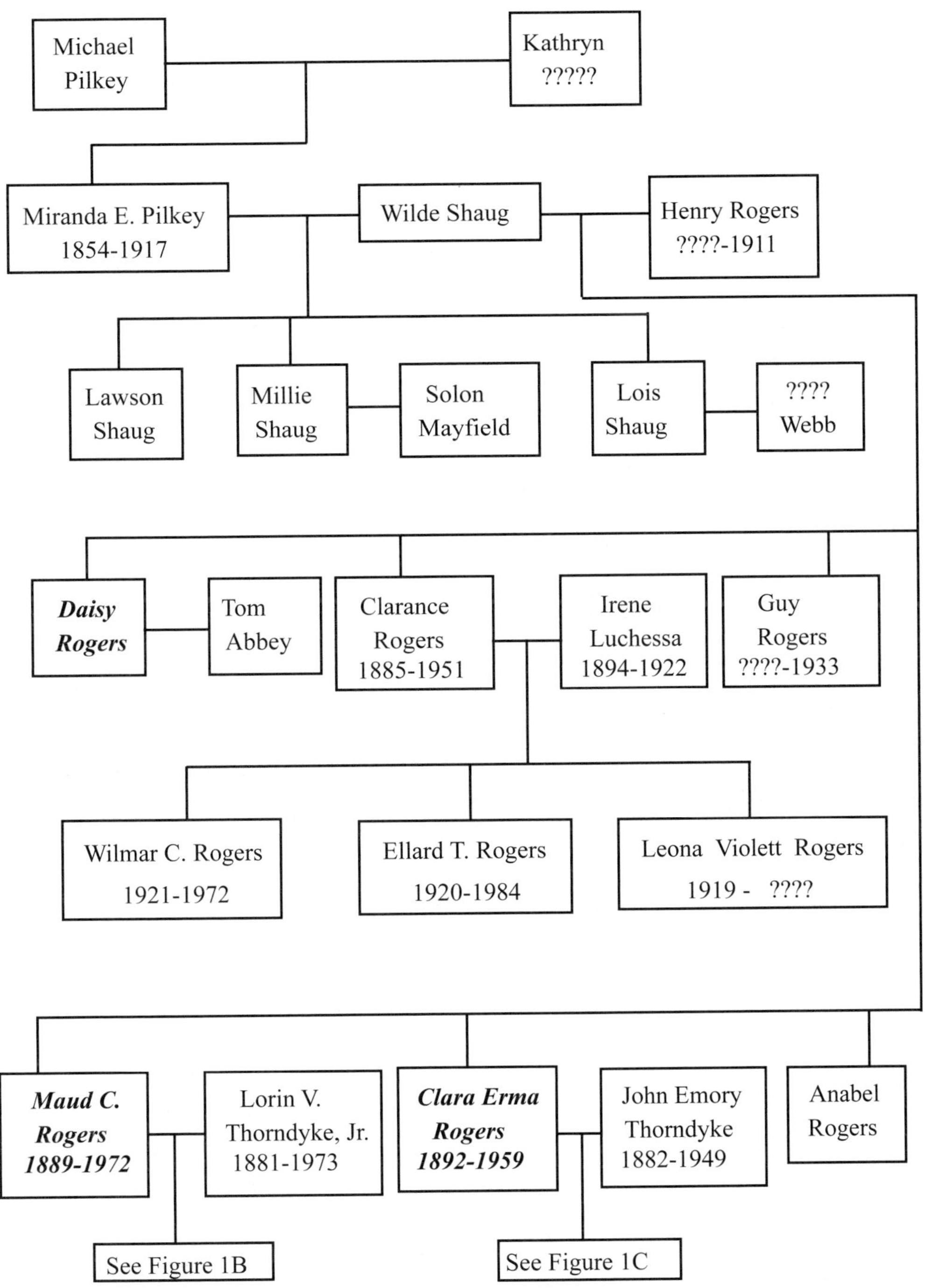

Figure 5. Rogers Family Genealogy

Piedras Blancas Light Station assistant keepers quarters circa 1934

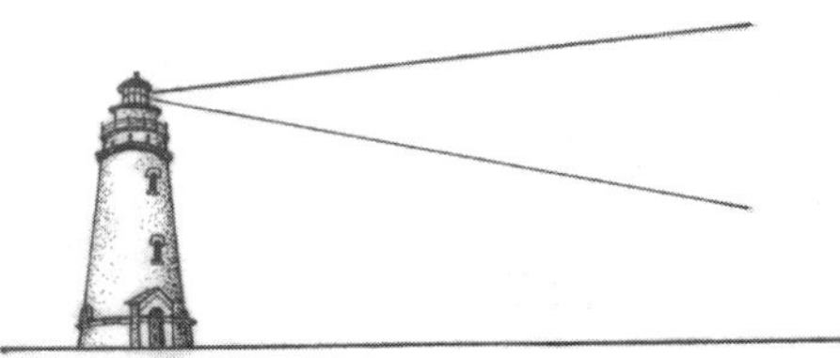

Corn	Desserts- Continued

Corn
Potato Chowder, **150**
Dried, with Pork, **151**

Cornmeal
Cornbread Casserole, **232-233**
Cornmeal Mush, **157**
Cornmeal Puffs, **54**
Fried Cornmeal Mush, **158**
Polenta, **254**
Scrappel, **158**
Tamale Pie, **173**

Crackers
Water Wafers, **63**

Desserts (also see Cakes or Pies)
Banana Nut Tea Bread, **242**
Brownies, **112**
Butterscotch Sticks, **128**
Chocolate Pudding
Steamed Balls, **131**
Cocoa,
Marshmallow Roll, **118**
Cream Puffs, **85**
Date Hermits, **120**
Doughnuts, **66, 129**
Dromedary Date Bars, **127**
Dromedary Date Torte, **99**
Gingerbread, **70**
Hermits, **121**
Ice Cream, **168**
Lemon Pie, **53, 68, 107**
Mollie's Receipt, **28**
Peculiars, **71**
Pineapple Lemon Pie, **52**
Rolpoly, **30**
Soft Gingerbread, **28**
Sour Milk Doughnuts, **66**
Sour Milk Gingerbread, **46**

Desserts- Continued
Sponge Gingerbread, **40**
Strawberry Shortcake, **83**
Tarts, **127**
Untitled, **66**

Eggs
Crispy Corn
Breakfast Burritos, **177**

Fillings
Cream, **35**
Chocolate, **32**
Feather, **170**
For Boston Cream Pie, **106**
For Cream Puffs, **85**
Lady Baltimore, **96**

Fish
Baked Rock Cod, **197**
Baked Steelhead, **144**
Cioppino, **247**
Codfish Cakes, **137**
Fried Steelhead, **143**
Rock Fish, **234-235**
Seafood Stew, **184**

Frosting
Boiled, **58**
Chocolate Icing, **51, 133**
Lady Baltimore, **96**
Mrs. Bostick's Boiled, **58**
Orange Icing, **43**

Gravy
Dried Beef, **138**

Home Remedies
Black Scale, **46**
Cleaning Aluminum, **49**
Head Noise Relief, **49**
Lemon Juice as Cure, **45**
Untitled, **61**

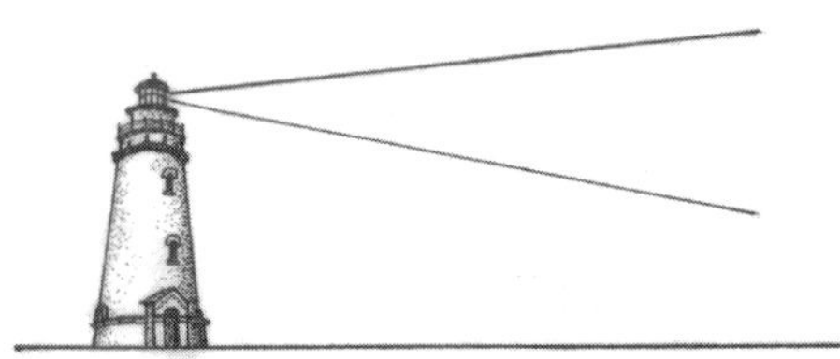

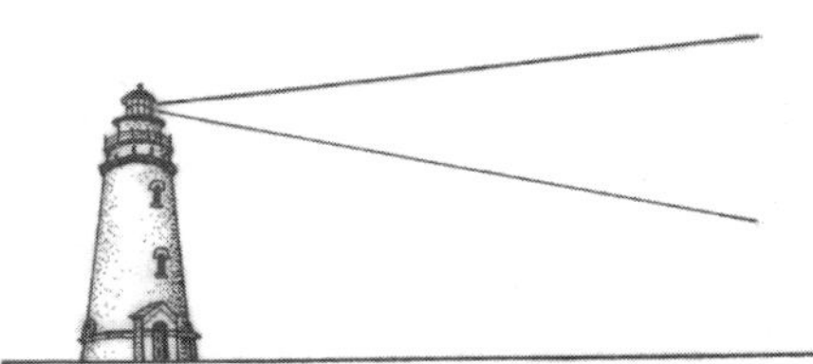

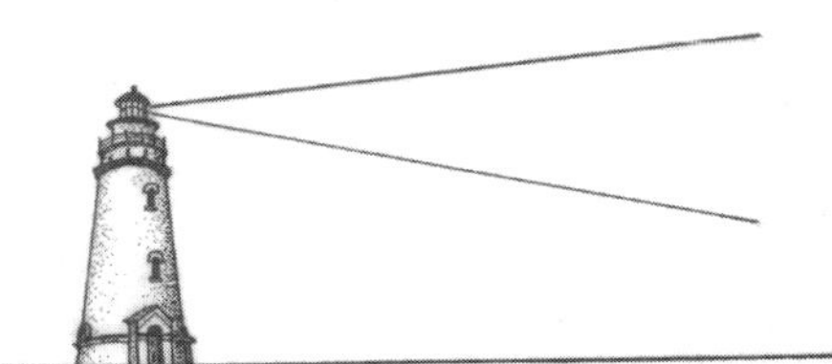

E

England, 13
Evans, Aldyth C., 272
Evans, Anabel, 272
Evans, Bruce, 272
Evans, Charles, 271
Evans, David E., 272, 273
Evans, Donald F., 273
Evans, Donna Mae, 273
Evans, Evan, 271
Evans, Gary, 273
Evans, George W., 272
Evans, Gordon, 271
Evans, Greg, 273
Evans, Howard, 273
Evans, James, 273
Evans, Jean, 272
Evans, John, 16, 270, 271
Evans, John C., 272
Evans, John C. Jr., 272
Evans, Judy, 273
Evans, Katherine, 272
Evans, Kathy, 273
Evans, Lillie, 70
Evans, Mary Jarmon, 4, 16, 21, 70
Evans, Merle J., 273
Evans, Mildred, 273
Evans, Patricia, 272
Evans, Richard, 272
Evans, Robert D., 272
Evans, Sue Jarmon, 273
Evans, Thomas C., 272
Evans, Thomas James, 16, 270-272
Evans, Vard, 273
Evans, Verna Mills, 273
Evans, Walter R., 272
Evans, Will, 271

Evans, William, 272, 273
Evans, William J., 271

F

Fairbanks Soap Company, 47
Ferndale, 125
France, 49, 53
Francis, Norman, 190-192
Francis, Norman Jr., 190

G

George, J.J., 270
Germany, 49
Gerring, Don, 269
Gerring, Ray, 269
Ghirardelli, 88, 90, 115, 129, 131
Ghirardelli, Domingo, 91
Gillespie, Evelyn, 273
Giurlani, Angelo, 132
Godsey, Jim, 199
Golden State Creamery, 125
Graham, Sylvester, 63
Gregg, Peggy, 273
Grindle, Lura Georgia, 268

H

Haas, Greg, 217
Hafley, Harvey, 272
Hampton, Linda Luchessa, 170
Hawley, Cynthia, 250
Harrington, Laura, 52
Hearst Castle, 207
Hearst Ranch, 191, 199
Hearst, William R., Jr., 199
Hernandez, Jean, 254-258
Hicks, Alice Cuthberston, 274

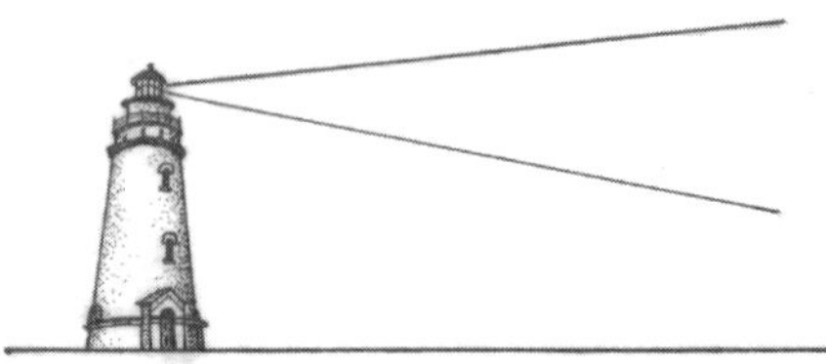

Hughes, Mrs. T., 148
Humboldt County, 125

I

Inabnit, Pat Smith, 2, 200, 201,208
Ingersoll, Majorie Jewell, 269
Ingles, Carol, 169
Ingles, Sissy, 169

J

Jannsen, Lena B., 272
Jarmon, 5
Jarmon, Ann, 16, 270, 271
Jarmon, Elizabeth, 15, 267, 270
Jarmon, John J., 270
Jarmon, Margaret, 9, 16, 267, 270
Jarmon, Martha, 16, 270, 274
Jarmon, Mary, 16, 270-272
Jones, Ann, 270
Jones, Gladys Dean, 268

K

Kane, Jackie, 261-262
Kansas, 238
Kraals, Martha, 272

L

Langworthy, Florence, 67
Lay, Robert, 272
Lee, Daniel Murray, 274
Lighthouse Service, 190
Lilly, Jim, 3, 191-197
Luchessa, Irene, 275
Lyon, Judy, 2

M

Macedo, Consuelo, 3
Maine, 15

Mathison, Wilfred, 272
Mayfield, Solon, 275
McCauly, Meta, 268
McQuaid, Mrs. M., 197
Merrill, Pam, 209-211
Millbrae, 88
Mills, Lula B., 272, 273
Muir, John, 175
Muir, Stephanie, 269
Mullen, Maryann B., 259
Muma, Ann Elizabeth, 274
Muma, Benjamin, 16, 270, 274
Muma, Irwin Johnson, 274
Muma, Jane Erskins, 274
Muma, John Rothbury, 274
Muma, Mattie R., 274
Muma, Susan, 274
Murphey, Tom, 236
Murphy, Anna Mae, 268
Murray, Mrs., 72

N

New Guilford Brethren in Christ
    Church, 216
New Orleans, 36
New York City, 45, 49
Noyes, Edith, 274

P

Paso Robles, 167
Patent, Greg, 92
Pfleghaar, Herman, 272
Pennsylvania, 216
Piedras Blancas Light Station,
    Title Page, 7, 8, 9, 15,161, 190, 199,
    200, 211, 214, 217, 250, 276

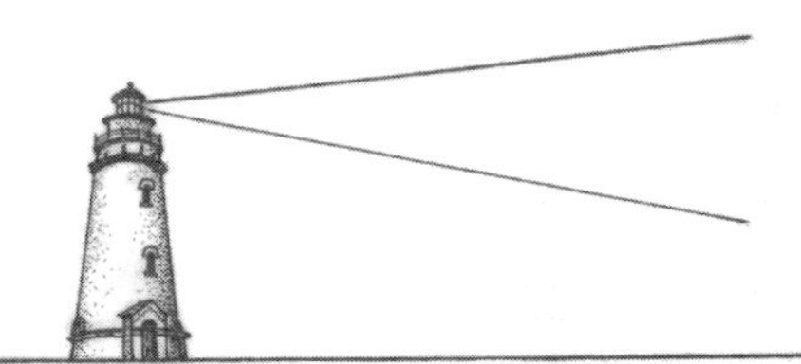

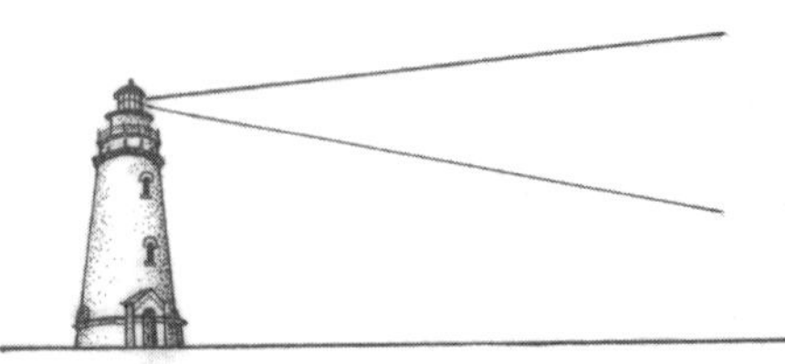

Thorndyke, Alena, 269
Thorndyke, Alta Margaret, 268
Thorndyke, Bonnie, 174
Thorndyke, Brian, 175, 188, 269
Thorndyke, Captain Lorin V., 9, 12, 15-18, 20, 23, 155, 163, 170, 175, 267, 270
Thorndyke, Carol Ann, 268
Thorndyke, Cyril, 269
Thorndyke, Dana, 269
Thorndyke, Donald, G., 268
Thorndyke, Donald G. Jr., 268
Thorndyke, Donna Jean, 268
Thorndyke, Elizabeth Jarmon, 6, 9,15-18, 22, 26, 34, 70
Thorndyke, Erma Rogers, 6, 65, 68,72, 163
Thorndyke, Frankie Ruth, 16, 267
Thorndyke, Gerald E., 268
Thorndyke, Gerald R. "Dick", 2, 155, 268
Thorndyke, Ione Elizabeth, 269
Thorndyke, Irwin Roger, 268
Thorndyke, Janet, 268
Thorndyke, Jim, 163, 269
Thorndyke, John Emory, 15, 17, 23, 65,72, 267, 269, 270, 275
Thorndyke, Judy Kay, 268
Thorndyke, Linda Buttke, 163
Thorndyke, Lorin, 268
Thorndyke, Lorin V. Jr., 10, 12, 15, 17, 23, 74, 134, 137, 149, 165, 267-268, 270, 275
Thorndyke, Margaret Jarmon, 4, 6, 10,12,16-18, 20, 21, 54, 70, 37, 267

Thorndyke, Marjorie Ingersol, 163
Thorndyke, Maud Rogers, 6, 10, 12, 67-68,74, 76, 77, 85, 95, 104, 111, 114, 122, 129, 161, 167, 170-171
Thorndyke, Mervyn Emory, 269
Thorndyke, Mike, 269
Thorndyke, Nancy Lee, 169, 170, 268
Thorndyke, Richard, 12
Thorndyke, Stephanie, 175, 188
Thorndyke, Tina, 269
Thorndyke, L.V. Store, 12, 171
Tift, Mayme, 272
Twain, Mark, 36

U

U.S. Coast Guard, 3, 7, 10, 189, 190-191, 199, 214

V

Valenzuela, Jesus, 211
Valenzuela, Mary, 211
Van Gordon, Clara Mae, 271
Van Gordon, Earl, 272
Van Gordon, Florence, 272
Van Gordon, Gladys, 4, 21, 272
Van Gordon, Helene, 4, 21, 272
Van Gordon, Kate Evans, 4, 21
Van Gordon, Mary Ethel, 272
Van Gordon, Vine, 272
Vreeland, Marion M., 268

W

Wagner, Larry, 191-193, 197
Wales, Wisconsin, 16

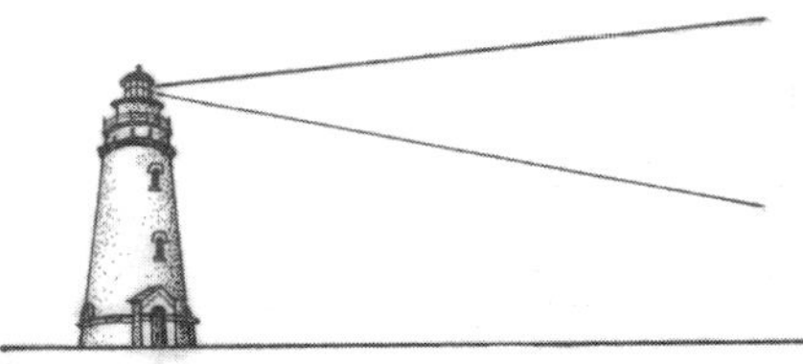

To order additional copies of "Dinner at The Light-house" as gifts for friends or family, please contact:

Piedras Blancas Light Station Association
P. O. Box 127
San Simeon, CA 93452
PBLS Association is a 501(c)(3) non-profit corporation.